D0780409

THEN WE'LL
SING A NEW SONG

THEN WE'LL SING A NEW SONG

African Influences on America's Religious Landscape

MARY ANN CLARK

ROWMAN & LITTLEFIELD PUBLISHERS, INC.
Lanham • Boulder • New York • Toronto • Plymouth, UK

Published by Rowman & Littlefield Publishers, Inc.
A wholly owned subsidary of The Rowman & Littlefield Publishing Group, Inc.
4501 Forbes Boulevard, Suite 200, Lanham, Maryland 20706
www.rowman.com

10 Thornbury Road, Plymouth PL6 7PP, United Kingdom

Copyright © 2012 by Rowman & Littlefield Publishers, Inc.

All rights reserved. No part of this book may be reproduced in any form or by any electronic or mechanical means, including information storage and retrieval systems, without written permission from the publisher, except by a reviewer who may quote passages in a review.

British Library Cataloguing in Publication Information Available

Library of Congress Cataloging-in-Publication Data

Clark, Mary Ann, 1949-
  Then we'll sing a new song : African influences on America's religious
landscape / Mary Ann Clark.
    p. cm.
  Includes bibliographical references (p.   ).
  ISBN 978-1-4422-0879-7 (cloth : alk. paper)—ISBN 978-1-4422-0881-0
(electronic)
  1. Africa—Religion. 2. Slavery—Africa. 3. Slavery—United States. 4. African
Americans—Religion. I. Title.
  B5310.C53 2012
  200.89'96073—dc23

                                      2012000653

∞™ The paper used in this publication meets the minimum requirements of American National Standard for Information Sciences—Permanence of Paper for Printed Library Materials, ANSI/NISO Z39.48-1992.
Printed in the United States of America

CONTENTS

Preface   vii

1   A Most Religious Nation   1

2   Jesus Is My Bosom Friend: The Development of
    American Religion   23

3   African Christianity: Kingdom of Kongo   47

4   The Dead Are Not Dead   67

5   Children of Oduduwa: The Oyo Empire   87

6   Then Why Not Every Man?   109

7   Children of the Leopard: Kingdom of Dahomey   131

8   That Voodoo That You Do   151

9   New African Branches   169

Notes   193

Glossary   199

Timeline   209

Additional Readings   215

Bibliography   219

Index   227

PREFACE

In 2004 I sat on a panel with Terry Rey at the African Studies Association conference in New Orleans. His paper, based on his chapter in Linda M. Heywood's *Central Africans and Cultural Transformations in the American Diaspora*, described the influence of Kongolese Catholicism on the development of Haitian Vodou. As I learned more about the Kongolese people I became more and more intrigued with the idea that such a large proportion of the enslaved brought to the Americas and to the United States came from a long-standing Christian culture. I began to wonder how these folks might have influenced the development of African American religion and American religions in general. Ideas and intuitions about these influences rattled around in my mind for several years until Sarah Stanton of Rowman & Littlefield contacted me to ask if I was working on anything interesting. I had just been putting together a proposed syllabus for a course on African American religions and found that there was little at the undergraduate level that described how the religions and cultures African peoples brought with them to the Americas might have influenced their approaches to religion during slavery and beyond.

This book is the result of pulling those ideas and more together into a text I hope undergraduates and amateur scholars will find as fascinating to read as it was to write. My original intuition that African-heritage peoples contributed more than fragmented "Africanism" to American culture has expanded to a great appreciation of the ways in which Americans have become more like Africans and less like Europeans in many of their religious sensibilities. The answer to my central question—why are Americans' religious sensibilities so different from those of their European cousins?—depends on the influence of the thousands of Africans transported here during the first two and a half centuries of the settlement of what became this great country.

I want to thank Sarah, her assistant Jin Yu, and the anonymous reviewers who helped me think through how to put these intuitions into a tangible form as well as the many scholars of African and American cultures whose work has been brought together on these pages. The fine folks at the interlibrary loan department of the Prescott Public Library have made it possible for me to access wide-ranging scholarly materials, and I thank them for their generous work. I want to especially thank Stephen Finley from Louisiana State University and Alice Wood from Bethune-Cookman University for their enthusiastic responses to my original proposal and their continued support of this project. Alice has been a good friend and colleague from the earliest years of my scholarly career while Stephen is a new colleague and I think a bright new star on the academic horizon. It was Alice's research on Howard Thurman that inspired the title of this work. Although she has passed from the world of the living, I want to acknowledge all the ways that Dr. Edith Wyschogrod has influenced my work. She first introduced me to the study of religion, including the work of Philippe Ariès, and consistently supported my rather eccentric way of thinking about these ideas. I also want to thank all of my friends for their patience as I refined my ideas in what they thought were going to be casual conversations. Thanks for listening or at least nodding wisely.

And finally, as always, I want to express my most heartfelt gratitude to my partner Art Gorski, who has unequivocally supported me through this project and others. I know you are my biggest fan and I appreciate your loving support more than I can say.

1

A MOST RELIGIOUS NATION

"On my arrival in the United States," the famous French traveler Alexis de Tocqueville observed in the early nineteenth century, "the religious aspect of the country was the first thing that struck my attention."[1]

Although it is common to think of the United States as a Christian country, its history is one of new and unconventional religions. Thousands of years before Columbus stumbled upon this "New World," people from northern Asia came across the Bering Strait to present-day Alaska to live in North and South America and the islands of the Caribbean. They settled everywhere from the windswept tundra of the Arctic to the steaming jungles around the equator to the tip of the southern continent. They developed diverse religious beliefs and practices. Later, people from Europe, Africa, and Asia added their own beliefs and practices to form the diversity of traditions we find today. Even in the twenty-first century, newly arrived peoples are adding their own beliefs and practices to the mix.

In the process of immigration and integration Americans have developed a unique religious culture by drawing on inputs from all of the people who have populated this country. Knowing something of the culture of those who came here helps us to understand the religious culture that has been developed here. For all people, their originating cultures form the warp threads upon which the weft threads of their experiences in the Americas are woven to create the whole cloth of their new lives. When we discuss our culture we tend to focus on particular originating cultures. However, it is also important to remember that for all immigrant groups what were local "ethnic" designations in their original areas became combined in the Americas. People who saw themselves as members of a particular group at home soon found that they were included in wider designations. Thus people who considered themselves Neapolitans and Sicilians became simply "Italians."

1

Diverse peoples from throughout China became simply "Chinese." People who were members of unique groups from the various city-states of Central West and West Africa became Kongolese, Fon, Yoruba, and others before they became simply "African Americans" (Brandon, 55). It is important to remember that just as many of the European nations we are familiar with today didn't exist during the colonial period, so also West and Central Africa were a mosaic of ethnic groups, city-states, and, in some areas, kingdoms. And just as we often conflate the different groups within European areas with their contemporary political organizations (countries) we often conflate African groups together, sometimes even treating Africa as though it were a single large political entity. As we shall see, sometimes we need to break open those larger designations in order to understand what a group brought with it across the oceans. This is especially true when we begin speaking about peoples from the many areas of Africa.

Each immigrant group has had a different experience of assimilation into American society. Each group, regardless of origin, initially attempted to re-create as much as possible its familiar patterns of life within the constraints of the new and generally hostile environment. None have been entirely successful, so out of this process new cultural realities have developed. This process is as true for Europeans as for Africans. Not only did members of different societies within similar ethnic and racial groups have to learn to deal with each other (Englishmen from different parts of the island with each other and the Irish, for example), they also had to learn to adjust across ethnic, racial, and religious lines in a process of creative cultural development. In addition, those arriving later had to adjust to the institutional structures developed by what T. H. Breen calls "charter" communities of those who had arrived earlier (Breen, 215–16). As a consequence of its immigrant population, America has become a mosaic of religious traditions, including Christian, African, Jewish, Asian, Islamic, and new religious traditions. When you look closely you can see all that differentiates these groups from each other. However, when you step back you can see their similarities. Those similarities are the common ways Americans have developed of looking at and being in the world. Those shared ways of looking and being form the set of behaviors I am calling *American religious sensibilities*.

In general, six such sensibilities typify American religion. *Individualism* is the tendency to construct one's own religious beliefs and a preference for a personal experience of the holy. *Fideism* is the belief in some sort of "God," whether or not one participates in any specific religious community. *Polymorphism* is the tendency to engage in several unrelated religious traditions at the same time or one after the other. *Experimentalism* is the willingness, even eagerness, to welcome new religious beliefs and practices. *Tolerance* is the willingness to accept that others are following a different spiritual path and a willingness to work with others for common causes, especially social causes. And, finally, *pragmatism* is the expectation that religion will provide practical benefits in one's daily life and the willingness to test religious beliefs and practices for one's self. While individually these sensibilities are not uniquely American, together they form an American way of being religious. New religious traditions that are brought to these shores by immigrants from around the world have generally shaped themselves to conform to this general sensibility so that within a couple of generations practitioners have formed an American variant of the religious traditions their grandparents brought here.

Many of the earliest European immigrants to the Americas were religious dissenters, people who left (or were run out of) their homelands because of their unconventional religious beliefs. Many of these early groups, once they had established themselves, tried to make theirs the only tradition allowed, banishing and even killing those who disagreed with them. The seventeenth and eighteenth centuries were also periods of religious excitement in the American colonies. Several new groups of dissenters made their home here, including the Quakers, the Shakers, the Mennonites, and the Amana society, as well as many lesser-known groups. American religious sensibilities have been deeply influenced by the utopianism and "enthusiasm" of these communities.

Because of its history of colonization by Europeans, generally we think that the culture of the United States is primarily based on that of Europe. However, in terms of religiosity in the twenty-first century, Americans are more like the highly religious countries of the Middle East and what is known as the global South (Africa, Asia, and Latin America) than any of the highly industrial countries of Europe. Since Columbus stumbled upon this so-called New World over five hundred years ago, Americans have become increasingly more religious than their European cousins. According to the World Values Survey[2] conducted between 2005 and 2007, almost 40 percent of Americans report they attended religious services weekly, placing Americans seventh behind Jordan, Indonesia, Poland, Egypt, Brazil, and India and ahead of Iran, Italy, Canada, Britain, China, Germany, France, Russia, Japan, and Sweden. Almost half of the Americans surveyed (47 percent) said that religion was "very important" in their lives while fewer than one in five of the Swiss (17 percent), Dutch (12 percent), and Swedes (9 percent) said the same.

Thus an important question is why religiosity in the United States developed so differently from religiosity in the nations of Western Europe.

Scholars offer many explanations for these differences. But they often ignore the influence of the many Africans brought to America between its founding and the Civil War that eventuated in the end of slavery in the United States. As we explore the ways Africans may have influenced American religious sensibilities we need to be careful not to simply look at those traditions and ideas that are distinctively African but to also look at the ways Americans have blended these cultural elements into their developing religious sensibilities and watch for what is distinctively non-European (Thornton 1992, 230; Gomez, 12).

Commonly when we think about the interactions between Europeans and Africans in early America we imagine that Africans were only the recipients of European culture. We think that they provided little to the great melting pot of ideas that became American culture. That distorts the picture. Actually West and West Central African religious sensibilities have formed the root of many current American religious beliefs and practices. Like the hidden roots of a large tree, these African religious sensibilities support and nourish the more visible portions of American religious sensibilities. As Jason Young argues, the slave trade brought not only men, women, and even some children to North America, but also African "cultural meanings, signs, and symbols" (Young, 3). Over its long history, the culture of what became the United States has incorporated many of these African ways of viewing and being in the world into its own worldview as it evolved from a set of European colonies to its own independent culture. In fact, it can be argued that it was these African contributions that made American culture distinct from its European antecedent (Gomez, 12). Although we can find African influences throughout American culture, in this book we will focus on American religious sensibilities and the distinctive form of religiosity found in the United States today. We will look at the ways in which it is radically different from that practiced in Europe today or even from that practiced by the earliest Europeans to reach these shores. We will explore the new religious song created in the United States, one that was made stronger and more enduring by the addition of these African contributions. My hope is to extend the analysis of art and philosophy begun by Robert Ferris Thompson in his *Flash of the Spirit* not only to religion but beyond African-identified cultures to American culture in general.

Peoples from Africa, most of whom came to the Americas as slaves, brought their own religious sensibilities with them. Those sensibilities were very different from the Christianity practiced in Europe at the time. Even the people from the kingdoms of Kongo and Angola, who had converted to Christianity in the late 1400s—before Columbus's voyage—brought their own unique set of Christian beliefs and practices with them as they made the journey from their homelands to the Americas. As we explore both African religious ideas and practices and the development of a distinctive American form of religiosity, we will see that West and West Central African religious sensibilities have heavily influenced what began as a European cultural tradition. Although we might expect to find these influences among African Americans, the descendants of enslaved peoples from Africa, we will also see the ways they were influential throughout American society. As African-heritage peoples converted to Christianity, for example, they also converted Christianity to a form more compatible with their own religious sensibilities. They were then able to share those religious sensibilities with their white counterparts. Consequently, American religiosity of the twenty-first century is much more similar to that of seventeenth- and eighteenth-century West and West Central Africa than that of European Christians of the same time frame or that found among European Christians today.

The West and West Central African societies that contributed the bulk of the enslaved who came to the United States have been described as "open, flexible, and incorporative rather than closed rigid, and conservative" (Drewal 1988, 132). Their flexibility served these African peoples well as they attempted to make a home in an extremely hostile environment. But cultural exchange was not a one-way street—Africans made their own contributions to American religious culture. Africans and Europeans were not alone on this continent, but for much of the early history of the American colonies the primary interactions were between Europeans and Africans—Native Americans generally did not live in the towns or work on the farms of European colonists and there were few if any Asians making their home here at the time. Thus we can say along with John Thornton, one of the premier scholars of the history of Africa and the African diaspora, that the culture that developed in these colonies was a Euro-African one. Many of the differences between it and its European and African counterparts were due to the interactions between the peoples from these two continents (Thornton 1992, 140).

ATLANTIC SLAVE TRADE

The earliest English colonists had no legal foundation on which to build a slave society, as there was no precedent for slavery in English common law. Colonists had to create for themselves the customary, judicial, and statutory practices and decisions necessary to create such a society in the New World.

In the beginning English colonists were indifferent, even hostile, to the idea of slave conversions. Colonists believed that the biblical injunction against Christians holding fellow Christians in bondage would require that when slaves converted they would have to be freed. In addition, many felt that conversion would make the enslaved proud, irascible, uppity, and saucy. In addition, the early Protestant idea of religion required at least a minimal amount of education. One of Martin Luther's primary complaints against the Catholic church of his time was that it kept individuals from reading the Bible for themselves. Believing that education would make slaves less docile and resigned to their position led to a fear of any slave education. This view ruled out the religious education necessary for an honest conversion. Eventually the Anglican General Assembly declared that slave conversions need not lead to freedom. However, colonists continued to be reluctant to provide religious instruction for their slaves. Consequently, very few Africans and their descendants converted to European-style Christianity during the early colonial period. The reluctance of slaveholders to provide religious instruction changed for a short time between 1782 and 1810, when many slaveholders in Virginia, for example, emancipated or at least afforded more humane treatment to the enslaved under the influence of religious admonitions and the high ideas of the American Revolution. However, after about 1830 such high-mindedness was quelled by the new militancy around slavery that developed in the south in the run-up to the Civil War (Gomez, 251–52).

The settlers in the early English colonies were a varied lot. Africans from Igbo, Yoruba, Kongo, Fante, Asante, Ibibio, Fon, and other ethnic groups mingled with Europeans from English, Scotch, Scotch-Irish, Huguenot, and other groups. Many of the non-English Europeans came as indentured servants. In the earliest years of the English colonial project the indentured were preferred over the enslaved. Slaves were much more costly to acquire but neither the enslaved nor the indentured tended to outlive the normal term of indenture. Later, when economic conditions in Europe improved, many of the European poor were able to stay home and no longer had to indenture themselves to the colonies. Around the same time living conditions in the Americas also improved such that colonists from all social groups tended to outlive the normal term of indenture. At the point when lifetime servitude became economically viable, slaves began to provide the primary workforce, particularly in the middle and southern colonies.

Detailed analysis of the patterns of both the acquisition of slaves along the African coast and the sale of slaves in the Americas shows the impact of specific African regions and ethnicities on particular places in the Americas (Hall). Both scholars and the general public have long believed that Africans from throughout Africa arrived willy-nilly in the Americas with no possibility of acknowledging their own cultural heritage or interacting with others from their own area or ethnicity. Closer analysis reveals that Africans were mainly taken from the western and central African Atlantic coasts, an area that extends from current-day Senegal in the north to Angola in the south, but not from too far inland or from most other areas of the vast African continent. African scholar John Thornton has said there were only three major cultures and seven subcultures that contributed African people to the New World (Thornton 1992, 186). People from these areas did not live in isolation from each other either. Rather they traded with each other, sometimes exchanged their children in marriage, migrated back and forth, and often spoke similar languages, learned each other's language, or developed a mutually understandable trade language. In addition, the slave trade followed a rhythm that accented one area over another at different times during its long existence. Many of the cultures along this coastline were empires whose rulers choose when and to what extent their people would engage in the slave trade. Thus, as circumstances changed along this long coast, people from the different areas became available or unavailable to the slave-trading vessels that sailed there.

Since the ships' captains preferred to spend the least amount of time possible anchored along the African coast, most wanted to pick up their cargo from one or two closely spaced ports where they had ongoing relationships with the sellers. Hence each ship would generally have people from one port or a single cultural area. In fact, since many ships were filled with people captured in local wars the entire cargo might be people from the same culture, or even people who grew up and went to war together. Similarly on the American side, ships generally unloaded their cargo at a single port, commonly the ports of Chesapeake Bay and South Carolina, especially Charleston (Gomez, 20), and many of the ships landing at a particular American port were arriving from neighboring African ports. Because the slave trade was controlled not only by the desires of buyers in the Americas but also by those of the sellers in Africa, at any place and time the variety of cultures represented was relatively small. Individuals often looked for and found others from their own cultural areas and many became more flexible about who they considered countrymen (Thornton 1992, 193, 195, 196).

In this book we will look specifically at three cultural groups that strongly impacted the development of religious sensibilities in North America and the Caribbean: the Kongolese and Angolans from the Angolan coast, the Yoruba-speaking people of West Africa, and the Fon peoples from Lower Guinea. Each of these areas contributed significant numbers of individuals to the slave trade and for each we can trace some of their cultural impact in the Americas. Of course, many other groups also contributed to the trade and impacted American culture, but to keep this project reasonable we will focus on these three. Although many Americans are enthralled with the Asante culture of West Africa, it appears that few people from that area arrived in what would eventually become the United States, so much to my regret I decided not to include them in this text.

During the earliest colonial period most masters and slaves worked together clearing the land, plowing, planting and harvesting the crop, and surviving the hardships of those times together. This was not the time of the great plantations and grand southern lifestyle we generally associate with American slavery. Many Africans were imported not for brute, unskilled labor but as the experienced workforce needed to tame the American wilderness. In many cases, Africans were able to contribute important skills needed for the development of the Americas, where they worked as

> blacksmiths, metallurgists, toolmakers, sculptors and engravers, silver-smiths and goldsmiths, tanners, shoemakers, and saddle-makers . . . coopers, draymen, and coach drivers; breeders, groomers and trainers of horses; and cowboys skilled in cattle rearing and herding . . . ship builders, navigators, sounders, caulkers, sail makers, ship carpenters, sailors, and rowers. They were indigo-makers, weavers and dyers of cloth, tailors and seamstresses. They were basket weavers, potters, and salt-makers. They were cooks, bakers, pastry chefs, candy-makers, street vendors, innkeepers, personal servants, housekeepers, laundresses, domestics, doctors (Hall, 20).

In addition to their labor, these people also contributed their religious ideas to the American mix. As we shall see, American religiosity became more like that of Africa over the long period between the time its first colonists set foot on what would become the United States and that time after the Civil War when the Christian churches became, as Martin Luther King Jr. said, the most segregated institutions in the country,[3] and even beyond that into the twenty-first century.

Unlike their European counterparts, the enslaved seldom came to the Americas in family groups. Families were broken up, and gender imbalances among the enslaved made it difficult to establish new family groups. However, both West and West Central African societies had other types of organizations that the enslaved could use to form themselves into cultural groups. The most prominent of these were the specialized groups often characterized in the literature as "secret" societies. Membership in these societies might be generational (age-group societies), occupational (market women or blacksmiths, for example), or religious (worshippers of a particular deity or followers of a certain religious tradition). Membership in these societies was often open and flexible as long as one met the primary requirements (Thornton 1992, 220–21). It appears that similar groups were formed in the New World. We know the enslaved in South America and the Caribbean used similar societies to organize themselves and eventually reconstitute portions of their own culture. It appears that such groups were also formed in North America. William Pierson, for example, documents the black culture based on African precedents that flourished in New England during the eighteenth century (Pierson). Certainly many slave rebellions were organized according to these principles, and the earliest congregations of enslaved Christians appear to have followed similar structures.

In her analysis of the social history of eighteenth-century Virginia, the largest and most populous of the original English colonies, Mechal Sobel suggests that the culture of America was deeply affected by African values and perceptions largely because during its earliest periods blacks and whites lived and worked closely together, often sharing their churches and their religious perceptions, generally for their entire adult lives (Sobel). The enslaved generally lived and worked in the centers of power as domestics and laborers in the homes and on the homesteads of the most elite members of society rather than in the more marginal or rural areas (Thornton 1992, 151). We must also remember that a great many of the enslaved brought to the Americas were prisoners of war. This included the soldiers who ended up on the losing side of the many conflicts in West and West Central Africa along with those supporting the war effort—all the people required to keep large armies in the field (Law, 104). In addition, throughout these areas, religious functionaries—priests and mediums of local deities—were often condemned to slavery in order to reduce the competition for the religious loyalty of the people. Similarly priests whose followers were on the losing side of a battle might be condemned to join them in enslavement (Thornton 1992, 264). Thus the majority of the enslaved were the finest their societies had to offer, rather than, as is often assumed, the dregs of their African cultures. In their new environment these young men and women were able to help build what would become American society and help develop a distinctive American culture, including its language, religion, food, aesthetic expressions, and political and social organizations (Walker, 3).

We also need to understand that although many scholars have suggested that the bulk of African American culture is based on the cultures of West Africa, as we shall see, more people who were brought to what is now the United States came from the Central African kingdoms of Kongo and Angola than from any other area or ethnic group.

AFRICAN CULTURE AND RELIGIOSITY

Conversion of the enslaved was spotty during the first 150 years of slavery in what was to become the United States. Missionary activities were hampered by the objections and indifference of the slaveholders as well as the paucity of missionaries available to serve in this cause. As we shall see, after 1740 and the mass evangelical movement known as the First Great Awakening, this all changed when missionaries from Methodist, Baptist, Presbyterian, and other groups began to invade the southern colonies and convert the enslaved. Most of these non-Anglican preachers were also bitter opponents of slavery. They welcomed slaves and former slaves into their churches and established black and biracial churches throughout the south as the enslaved began to embrace these new forms of Christianity. At the same time, astute missionaries suggested to the master class that under their guidance Christian slaves would learn the catechism of honesty, faithfulness, chastity, and discipline.

But not all of those brought from Africa to what became the United States were ignorant of Christianity. Thirty to 40 percent of the enslaved came from West Central Africa where Christianity had been introduced before the discovery of the Americas. By the early 1700s, when people from this area were being imported in great numbers, they were coming from a culture that had been developing its own form of Catholic Christianity for over two hundred years. In addition, from the mid-fifteenth century forward, even before the earliest voyages to the Americas, Africans along the whole western coast of African had been exposed to the Catholic missionaries that sailed with the Portuguese exploring these areas. Although nowhere were missionaries as successful as in the kingdoms of Kongo and Angola, there were Portuguese trading outposts all along the West and West Central African coasts and Catholic Christian ideas were spread by Africans trading inland. Thus, as John Thornton documents, throughout this area there were sizable Christian communities supplemented by Africans who were aware of Christianity, perhaps even sympathetic to its ideas and ideals, although not willing or able to partake in baptism. In fact, Thornton suggests, many Africans arriving in the Americas were baptized Christians or were familiar with, and perhaps sympathetic toward, Christian beliefs and practices (Thornton 1988, 262–66, 268). As we examine the African influences on the development of American religions we will consider what this meant for the development of American Christianity.

However, the Christianity found in Africa was different from that of early modern Europe. As we will discuss in more detail when describing Kongolese Christianity in chapter 3, the practice of Christianity in West and West Central Africa throughout this period was highly mixed with the African religious traditions. Unlike the Catholic church's position in South America, where all vestiges of indigenous religious practices were severely persecuted, in Africa the church took a more tolerant stance, accepting a certain level of religious mixing. For example, early catechisms for Kongo, Angola, and other areas accepted by the authorities in Spain and Portugal used indigenous expressions for Christian concepts and explained theological ideas in terms of local cosmologies (Thornton 1988, 267).[4] This means that those Christian religious concepts and ideas also carried local religious associations.

The nature of African societies also meant that Africans from these areas along the western coast of Africa were used to integrating alien religious ideas and concepts into their existing traditions. In areas such as the Kingdom of Dahomey that easily assimilated people from among neighboring groups it was common for such people, whether they were slaves forced to work for the king and his noblemen, women marrying into local families, or traders engaging in commerce across ethnic and political barriers, to bring their own religious beliefs and rituals with them. And these newcomers often taught their religious beliefs and practices to their new associates or family members. We should not be surprised when we find that Africans continued this religious flexibility in their New World environment.

HERSKOVITS/FRAZIER DEBATE

There has been much discussion among scholars of how much of their own cultures enslaved Africans were able to preserve in the Americas, particularly in North America. Many early researchers believed that the Middle Passage and slavery were so traumatic that black Americans lost their entire African cultural heritage. Consequently, all that remained for them was to attempt to interpret the European culture they encountered (Frazier). Others have suggested that Africans lived in such dissimilar groups that they had to rely on the surrounding European culture to provide the basis for their own societies (Morgan). While scholars have generally refuted the idea that Africans lived in significantly more primitive societies than their European counterparts or were essentially passive in the face of their enslavement, such ideas still find their way into works for both scholars and the general public. Many writers have suggested that African American culture can only be explained in terms of European culture because Africans either had no culture of their own or they were completely stripped of their own culture and heritage. Thus it is sometimes suggested that Africans were unable to contribute anything to the development of a new culture for themselves, let alone contribute to the larger American culture. However, other scholars have suggested that even though much of their cultural heritage was destroyed by the rigors of slavery, certain African cultural elements, sometimes called "Africanisms," were retained (Herskovits 1990). Some scholars have even taken a stronger position, arguing that there were often enough people from a particular linguistic and ethnic group in an area to enable them to remember, reconstruct, or maintain portions of the cultural heritage and, in fact, that they not only remembered Africa but intentionally and deliberately used those memories to create new and vibrant cultures (Thornton, 1992; Young).

These two positions, that Africans lost everything on their way to the Americas (as Frazier argued) or that Africans have been able to retain at least a portion of their own cultures (as Herskovits said), are known among scholars as the Herskovits/Frazier debate.[5] Although a myriad of scholarly texts have been published outlining the specific contributions Africans have made to American culture from language to music to building styles, the contributions made by Africa to America's religious culture remain obscure.[6] While African contributions to American religious sensibilities in general have been ignored completely, even the contributions of African beliefs and practices to African American religions are generally downplayed or ignored. Like Albert Raboteau in his superb book *Canaan Land: A Religious History of African Americans*, most scholars of African American religions begin their histories with European missionary efforts. These histories are written as though the enslaved brought nothing to the process, as though Africans arriving on the shores of North America had lost all of their own cultures, beliefs, and practices due to the trauma of the Middle Passage between Africa and the Americas (Raboteau).[7]

However, assertions that Africans had no culture of their own, retained nothing of their home cultures, or were unable to contribute to American culture in general are incorrect. As we shall see, many of the enslaved came from cultures that were as highly developed as those found in Europe at the same time. The enslaved were more often purchased from factors along the African coast than captured by Europeans.

In most of the African ports of call it was the African partners who controlled the slave trade. The king or his representatives made the European ships' captains follow their rules in order to engage in the trade, opening and closing their ports to Europeans and in some situations forcing them to take their business to other areas or to trade in other commodities. As John Thornton says, "Europeans possessed no means, either economic or military, to compel African leaders to sell slaves" (Thornton 1992, 125). From the African side, the trade was mainly one in luxury goods, since the Europeans couldn't provide anything not already available in the African homelands (except guns, which John Thornton asserts were also luxury goods since they did not provide any advantage on the battlefield[8]). These luxury goods often supplemented rather than supplanted a vibrant domestic trade throughout the Atlantic African coast, although in some cases cheaper European goods of lesser quality replaced the better-quality but more expensive domestic African goods (Thornton 1992, 7).

John Butler is one of the preeminent scholars of American religious history. In his classic *Awash in a Sea of Faith* he says that the system of slavery in the United States essentially destroyed any religious system the enslaved might have tried to establish, that during the earliest period (1680 to around 1760) the system of slavery was so brutal and the number of slaves in any one location so small that enslaved Africans suffered a spiritual holocaust. He suggests that it was only after the mid-eighteenth century, when the enslaved were able to reestablish family life and kinship systems, that they were able to develop a sustained religious life. Because of the destruction of their African spiritual systems, that religious life had to be based on the forms of Christianity they found around them, with few African cultural elements (Butler 1990, 154).

New research is suggesting a more nuanced view of African American religious life during the first couple of generations on the American continent. The early neglect of Africans' spirituality meant that the enslaved and the small number of African-heritage freedmen could craft their own religious systems away from the influence of either their masters or the Christian clergy. In addition, since Africans and Europeans had very different views of what constituted "religious activity," African religious rituals were probably often invisible to European eyes. In fact, Michael Gomez suggests that as many as 92 percent of the enslaved maintained some portion of the African religious beliefs and practices on American soil, as throughout the eighteenth century, clergymen were continuing to complain about the "idolatrous dances and revels" of the enslaved (Gomez, 254). In addition, archaeologists are discovering objects buried in slave quarters throughout the colonial areas that indicate that African culture and religion persisted from the earliest colonial period. For example, scholars and students from the University of Maryland–College Park excavated the home of Charles Carroll, one of the signers of the Declaration of Independence, while looking for clues about the daily life of African Americans. They discovered that a black slave had buried a collection of quartz crystals, polished stones, bone disks, and pierced coins in a dark corner of his or her basement workshop. The objects were covered by a bowl with a symbol that looked like an asterisk painted on the inside (Adams). Robert Farris Thompson, a scholar specializing in the cultures of Central Africa, including the region in southwest Democratic Republic of the Congo (formerly Zaire) and northern Angola, known in colonial times as Kongo, recognized the items as similar to items still used in that area today. Like all cultures, the Kongolese had a way of miniaturizing their religion. He suggests that these items represented the irreducible essence of Kongolese religion in the same way a miniature crucifix might represent the essence of Christianity. This dig and others like it are leading scholars to suggest that rather than repudiating their own culture in favor of the surrounding white culture, early African Americans appropriated European artifacts to perpetuate their own religious traditions (Adams).

Similar finds have been recorded at the colonial African Burial Ground of the City of New York, which was used by the black population between the late 1600s and 1796. The site was excavated by researchers from Howard University in the early 1990s. Early reports from that site list a string of glass beads and cowrie shells around the waist of one woman; a heart-shaped symbol believed to be the Adinkra (Akan) symbol for Sankofa, the link between generations, used to embellish the coffin of a man; and quartz crystals and beads in many of the graves (Blakey). The Levi Jordan Plantation in Brazoria, Texas, built a century later in 1848 and abandoned in 1891, was excavated by students from the University of Houston in the 1980s. This site shows how African American culture continued over time and through space (Brown and Cooper). Artifacts from this site suggest that the enslaved and later the black tenant farmers living at this site were involved in activities that the scholars say were African-identified. They come to this conclusion based on the way artifacts were found within the sites and the ways they were modified. These artifacts include drilled shells, carved bones, store-bought jewelry, and coins. In a cabin believed to have been occupied by a traditional healer/magician, the archeologists found paraphernalia associated with the healer's art, including the remains of an anthropomorphic wooden figure they characterized as an *nkisi*, a Kongolese ritual object.[9]

This was part of a ritual "tool kit" that is similar to items used by traditional West and Central African healers and religious leaders (Brown and Cooper, 16–17). Comparisons between these objects and similar objects used in West and Central Africa tie them back to their African origins (Brown and Cooper, 17–18).

Important in this analysis is the understanding that most of the objects found at all of these sites were existing Euro-American objects adapted for African and African American uses and invested with new beliefs and symbolism (Brown and Cooper, 17–19). Such adaptations allowed black users to hide these ritual uses from the prying eyes of the master class. I believe that such attempts to hide in plain view have hindered historians such as Butler from recognizing the ways the enslaved were able to maintain their own culture and cosmology within the brutal demands of American slavery.

DEFINITIONS OF "RELIGION" AND "RELIGIOUS ACTIVITY"

This brings us to the highly contested question of what constitutes "religion" and "religious activity." The fragmenting of Christianity into a myriad of forms after the Protestant Reformation affected the way Europeans of the time thought about religion or, as they were beginning to think of it, one's "faith" or "belief." As a consequence, "true religion" came to be associated with one's own tradition while "false religion" or "atheism," a lack of religion, was ascribed to those outside one's tradition regardless of their beliefs and practices. However, it really was when the age of exploration brought Europeans face to face with peoples from Africa, Asia, and the Americas that "religion" became an important category of analysis. Of course Europeans were already familiar with the non-Christian traditions of Judaism and Islam, but it was the discovery of vast groups who had never been exposed to any of the great monotheisms that caused scholars to rethink these terms. Early explorers were notorious for suggesting that native peoples, especially in the Americas, were without any religion or knowledge of God (Smith, 269). Although many writers came to recognize certain buildings, rituals, and functionaries among the great civilizations of South America, for example, as religious in nature, these persons, places, and activities were generally characterized as "idolatry," or "superstition," thus separating them from "true" religious activity (Smith, 270). Similarly, when describing African religious activities, writers are more likely to describe them as idolatrous or superstitious than religious. Gradually, the categorization of religion in both scholarly works and popular culture became dualistic: "our" (correct or true) religion and "their" (false, heathenistic, or superstitious) religion (Smith, 276). Scholars continued to attempt to categorize beliefs and practices. These categories included natural as opposed to institutional religions, or natural as opposed to ethical traditions, or world religions as opposed to local, ethnic, primitive, or minor traditions (Smith, 276–80). In attempting to find an overarching description of religion that doesn't privilege certain traditions over others, scholars sometimes suggest that religion is that which provides a worldview, or as Ninian Smart says, a system "of belief, which, through symbols and actions, mobilize[s] the feelings and will of human beings" (Smart, 2–3, as quoted in Smith, 281).

The challenge for all scholars of religion is in classifying and evaluating the different ways the ideas embedded in the terms "religion" and "religious activity" can be defined and described. The terms themselves are not native to any language or cultural group but have been created by scholars in order to develop the boundaries of their disciplines. There is no single overarching definition that works for all levels and types of analysis. Rather scholars use the model that works best with the phenomena they want to explore while acknowledging that many other such models exist. All such models of "religion" are incomplete and none account for all the behaviors we might identify as religious. However, the hope is that the chosen model provides an adequate description of the types of behaviors being analyzed. Horton's model, below, works for the thesis of this book because it doesn't depend on how similar the described religious activity is to Christian beliefs and practices and instead uses religious activity in Africa as its starting point. By using this model we can open up our view of what constitutes religious activity.

Along with scholars of religion, sociologists and anthropologists have had to develop their own models of religion in order to analyze non-Western groups and cultures. In *Patterns of Thought in Africa and the West* Robin Horton suggests that from an anthropological point of view religious activity can best be defined as an extension of human social relationships to interactions with certain classes of objects, often called "spirits" or the supernatural (23). These interactions are modeled on similar interactions between human beings with the limitation that when people interact with spirits they often must rely on the *effects* of their interactions rather than direct experience. Horton compares these interactions with the interactions we have with certain kinds of physical entities such as atoms, molecules, and subatomic particles, as well as germs and viruses (25). We can't directly see, touch, smell, taste, and so on germs, but we know them by the effects they have on our bodies—cold germs give us the sniffles, for example. He says that often people's interactions with spirits, gods, or the dead are ritualized since these entities, too, are invisible. Additionally, any feedback from the spiritual entity happens long after the event. There is none of the give and take found in normal human-to-human interactions—what we pray for may materialize long after the time of our prayer, or perhaps never.

Different cultures develop explanations for why one's prayers are not answered. For example, in polytheistic traditions, it might be believed that the actions of one deity counteracted those of another (god X prevented god Y from answering your prayer). In both polytheistic and monotheistic traditions, the deity may choose for his or her own reasons to deny one's request. In addition, in traditions such as the African traditions we'll be considering, there is a belief that a god or other spiritual being can possess a human medium and speak through him or her. Such interactions are more like the flexible give and take of typical human-to-human communications, but in these cases, too, the spirit may choose to refuse a request just as one's parent, child, or friend might (27–29).

Horton also suggests that there are two poles of human interaction, which he characterizes as pure communion and pure manipulation relationships. Pure communion relationships are those found between two equal partners where each person's actions are directed solely to obtain certain intrinsically valuable responses. The partners help each other for the pure joy of doing so, not because one or the other is in a more or less powerful position. Horton uses the example of partners with equal financial and social standing. Pure manipulative relationships are based on each person treating the other as merely a means of arriving at a goal without any reference to the relationship itself. The example Horton suggests is two financiers who are merely trying to take advantage of each other. Most interactions fall somewhere between these two extremes. In terms of religious relationships, Horton suggests that different traditions tend toward one pole or the other. Using William James's analysis of American and European religiosity of the late nineteenth century described in his *Varieties of Religious Experience*, Horton says that relationships among Americans and Europeans are typified by "an extreme character in which sheer communication with God is stressed to the virtual exclusion of benefits accruing either in life or after death"—a communion relationship. He contrasts this with emphasis among many African groups "on the manipulation of God for this-worldly benefits of health, wealth and increase"—a more manipulative type of relationship (33).

Individuals balance human-to-human and human-to-spirit interactions along this communion/manipulative continuum. In the absence of rich human-to-human relationships one might turn toward communion with a god or spirit. Conversely, when human relationships fail to provide for one's worldly needs, a manipulative relationship with a spiritual being might be considered (44–45). In addition, according to Horton, "Variation of religious relationships along the communion/manipulation dimension could be connected with changes in the importance of scientific thinking" (45). According to this hypothesis, as science accounts for more of the uncertainty in the material world, the manipulative aspects of religions become less important. However, often religious behavior does not disappear in the face of increased scientific knowledge. Rather, individuals appear to move toward the communion pole, depending less and less on the gods for "health, wealth, and increase" and more on the communion aspect (45–46). These frameworks provide important ways to view the changes to religious beliefs and practices undergone by both Euro- and African Americans during the development of American religious culture. African Americans moved from a more manipulative relationship toward the communion pole. At the same time, Euro-Americans moved from communion toward the manipulative pole.

Another way to look at the differences between African and European religious sensibilities is to look at the way each group of cultures dealt with revelations. As John Thornton explains, in both sets of cultures there was an understanding that outside of the visible everyday world we can all perceive there is another, invisible world that is the home of both spiritual beings and those who have died. Both sets of cultures agree that we know about this invisible world through revelations, communications of some sort from the spirits of the dead and from the other inhabitants of this invisible world. While the two cultures might disagree about the validity of particular revelations, both accepted that certain people received messages from this invisible world that could be reported back to those of us without such contact. Both also accepted other types of communications, including dreams and certain forms of prognostication. Messages from the realm of the spirits and the dead included information about the nature of that world and its inhabitants (philosophy), a clear understanding of the desires of the denizens of that world (a religion), and an explanation of the workings of both worlds (cosmology). These messages formed the basis of religion and also provided a mechanism for religious change (Thornton 1992, 238).

Christianity, of course, is based on a series of revelations recorded in the Jewish and Christian scriptures, the Bible. Catholics have accepted additional revelations provided to later individuals, including certain theologians and saints. Protestants, while denying some of these later revelations, also have left open the possibility that certain people can have access to revelations that can modify religious belief and practices. Both groups also accepted lesser revelations provided to individuals through dreams, the conjunction of certain events, apparitions, and the like. However, all these types of revelations were subject to the primacy of the Bible. Any revelation that contradicted the Bible directly or indirectly was ascribed to diabolic powers (Thornton, 239, 249). Thus revelations from unorthodox sources (nonclergy, for example) were often generally disregarded or, more seriously, labeled as heresy or witchcraft and severely punished.

Africans in the areas impacted by the slave trade also had a concept of revelation from the invisible world. Typically African revelations were gained by way of augury and divination, dreams, visions or hearing voices, and spirit possession (Thornton 1992, 39). West and Central African societies had a wide range of such types of revelations, and in many societies individuals were designated as recognized mediums for such messages. We will consider several of these types of revelations, including Ifa, a very popular form of divination that originated among the Yoruba people, and different types of spirit possession. Because such revelations were so common any individual revelation, even one from an important person or well-respected priest, did not usually give rise to any form of orthodoxy. Rather each revelation was seen as important for the person or community to which it was given but not necessarily for the wider community. In addition, any revelation was likely to be modified, overridden, or completely negated by a later revelation. Thus Africans from these areas tended to view any revelation as part of an ongoing communication stream from the invisible world to individuals and communities rather than a single absolute doctrinal statement.

Europeans observing these types of revelations in Africa did not doubt that they were genuinely from the invisible world. However, they generally classified them as diabolic and not to be adhered to. Africans similarly regarded European revelations as genuine but questioned the validity of revelations from the ancient past for contemporary people. Both groups also recognized that revelations needed to be evaluated, since insane people could receive apparent revelations, or those with certain ambitions could feign revelations (Thornton 1992, 239). An important difference between European and African views of revelation was the types of proofs required to make a revelation valid and acceptable. For Europeans a prophet should be able to demonstrate a power or knowledge not available through normal means. Thus miracles formed an important ancillary to Christian revelations, especially Christian scripture (Thornton 1992, 246). For Africans miracles were not the most important proof of the validity of a revelation. Instead, they judged a revelation by how well it worked to predict the future, cure an illness, or locate a guilty party. Among Africans, priests and mediums were constantly challenged to provide proof of the accuracy of their revelations. Anyone whose revelation fell short would be abandoned or perhaps even punished (Thornton 1992, 247). In cases where new revelations contradicted previous revelations, Africans assumed that some circumstance in this world or the world of the spirits had changed. For them no single revelation or series of revelations was considered a final, orthodox statement. Instead the latest revelation was deemed merely an analysis of the current situation and was always subject to be superseded by a still later revelation.

Thornton argues that this last issue led to a different place of the clergy in European and African societies. European clergy depended on an ancient set of revelations that could not be questioned. Strong political powers, kings, and other civil authorities backed up their pronouncements. African clergy, on the other hand, lived at the pleasure of their clients and the accuracy of their latest revelation. They had no power to enforce any strictures or recommendations given in their revelations. These two views of revelation came into conflict when African and European religious views collided, especially in Kongo and Angola. In addition, these conflicts affected the relationship between Africans and the clergy in the Americas (Thornton 1992, 248). Revelations accepted as valid by both Christian missionaries and the local people led to the conversion of the king of Kongo and eventually the wholesale conversion of his people. Much later the Kongolese visionary Dona Beatriz Kimpa Vita's revelation, although accepted by the people, would be called into question by the Christian authorities, leading to her eventual execution as a heretic. And in the mid-eighteenth century, as we shall see, one of the major factors that led to conversions among African Americans was the incorporation of a form of ongoing revelation into the American Christian religious experience.

LOOKING AHEAD

We cannot make a direct connection between the African religious sensibilities in our target cultures and many of the religious sensibilities that developed in what became the United States. We can, however, watch American religious sensibilities change between the colonial and antebellum periods to become more like those of West and West Central Africa and less like those developing in Europe at the same time. We can also suggest that the African beliefs and practices that have become embedded in the wide swathe of American religious sensibilities form a kind of root system that is foundational to the religious sensibilities of the United States. These influences began early in the colonial period and became more visible during the revival period immediately before and after the Civil War. The song of American religious sensibilities began to develop and evolve during the earliest periods of our history, influenced by the tunes and rhythms of Africa. Even into the twentieth and twenty-first centuries, African religious sensibilities continue to influence the larger American religious culture.

The remainder of this book is divided into two interconnected parts. One is an introduction to the cultures of three groups of African peoples that made major contributions to the North American slave trade. Each of these groups was an important player in the trade and each has a fairly well-documented culture. Consequently, we can get a good view of the religious beliefs and practices their people brought with them through the Middle Passage. In chapter 3 we will look specifically at the Kingdom of Kongo in West Central Africa, with brief forays into the neighboring Kingdom of Angola. As several authors have suggested, the influence of Central African cultures in the United States has been largely ignored in earlier explorations of slave culture, perhaps because of its mixed Afro-European heritage (Sweet, 71; Heywood, 13). In chapter 5 we will consider the inland Oyo Empire that some scholars say has produced the newest world religion. In chapter 7 we will look at their cousins in the Kingdom of Dahomey in Western Africa along with its subkingdom of Allada.

Before we begin looking at possible African influences, in chapter 2 we will do a brief survey of the development of American religion from the time of the earliest colonists to the antebellum and Reconstruction periods and beyond. Then, alternating with our forays into African culture, we will trace the development of certain American religious sensibilities. We will focus on religious beliefs and practices that are significantly different from those brought by European colonists and those that developed in Europe during these same time periods. In chapter 4 we will consider attitudes about death, dying, burial practices, and relationships between the living and the dead and the way these practices evolved away from a European style to become more like those found among the Kongolese peoples. In chapter 6 we will look more closely at the history of religion in America and how worship styles and views of God and his relationship to both the saved and the unsaved developed. In this chapter we will also look at how African-heritage peoples were drawn to the Christianity of the First and Second Great Awakenings and the ways in which they influenced the religious beliefs and practices that developed during that period. We will also look at the ways women's place in American religious life has changed. In chapter 8 we will look abroad at Haitian Vodou, a new American religion that drew on religious sensibilities from each of our African groups. We will also consider the ways in which Vodou influenced the similar tradition that developed in the city of New Orleans as well as the magical tradition known as hoodoo.[10] Finally, while we are looking at magical traditions we'll consider the forms of magic and magical thinking known as witchcraft and consider the differences between African and European ideas of witchcraft. Finally in chapter 9 we will look at the new African-based religion of Santería, which arrived on American shores in the mid-to-late twentieth century, and the twentieth-century religious tradition known as Pentecostalism. In that chapter we will also consider what African religions might teach us about religious tolerance. As we shall see, between the colonial period and the dawn of the twenty-first century American Christians saw their relationship with God, and the ways they manifested their beliefs in religious rituals changed significantly. This movement was away from the forms of Christianity colonists brought with them from Europe and toward a more Africanized version of Christianity. Throughout we will look for those deeply rooted African beliefs and practices that have informed and continue to inform Americans of all religious persuasions.

Absent from this book is any analysis of the contributions of African Americans to American music both sacred and secular. These contributions have long been recognized by scholars and others, while the goal of this book is to expose less well-known contributions. Also absent will be consideration of such African-inspired traditions as Rastafari, Garveyism, the Moorish Science Temple, and the Nation of Islam. Although each of these has developed strong followings within the African American community, they have not (yet) had discernable influences on wider American religious sensibilities. I leave the analysis of the future effects of these traditions to others.

2

JESUS IS MY BOSOM FRIEND

The Development of American Religion

When I get dar, Cappen Satan was dar
Says young man, young man, dere's no use for pray,
For Jesus is dead, and God gone away,
And I made him out a liar, and I went my way.

O Satan is a mighty busy old man,
And roll rocks in my way;
But Jesus is my bosom friend
And roll 'em out of de way.[1]

Before we can delve into the ways in which African ideas changed American religious sensibilities we need to review the religious ideas the earliest American colonists brought with them across the seas. In this chapter I will outline a short history of European theological ideas and the development of European religiosity. Then we will turn our attention to the American colonies and look at the history of religion in America, focusing specifically on the development of American religiosity. Finally we will discuss how African Americans may have influenced the ways American religiosity diverged from that of its European counterparts.

HISTORY OF GOD AMONG EUROPEAN CHRISTIANS

As early as AD 320 Christians began serious discussion about the nature of their God and the relationships between that God and his worshippers. At that time a presbyter (local congregational leader) from Alexandria named Arius began to ask difficult questions about the nature of Jesus

23

Christ and his relationship to God the Father. Without denying the divinity of God, Arius suggested that it was blasphemous to think that Jesus was divine by nature and the equal of the Father. As the religious scholar Karen Armstrong says, "Today Arius's name is a byword for heresy," but in his own time there was no official, orthodox position on his questions and no reason to think that his position was inherently wrong (Armstrong, 107–8). Many of the basic theological concepts of Christianity were developed during this time, including the notion that God created the universe ex nihilo, out of nothing, thus constructing a vast chasm between God and the created world. In this view, God "summoned every single being from an abysmal nothingness, and at any moment could withdraw his sustaining hand" (Armstrong, 108). According to the theology developed and refined at this time, Jesus through his death and resurrection redeemed humanity from extinction and enabled humankind to cross that cosmic gulf. Jesus's divine nature became theological fact at the Council of Nicaea in 325.

European ideas about the nature of God and his relationship to humanity continued to develop during the medieval and early modern periods. In the sixteenth century the movement that became the Protestant Reformation again raised these important questions. Martin Luther's God was characterized by his wrath. According to Luther's thinking, no one could endure God's divine anger and there was nothing one could do to appease him. Good works and observance of God's law could not cause one's salvation, could not restore one's relationship with God. People are only able to observe the precepts of religion because God has already saved them. The best that people could do was to surrender to God's will. Calvin expanded and refined Luther's idea to profoundly affect the European Christianity that the first colonists brought to America. Calvin based his theology on his understanding of God's absolute rule. In Calvin's thought, conversion is entirely the work of God, he alone is in control, and individuals were absolutely powerless. Eventually this Calvinistic viewpoint became embedded in the doctrine of predestination, the idea that God has decided for all eternity who will be counted among the elect (who have been saved) and who will be damned to hell for all eternity (Armstrong, 275–82). Such a view of God depends on his description as an all-powerful and changeless being whose decrees are both just and eternal. Such a God was terrifying, a distant sovereign without mercy or compassion. Such a view of God led not only to anxiety among Calvinists such as the American Puritans, but also to what Karen Armstrong characterizes as "a harsh intolerance of those who were not among the elect" (Armstrong, 284). Most of the earliest American colonists, not only the Puritans, followed some version of this Calvinistic viewpoint.

ENLIGHTENMENT RELIGION

Although earlier polemicists hurled the epithet "atheist" at each other, it was only in the seventeenth and eighteenth centuries that Europeans began to cultivate an attitude that would make the denial of God's existence not only possible but also desirable (Armstrong, 288). Around the time the first colonists were landing in North America, European thinkers were reexamining Christian doctrine in the light of the developing scientific method. A new religious viewpoint about the nature of God and his relationship to humanity based on a scientific, rational view of God known as Deism developed. Deism was not a religion in the way that Catholicism, Lutheranism, or the various types of Calvinism were; instead it was a new way of answering philosophical and theological questions. Deists turned their back on the mysticism and mythology of earlier Christianity to declare their allegiance to an impersonal God whom individuals could discover through their own efforts without the necessity for revelation or organized religious hierarchies. Deists refused to believe, as Voltaire, an important spokesperson for this movement, said, "in things that are impossible, contradictory, injurious to divinity and pernicious to mankind, and which dared to menace with eternal punishment anyone possessing common sense" (Armstrong, 310, quoting Voltaire). These philosophers rejected the cruel idea of God that had developed during the Reformation, that he was capable of threatening all of humanity with eternal fire. These thinkers didn't reject the idea of a Christian God (they were not true atheists); rather, they rejected many of the ideas about God that had developed during the previous centuries that they felt led to superstition and fanaticism. They believed that all the trappings of religion were not necessary to come to knowledge of God. It was a short step from this rational understanding of God to the more radical position of Emmanuel Kant that there was no way to prove or disprove the existence of God and that our ideas of God are only a convenience in developing a moral culture, a strategy enabling us to function more efficiently and morally. The final step away from a religious worldview was to dispense with this tenuous idea of God completely, to move to true atheism.

Alongside this developing atheism another religious sensibility that relied on neither traditional doctrines nor rationalistic ideas but on personal religious experience, a "religion of the heart," was developing. In eighteenth-century England, John and Charles Wesley and their followers were attempting to shake off centuries of religious dogmatism and ritualism to return to what they saw as the original plain and genuine Christianity of the first Christians. For these so-called Methodists the experience of being "born again" was crucial in order to *experience* God and his eternal love. This was an intensely personal, internal religious experience that depended not on doctrines but on each individual's own emotional, ecstatic religious experience. About the same time the Wesleys were preaching this new approach to religion, the first Quakers, George Fox, James Naylor, and their disciples, were suggesting that all people, men and women of all social classes or statuses, had an inner light that could be discovered and nurtured. With the help of this inner light one could approach God directly and achieve one's own salvation here on earth. These internalized, emotional religious sentiments often led to emotional and even violent religious expressions. However, when the emotional enthusiasm passed, as it generally did, the people were often left in a state of suicidal dejection. Those who survived both the heights of ecstasy and the depths of despair were left in a more joyful and calmer state than before their awakening (Armstrong, 324).

By the beginning of the nineteenth century, the Deism of the elite had begun to transform into an atheistic religious viewpoint. The century would give Europeans Ludwig Feuerbach, Karl Marx, Charles Darwin, Friedrich Nietzsche, and Sigmund Freud, who would propel many to replace theological explanations of reality with scientific ones. Soon it would appear that rational human beings would find traditional ideas of God inadequate, the cause of centuries of superstition and bigotry. Even the Romantics, who found rationalism reductive and unimaginative, reinterpreted the myths and mysteries of Christianity in a more secular way, translating heaven and hell, rebirth and redemption into a more intellectually acceptable idiom. The Romantics, who were poets and novelists rather than theologians and clergymen, proclaimed a return to mystic, intuitive activities outside the confines of church or religious institutions. Nineteenth-century philosophers rebelled against previous notions of God as an otherworldly being who watched like a celestial Big Brother, condemning humanity to servitude and utter dependence. As political liberation swept through Europe, so did concepts of psychological and spiritual freedom. Secularism began to hold sway throughout the continent. Many of the best and brightest of Europe's nineteenth-century thinking lamented the denial of God and the withdrawal of faith from the culture, but by the twentieth century European religious sensibilities could only be described as "the cult of secularism that claimed independence from God" (Armstrong, 325). European secularism and atheism seemed to spell the end to religiosity on the continent. Atheism was no longer the ideology of just the intellectual elite but the prevailing mood of common people. For many people freedom from the vengeful God of the past was a welcome relief; for others what Sartre called a God-sized hole in human consciousness left desolation. In either case, one was counseled that only through freedom from God could humanity become fully human. Many agreed with Freud that religious belief was part of an immature stage of human development that reason and modern scientific knowledge have overcome.[2]

A SHORT HISTORY OF RELIGION IN AMERICA

The earliest Europeans in what is now the United States were the Spanish conquistadors and their Catholic priests, who arrived from the south and traveled along the western coast of what is now California and southwestern regions of Arizona and New Mexico. They established missions throughout this area in an attempt to convert the indigenous people, which met with mixed success. However, they had little influence on the development of American religious sensibilities until much later in their history. The primary influences were the Protestant dissenters who populated the northeastern coastal areas and the Anglicans who established the first plantations in what became known as the middle and southern colonies. Although these people came from several different European countries, it was the British who formed the cultural core of what would become the United States. The English church separated from the authority of the Pope in 1534 during the reign of King Henry VIII. Although Henry himself maintained a strong preference for traditional Catholic practices, after his death Protestant-influenced forms of worship began to be adopted and a strong anti-Catholicism developed. This movement toward Protestantism was interrupted during the reign of the Catholic queen, Mary I, but was continued and solidified during the long reign of her sister and successor Elizabeth I (1558–1603). Under Elizabeth the Church of England developed its own middle way of religious sensibility, emphasizing its continuity with the Catholic and apostolic church fathers while expressing a moderately Reformed doctrine.

Within this structure several dissenting groups who opposed state interference in religious matters arose, including the Puritans and Pilgrims, who fled England for the Netherlands and later immigrated to the American continent, where they established colonies in what is now known as

New England. The Pilgrims arrived at Plymouth Colony in 1620, and the Puritans migrated to the Massachusetts Bay Colony between 1620 and 1640. The earliest religion culture of the American colonies was Calvinistic, as represented in the Congregational north by these English Separatists and in the Anglican south by the inhabitants of Jamestown, Virginia, founded 1607, and the surrounding settlements. The Calvinism they espoused is based on two main ideas: that God is able to save every person he chooses and that his efforts to do so are not affected by the good or evil actions of those individuals. These ideas are based on a doctrine of total depravity, the idea that people are naturally sinful and inclined to reject the rule of God. Individuals cannot choose to follow God and are unable to make any efforts toward their own salvation. Instead, God has chosen from all eternity those whom he will save through the sacrifice of Jesus Christ. This election is based on God's own mercy, not the virtue, merit, or faith of the individual. Those who have been chosen for salvation and those who are condemned to damnation cannot change their status in any way. People are expected to worship God and live good lives because they are dependent upon God, not because doing so has any influence on their chances for salvation.

According to these early American Calvinists, everyone is born ignorant of his or her status with respect to salvation. However, it was expected that one would have a conversion experience, generally during adolescence, that illuminated one's status. Thomas Hooker, founder of the Connecticut Colony in 1636, identified seven stages of this conversion: (1) contrition for one's sins, (2) humiliation at one's sins, (3) a call from God, (4) justification, by imputation of Christ's merits, (5) adoption by the Spirit, (6) sanctification, producing virtuous acts, and (7) glorification, the complete salvation in heaven (Wills, 56–57). Once individuals became convinced that they were truly converted and had reached at least the first five of Hooker's stages, they went before the religious congregation, the "saints" who had themselves already been converted, to testify as to their conversion. Members of the congregation validated that one had really been saved and welcomed the newest saint into full communication with the congregation (Wills, 55). Regardless of one's deeply felt conviction of salvation and the assurance of the other members of the congregation, one's conversion could always be called into question. What if the individual was fooling himself, or the other "saints"? What if one fell into sin? Had he or she really been converted in the first place? Puritans, the most severe of the Calvinists, lived in a constant state of uncertainty, never fully assured that their conversion was authentic. As Willis says, "Puritanism required a believer to find certainty in uncertainty—required him (or her) to rely for salvation on unmerited, predestined saving grace while spending a lifetime doing unrewarded good works; required him to search his soul for the Holy Spirit but denied him access to direct revelation; required him to be pure but told him he could not be" (Wills, 54). And those who had not (or not yet) experienced conversion were still expected to support the church, attend services, and live virtuous lives with both civil and religious authorities enforcing the religious moral codes.

Although this extreme view of salvation was different from the more moderate views of congregations in the middle colonies and the south, it became the model of American religiosity and, as we shall see, has been extremely influential in the later development of the American religious sensibility. However, Anglicans in the middle and southern colonies followed an Arminian form of Calvinism. According to the Dutch theologian Jacob Arminius, God knows but does not control whether or not an individual can achieve salvation. According to this view individuals have the free will to affect their own salvation by making appropriate ethical and moral choices. Colonists in the middle and southern colonies, however, were notorious for their lack of religious fervor in spite of the fact that during the first meeting of the Virginia House of Burgesses, the colonial legislative assembly took up religion as a major task and "passed laws to uphold 'God's service' in the new world" (Butler 2008, 49). Churches were established in the towns, and laws were passed requiring colonists to attend services regularly as well as to support the local congregation with their taxes. However, the settlements in these areas were geographically isolated and it appears that when they did get together, colonists were more interested in social activities than attending church services.

Puritan colonists brought what would become Baptist sentiments to the American colonies in a search for religious freedom. Roger Williams, a British separatist, landed in Massachusetts in the mid-1600s but was exiled by 1635. Sent out into the "howling wilderness," he soon established the Providence Plantations in the colony of Rhode Island, where religious liberty was granted to all. There he established the first Baptist church in America in 1638. Baptist churches were soon spread through the colonies to as far south as Charleston, South Carolina (B. Leonard, 13–14). By the eighteenth century Baptist churches in Virginia and throughout the south were beginning to challenge the religious domination of the Anglican establishment (B. Leonard, 15). Early American Baptists encompassed both Calvinist and Arminian theologies, generally distinguished as Particular and General Baptists (only certain, particular people have been saved, or all have the potential to be saved).

Both in the north and south religiosity declined throughout the later half of the 1600s. Colonists became increasingly lax in their own religious observance while also becoming more intolerant of the observances of others. Even in areas with little religious diversity disagreement arose among the colonists, raising the level of religious intolerance (Butler 2008, 50–51). Puritanism began to fail when people no longer felt constrained by the discipline of a godly life that was, according to their Calvinist beliefs, unlikely to grant them salvation (Butler 2008, 55). Baptist, Presbyterian, and Quaker congregations as well as non-English congregations competed with established Puritan and Anglican congregations for members (Butler 2008, 59). During the late seventeenth and early eighteenth centuries and the run-up to the Revolutionary War, the American religious scene showed two competing movements. On the one hand, religious diversity was increasing exponentially, so that by the eve of the Revolution variety had become one of the hallmarks of the American religious scene. In addition to the Puritans in the north and the Anglicans in the south, the colonies were home to Scottish and Scotch-Irish Presbyterians, English and Welsh Baptists, Quakers, German Lutherans, German Reformed and Dutch Reformed congregations, Mennonites, Moravians, Catholics, English Methodists, French Huguenots, Jews, and others. On the other hand, in spite of the wide range of religious choices around them, many of the American colonists were moving toward the same sort of religious indifference found among European intellectuals of the time (Butler 2008, 72–73).

An important religious innovation brought about by the American colonists was the idea of congregational independence, sometimes characterized as congregational polity. From the earliest years of Christianity until late in the Reformation, individual congregations were organized in a hierarchical structure in which every church was under the authority of a higher-level religious leader such as a bishop. In the Roman Catholic church, bishops were under the authority of archbishops who were under the authority of cardinals who were under the authority of the Pope. Although Protestants eliminated some of these positions, individual congregations continued to be under the authority of higher-level functionaries. In the Church of England the highest authority rested with the king, but practically the church was governed by a synod of bishops each of whom was responsible for all the congregations within a certain geographic area.

Although the northern American colonies were generally independent of the Church of England, in Virginia and later throughout the south, the colonial congregations were tightly linked to the Anglican church back home and its synod, with each congregation under the authority of a bishop, generally the bishop of London. The bishop was responsible for the training and ordination of ministers in England and their assignment to congregations. In England, generally these assignments were lifetime appointments, with ministers' salaries often paid for by benefactors who may or may not have been part of the congregation. In the American colonies both north and south, the support for the church and its ministers fell to the colonists themselves. Since there were no seminaries in the colonies, Anglican groups looking for a minister had to petition their bishop to send someone to them. The cost of the minister's transportation to the colony and his maintenance once he arrived was the responsibility of the colonial group. Although the British bishops tried to maintain control over the colonial churches, it soon became clear that the bishops back in England had little power to enforce their will on the distant colonies. The day-to-day operations of the colonial Anglican churches became the responsibility of an all-powerful, locally elected vestry or governing board. Very quickly the vestries took over control of the churches, maintaining the church buildings and property, hiring and firing ministers, and taxing members for the support of the church and its minister. The vestry was also responsible for the maintenance of church doctrine, conformity to orthodoxy in ritual forms, and the use of orthodox hymnals and prayers books (Klein, 151–53). Although the Virginia vestry was originally established as an elected body, by the mid-1600s the electoral system was abolished and vestries became autocratic, self-replicating bodies (Klein, 153–55). In spite of the fact that British bishops continued to train, ordain, and appoint ministers, vestries held the purse strings, and ministers who fell out of favor with their vestrymen soon found themselves out of the pulpit. For this reason, Herbert S. Klein suggests, ministers in Virginia often found themselves questioning and modifying standard church dogma, discipline, and ceremonies in order to satisfy their parishioners as represented by their vestrymen (Klein, 154–55).

EARLY AFRICAN AMERICAN RELIGIOSITY

Blacks first arrived in New Amsterdam (soon to become New York) in 1526 as indentured servants. Around 1677 perpetual enslavement became the rule and by 1700 black slavery had become legal throughout the Eastern Seaboard and in all of the thirteen original colonies. During this earliest period, colonial slave owners thought that converting and baptizing their slaves would lead to their emancipation, as it was believed that Christians should not own one another (Butler 2008, 101). Thus there was little effort to convert blacks or give them any sort of religious instruction, even those who might have been baptized either in their homelands or along their journey to the American colonies. There was, however, ambiguity among the master class concerning the enslaved. According to the European clergy and their white congregants, whatever religion the enslaved brought with them from Africa (even Kongolese Christianity) was a form of idolatry that ought to be suppressed (Wills, 42). On the one hand, the enslaved ought to be converted, since allowing this "devil worship" to continue on what was considered the religiously pristine new continent was dangerous. As Cotton Mather says in his *The Negro Christianized*, Africans were "vassals of Satan" and "servants of Iniquity," who "do with devilish rites actually worship devils or maintain a magical conversation with devils" (Mather, 3, 8, 15). Thus conversion was imperative to protect the people and the land. However, from the colonial period until the Second Great Awakening in the early nineteenth century, even when they had convinced themselves that conversion need not lead to emancipation, few clergymen and fewer masters were willing to engage the enslaved in efforts toward conversion. Consequently, few African-heritage peoples were converted to the forms of Protestant Christianity around them.

Forms of African Christian religiosity were not completely absent during the colonial period either, particularly among the more elite African-heritage peoples of the northern areas. Liam Riordan documents the establishment of an African American denomination independent of white control in the Delaware Valley soon after the end of the Revolutionary War. Taking advantage of a 1787 law that permitted all Christian groups to incorporate their own congregations, free blacks in this area asserted their own right to worship separately by establishing the Union Church of Africans (UCA). In their own church UCA members were able to embrace Christianity on their own terms while also celebrating their African heritage (Riordan, 207, 222). Similarly Richard Allen, a former slave turned Methodist minister, established the first black church in Philadelphia, Bethel Church, in 1787, as well as the first independent black denomination, the African Methodist Episcopal Church, in 1816. Allen was elected the first bishop of the new denomination, thereby becoming the first black bishop in the Americas (Newman, 173, 130, 177). Although Newman's outstanding biography of Allen gives few examples of direct African influence on Allen's religious and political activities, hints show through. As Newman remarks, Allen constantly "embraced his identity as a former slave and person of color" (Newman, 111). Importantly, he also consistently included "African" in the names of the many organizations he founded during his extremely busy life, including, as Newman outlines, "the 'Free African Society,' a black mutual-aid group formed in 1787; the 'African Methodist Episcopal Church,' an autonomous African American religious organization, formed in the early 1790s; the 'African Society for the Education of Youth,' formed in 1804. When Allen discovered in 1807 that white religious leaders had craftily conceived legal documents undermining his own church's autonomy, he wrote a rebuttal of their actions entitled simply the 'African Supplement'" (Newman, 33).

In addition, anyone familiar with the important role blacksmiths and their smithies served as religious space throughout West Africa (Barnes) is struck by the fact that not only did Allen drag a former blacksmith shop to the plot of land he bought for Bethel Church to serve as the church's first building in 1794, but "The Roughcast," as the building was called, continued to be valorized for its original usage. An 1876 painting of the early church shows a small group listening to a preacher who is standing on a slightly raised platform in a space devoid of any other features except a door opening to the outside on the far right and a blacksmith's anvil set in an alcove on the left (Newman, 71, 76). Newman says that Allen "loved" the idea of conversion, including his own conversion from a suffering slave to a free person of color and from a nonbeliever to a Christian (71). He may also have loved the idea of converting an African sacred space into a Christian one.

Other attempts at conversion were not entirely absent. However, the earliest attempts by the European master class to convert their African bondspeople or the few free Africans in the colonies were generally dismal failures, especially in the Anglican south. As Sylvia Frey and Betty Wood suggest in their text *Come Shouting to Zion: Protestantism in the American South and British Caribbean to 1830* (Frey and Wood), Anglicanism held little appeal for Africans and their early descendants. Anglican owners thought that the few who converted were attempting to soften the conditions of their enslavement or even to sue for freedom, which may have been partially true, but comparing colonial Anglicanism to the religious traditions Africans would have left behind suggests that there was little that Anglicanism could offer to entice or encourage conversion (Frey and Wood, 75). Protestant Christianity was born from Luther's idea that every person should be able to read and interpret the Bible for themselves. As the Protestant movement developed, the reasons for choosing one denomination over another were deeply theological. Such religiosity demanded a certain level of theological knowledge and biblical literacy. Those few Anglican clergymen who attempted to convert the enslaved modified ideas about personal religious responsibility to better conform to the needs of the master class for docile servants and the assumed intellectual inferiority of the enslaved. Thus the enslaved were taught a type of Christianity that focused on blind unthinking submission in this life and freedom and the good life only after death. According to these teachings, the Christian slave who was not submissive but engaged in "roguery, mischief, and lying," "knavery or murmuring," could be punished by the master while alive and by the devil after death (Frey and Wood, 76).

Africans, even those exposed to Christianity in their homelands, would have found little reason to explore Christian conversion in the American colonies. In the Anglican south the central goal of ministerial work among the colonists was to encourage adherence to Christian practice through leading Sabbath services, performing marriages and funerals, and catechizing throughout the parish. Parishioners were encouraged to attend Sabbath services regularly and to lead well-regulated Christian lives. Services were sober events with little of the public ceremonialism so bitterly criticized as typical of Catholic practice. Services consisted principally of extended sermons focused on a theology that combined rationalism, moralism, and piety. Outbursts of what was called "enthusiasm" were soundly censured as morbid and pathological. Sabbath services were also an opportunity for the laity to gather for secular social activities such as gambling and horse racing (Butler 1990, 166–67). None of this would have seemed particularly religious for Africans who were used to extravagant public rituals that often included drumming, dancing, and the injection of spiritual beings into the event through the phenomenon of possession trance. Anglicanism had no place for the honored ancestors and offered little hope for any softening of the blows of everyday life. In addition, the enslaved would have noticed that the same people who proclaimed Christian virtues on Sunday engaged in extreme acts of brutality towards their bondspeople during the week.

This lack of interest in conversion from either side left an opening for Africans and their descendants to continue the religious and spiritual activities of their homelands, including secret meetings to engage in healing and prophecy, rites of passage including funerals and perhaps weddings, and those public rituals often characterized as "devil dances" by European observers. Important to these meetings and rituals were the African concepts of spirit and the ability of spiritual beings to possess and speak through selected human beings (Pitts, 36–38). Much of the religious activities of non-Christian African Americans remained hidden from their European masters and even their indentured counterparts. We can suggest two reasons for this. First of all, African religious sensibilities were so different from those of

Europeans as to be unrecognizable as religious. While Europeans expected to sit for long hours in churches and chapels listening to emotionally sterile sermons and singing ponderous hymns, the public face of African religiosity would have been exhibited through a livelier musical form and a dancing style that often led to the voice of deities or ancestors spoken through possessed individuals. Secondly, much African religious activity on both sides of the Atlantic was secret or at least private. Individuals engaged priests and diviners in identifying and healing personal and familial dis-ease, and many religious functionaries were available to help individuals and families maintain relationships with the denizens of the invisible world. In general Europeans would not have noticed many of these activities, and even when they became visible to non-Africans they were often ignored or characterized as "superstition" or consorting with the devil.

However, we know both from the archeological record and because certain of these activities persisted into later generations that Africans did not lose or forget their indigenous cosmological worldviews, their ways of worship, or their techniques for interacting with otherworldly beings. In fact, as Mechal Sobel says, when the spiritual revivalism of the First Great Awakening reached Virginia after 1750, it only took root where "whites were in extensive and intensive contact with blacks," so that over the next fifty years, this phenomenon was a shared black and white experience in which the worldviews of generally lower-class whites and both free and enslaved blacks were "stimulated, permeated and invigorated" by interaction with each other (Sobel, 180). Blacks learned the Christian story through preaching, hymns, and bible classes while their white counterparts became more open to ecstasy and an intense spiritual life, willing both to have religious experiences and share those experiences with others (Sobel, 203). In addition, Africans shared their views of death not as a terrifying unknown but as a gateway to a continuation of this visible world and a place where one could reunite with family and friends (Sobel, 203). It was during this period that blacks began to meld their African religious ideas with Christian beliefs and practices to create a uniquely African American religiosity that became the black church, and whites modified their religiosity away from its European base.

FIRST GREAT AWAKENING

The American colonists were pre-Enlightenment thinkers, and Gary Wills suggests that the First and Second Great Awakenings (1730s and 1740s and about 1800 to about 1860) were partially dependent on and the results of the Enlightenment and the growth of Enlightenment thinking in America. Among the American Enlightenment thinkers were the Deists, who were among the founding fathers of the United States, including Benjamin Franklin, Thomas Jefferson, James Madison, Thomas Paine, and George Washington. Deists thought that reason and observation of the natural world, without the need for any organized religion, could be used to determine that there was a supernatural being that created the universe. They rejected supernatural events such as miracles and prophecy, believing that this supernatural being (God) did not intervene in human affairs or suspend the laws of nature. Another important influence on American religious sensibilities was the Romantic movement. Romanticism developed in the second half of the eighteenth century as a reaction against scientific rationalism and the social and political norms of the Enlightenment. The Romantics said that Enlightenment thinkers overvalued rationality and undervalued nonrational human experience such as the emotions, intuition, and the like. In the American religious landscape Romanticism was expressed in two different ways. Among the elite in the northeast, the Transcendentalists found God in nature and in the sacred texts of Eastern traditions, particularly the Bhagavad Gita, a small part of the much larger Hindu epic the Mahabharata. Transcendentalists found salvation not in church but in the "cathedral of nature." However, they also carried forward many of the Congregational tenets of earlier times, especially an individualist spirit of salvation, the dichotomy between what the Congregationalists called the "regenerate" and the "unregenerate," and the vision that they had a special responsibility to transform history (Wills, part two and part three).

However, Transcendentalism was an intellectual movement primarily limited to the educated elite of New England. In the rest of the country (remembering that the rest of the country in the mid-eighteenth century was the Atlantic seaboard, with some frontier settlements in Kentucky, Ohio, and Tennessee), Romanticism gave rise to the Second Great Awakening (about 1800 to the 1860s) and the so-called Methodist explosion. By this time, blacks were beginning to have a noticeable effect on the American religious landscape. According to the first national census of 1790, a fifth of the country's population was black, with the majority of those enslaved, generally but not exclusively in the southern states. As we've discussed, during the early colonial period little effort was made to convert blacks to any form of Christianity. It was only during the First Awakening in the 1730s and 1740s that the work of black conversion began. As Sylvia Frey and Betty Wood say, "The growth of the enslaved African population and its geographic concentration coupled with a general lowering of linguistic barriers, especially in the older plantation societies, created conditions uniquely favorable to the evangelical missionaries who made their first appearance in the late 1730s" (Frey and Wood, 82). These early missionaries to the slave quarters presented a view of Christianity different from that found in the local Anglican churches. They put an emphasis on spiritual equality dependent not so much on a literate understanding of the Bible and theology but on a direct communication with the supernatural. Although conversion could not provide any relief from the rigors of southern slavery, it did promise an afterlife freed from want, illness, and fear for those who converted (Frey and Wood, 90). Methodist and Baptist missionaries were the most influential in this effort.

The Methodist movement begun in England by the Wesley brothers, John and Charles, was decidedly Arminian in its outlook. According to this position, although humans are naturally unable to make any effort toward their own salvation, and that salvation is predicated on the sacrifice of Jesus Christ, individuals have the responsibility for accepting or rejecting the salvation offered by God. Salvation is only possible through God's grace, so that no work or human effort can cause or contribute to one's salvation. However, one is free to reject that saving grace and it is possible to lose one's salvation through persistent and unrepented sin.

John Wesley and those preachers who followed him became notorious for their enthusiastic preaching style. Such preaching was completely different from the dry intellectual style of the Anglicans and other British denominations. Many observers felt that enthusiastic responses to such preaching were dangerous, leading people into madness or at least credulity, superstition, and fanaticism. However, early enthusiasm was very low-key according to the standards that would develop later. John Wesley's earliest British converts exhibited merely warmth and earnestness, although some would shout out, faint, or fall. The convulsions, holy laughing, and other spectaculars typical of later American Methodist services were very unusual (Beckmann, 16). John Wesley himself interpreted this enthusiastic behavior not as evidence of the Spirit's presence but as the last throes of the devil being ejected from one's soul, the violent struggles of one grasping toward repentance and peace with God (Beckmann, 16). It wasn't until the Second Great Awakening, the first major success in evangelism among African Americans, that the full force of these phenomena was exhibited.

In New England, it was the preaching of George Whitefield, a disciple and colleague of the Wesleys, and of the American preacher Jonathan Edwards that inspired the waves of emotional religious fervor known as the

First Great Awakening (1730–1755). This short-lived revival foreshadowed the Second Great Awakening, which would take Americans on a completely different religious trajectory from their European counterparts. George Whitefield (1714–1770), who attended Oxford with the Wesley brothers, was instrumental in the development of American Methodism and African American Christianity. He was one of the founders of Methodism and became one of the best-known preachers in eighteenth-century America. In 1740 he preached series of revivals that became known as the Great Awakening. Although the majority of his evangelical work was in New England, he traveled as far south as Charleston, generally preaching in open-air venues, rather than stuffy churches. Whitefield developed a special relationship with a handful of African men and women who helped him establish his ministry (Frey and Wood, 91), and for a short period between 1782 and the early 1800s Virginian slaveholders under the influence of Methodism liberated nearly six thousand of their enslaved bondspeople (Newman, 143–44). While Whitefield himself was more purely Calvinistic in his outlook, American Methodism would eventually take a decided Arminianist turn. Caught up in the religious fervor that swept through their area, the good, sober, orderly people of Edwards's parish soon became "born again" after being broken by the fear of God and then experiencing a sudden wave of elation as they felt they had been saved by his mercy. A whole range of intensely emotional expressions, including laughter, tears, and loud cries, expressed these internal experiences.

SINNERS IN THE HAND OF AN ANGRY GOD

In July 1741 Jonathan Edwards, an early American theologian, delivered one of the best-known sermons of his time. Entitled "Sinners in the Hands of an Angry God," its vivid imagery of hell and observations about the secular world show the theology of the First Great Awakening (Edwards et al.).[3] Edwards's Arminian form of Calvinism suggested that individuals needed to make the appropriate ethical and moral choices in order to achieve the salvation promised by God and won for them by Jesus Christ. Edwards's sermon spoke directly to those who had not yet realized their own depravity and had not yet made the choice to mend their evil ways and turn to Christ. According to Edwards the wicked were already under God's condemnation and might at any moment be given over to Satan and cast into hell. Simply because one was not in hell at this time, simply because death seemed like a distant and unlikely future, simply because one felt as though one was able to care for oneself or that another would care for one, one was *not* safe from God's eternal damnation. Only by waking up to one's plight and fleeing to Christ could one escape the horrific fate outlined. According to Edwards, God was as angry with the living wicked as with those he was currently tormenting in hell at that very moment. If those listening did not feel the fierceness of his wrath, it was only a matter of time before they would. In one of his most famous images, Edwards characterizes God as one who holds a noxious bug over the flame of a fire by a single thread. At any moment his hold may be loosened and the pitiful insect dropped to its fiery doom. While Edwards's God was described as "angry," in much of the imagery he appeared cold and impassionate, neither vengeful nor caring. God had chosen not to cast the wicked in the fire of hell immediately but instead was waiting for the appointed time of their deaths, when they would fall to the fiery punishment by the weight of both their own sinful nature and their natural depravity. This sermon and others like it led New Englanders and others to a new type of religious "enthusiasm" characterized by swooning, outcries, and convulsions.

While many of the founding fathers of the United States were self-proclaimed Deists, the Awakening appealed to the poorer, lower-status members of the new nation. These were the people who would have found little consolation either in the cool rationality of Deism or in the harsh doctrines of Puritan Calvinism. For them the feelings of joy they felt as part of their conversion gave them something new, a God-given experience of enlightenment that was available to all, even the lowest members of society, many of whom had previously been barred from religious participation. Karen Armstrong argues that both the Deism of the elite and the revivalist spirit of the lower classes helped to fuel the impending American Revolution as both groups believed that human effort could "hasten the coming of God's Kingdom, which was attainable and imminent in the New World" (Armstrong, 325). This emotional form of religiosity was short-lived, but it set the stage for a second, greater awakening a generation later.

SECOND GREAT AWAKENING

The Second Great Awakening, begun in 1790, was the evangelical movement that continued Whitefield's method of bringing salvation to the people instead of expecting the people to come to the church seeking salvation. Missionaries, principally Methodists but also some Baptists, spread throughout the mid-Atlantic and southern states preaching not only in churches and town squares but on farms and plantations. These circuit riders soon began to gather people together in revivals where, through preaching and exhortation, they could convert masses of people and bring them into the assembly of the saved. Typically revivals brought people to the conversion experience that Ann Taves typified into two movements: a downward movement that was an "internalization of the Calvinist view of God as judge and humans as totally sinful or depraved, in need of salvation, and yet unable to save themselves," and an upward movement "centered on the internalization of the view of God as gracious and loving" and the realization that one may indeed have been saved (Taves, 22). Important to these movements was the outward physical expression of one's inward spiritual journey. Just as Wesley had interpreted the milder forms of enthusiasm as one's struggles toward repentance, the phenomena of shouting, falling, and even convulsions that exemplified revivals and early Methodist and Baptist services were interpreted as the last violent struggles with the devil as the sinner moved toward repentance and peace with God (Beckmann, 16). Another important change exhibited during this period was that the newly converted could join together to form congregations or could join existing congregations without gaining the permission of any other ecclesiastical authority. One's own spiritual experience was sufficient (B. Leonard, 19).

African religiosity played an important part in the development of these spectacles. Although since the early beginnings of slavery in the American colonies Anglican churchmen had delivered assurances that the conversion of African and African American bondsmen and bondswomen would not require that they be freed, there had been little incentive for the master class to offer the fruits of Christianity to the enslaved. However, by this period preachers took a different tack in offering their services. They were beginning to suggest to the master class that conversion would make the enslaved more compliant and accepting of their situation. Christianized slaves, it was suggested, would be less likely to engage in activities opposed to the best interest of the master, such as stealing, malingering, running away, or rebelling. At the same time conversion in these settings didn't require any knowledge of Christian ritual and dogma but instead was based on a personal experience of repentance and conversion. The lack of requirement for any type of religious education meant that missionaries could honor the law prohibiting slave literacy. And as Christian rituals became more like the African ones that Africans and African Americans were already familiar with, including the possibility for a type of possession experience, they were drawn toward these forms of Christianity.

The focus of most of the efforts of the circuit riders was toward the middling and lower sort, including the enslaved. Many prided themselves on their willingness to preach in the slave quarters. As the movement grew and spread, blacks became an important part of local congregations and revivals. For a short time during the antebellum period blacks and whites worshipped together. Because the Baptist and Methodists tended to have an open organizational structure both black and white members could take leadership positions, and independent black religious associations could operate outside the direct purview of the master class. There are records of black church members and leaders both among the laity and the ministry, and it was during this time that African ideas of religiosity were directly incorporated into the developing American religious sensibilities. Free black Methodists and Baptists also served as missionaries to their enslaved brethren. Many black churches were founded during this period. Often they were mixed-race churches or members of mixed-race denominational structures. As early as the late eighteenth century, many of these churches separated from the white-dominated denominations to form their own independent African American congregations and denominations (Butler 2008, 105).

For many, both blacks and whites, conversion during this period was often preceded by great distress, an illness or weakness followed by a vision or dream where one is shown both the fires of hell and the beauties of heaven. Sin was seen as a sickness, the cure for which was baptism. Such visions were a prerequisite for conversion—until one had such a vision one was not considered ready for baptism. Whites had little cultural experience with the "fits" enthusiastic preaching and such visions engendered and tended to merely endure them as part of the necessary movement from sin to salvation (Gomez, 253). However, among black converts the "dreams, visions, trances, voices" required for conversion were welcomed and generally continued after baptism. Among blacks such communal visionary experiences came to form the basis of worship. As Beckmann suggests, this type of trance experience would reshape American Christianity as blacks taught their white counterparts this religious technology.

By 1801 when nearly 10 percent of the population of Kentucky met at Cane Ridge, the revival movement had come into its own. Thousands were converted during that single event. Many exhibited the most extreme forms of trance behavior, including spasmodic jerking, holy laughter, barking, hysterical dancing, shouting, or sobbing. For those familiar with West African–style possession trance the similarities are stunning. Subsequent revivals replayed the events of Cane Ridge until sinners were exhibiting these phenomena throughout Tennessee, North Carolina,

Georgia, Ohio territory, western Pennsylvania, and Maryland (Beckmann, 18). Blacks generally had an independent role at these revivals. They set up separate encampments and often had their own preachers and exhorters. When left to their own devices blacks tended to engage in more extreme convulsive outbursts, often to the consternation of white officials. However, when blacks and whites mingled together in a single service, the general consensus was that the meetings were more exciting and powerful (Beckmann, 19).

Theological understanding and knowledge of basic Christian dogma were not very important to revivalists. The enslaved themselves seemed to feel that a relationship with God was most important, and missionaries were often astonished at their lack of basic Christian education. The same tended to be true among lower-class whites who suffered a similar lack of education and literacy. Masters wanted their slaves to learn obedience and passivity, while the enslaved focused on ideas of freedom and eventual liberation. Neither was sufficiently interested in a systematic teaching of Christian theology. However, not all of the enslaved were caught in the large plantation system that typifies our view of southern slavery. Along the western frontier, for example in Kentucky, most of the enslaved were domestic workers or skilled laborers who worked alongside their masters and mistresses in taming the wilderness (Beckmann, 18). In these areas the enslaved tended to be more respected and better treated than on the larger more impersonal plantations in the Deep South. Both situations were instrumental in the development of American religiosity. In areas where blacks and whites lived and worshipped together, whites were able to share their knowledge and understanding of the Bible and Christian theology, while blacks shared the technology of trance and contact with the invisible world. In areas where blacks were sequestered into slave quarters that were often the size of small villages, the enslaved were able to worship in the manner they found most satisfying.

By the 1860s Evangelicals, principally Methodists and Baptists, made up at least 85 percent of the American church population. This is astonishing considering that there was also a population boom during this period. In 1775 the population of the entire United States was less that half that of England, yet by 1845 Americans outnumbered the English by five million (Wills, 288). Between 1800 and 1860 the Methodists went from 65,000 members to 1,744,000 (or more, since these statistics are notoriously unreliable) (Wills, 288). Missionaries from these two denominations had managed to convert a huge percentage of a much larger American population. As early as the 1830s blacks and whites had begun the process of creating segregated spiritual communities. But both groups continued to include the trance behavior they had developed during their time together.

AFRICANISMS IN AMERICAN RELIGIONS

There has been a long-standing assumption among scholars that Africans brought to South America and the Caribbean were more able to retain their cultural heritages than those brought to North America. In terms of religion, proof of this assumption is generally seen in the development of African-influenced religions such as Vodou in Haiti, Santería in Cuba, and Candomblé in Brazil, while no such corresponding development is found in North America. In his 1978 text *Slave Religion: The "Invisible Institution" in the Antebellum South*, Albert Raboteau critiques Herskovits's suggestion that not only the "shouting" that is so characteristic of black churches but also the theological view that "God, Jesus and the Holy Spirit are all concerned with the immediate fate of those who worship them" reflect the retention of a certain "Africanism" by their participants and are "deviations from the practices and beliefs of white Baptists." Raboteau says that this is not a convincing argument since both this theology and these ritual practices were commonly found in the white Holiness and Pentecostal churches of his day (Raboteau, 56–57, quoting Herskovits's *Myth of the Negro Past*). However, as we shall see, these beliefs and practices seem to have actually originated in black and biracial congregations and migrated to white congregations. As we have suggested, African-style religious activities were Christianized and continued during the revival period between 1750 and 1822. Africans and African Americans who were already well versed in the movements of the spirit were drawn to the emotional Christianity of the revivalist traditions of this period. According to the doctrines developed at this time, salvation was available to everyone regardless of class, skin color, or economic status, rather than to the select few of earlier Calvinistic preaching (Pitts, 42). All that was required for salvation was a direct conversion experience, that is, becoming overwhelmed by the Holy Spirit. For a short while during this period those drawn to this new type of Christianity, generally poor whites and both free and enslaved blacks, attended revivals and formed congregations together. In those situations where blacks and whites worshipped together, blacks taught whites their ecstatic worship style. Later, when these congregations segregated themselves by race, many whites continued in the worship patterns taught to them by their former black coreligionists. As we shall see in chapter 9, blacks and whites came together again in the early twentieth century in Pentecostal churches and again the movements of the spirit were important characteristics of worship. Consequently, it is probable that Raboteau has his causation wrong. There is good evidence that whites in Holiness and Pentecostal churches learned these beliefs and practices from their African-heritage coreligionists and remembered them when their congregations dis-integrated. In addition, African spiritual beliefs and practices didn't just flourish in South America and the Caribbean. Rather, many beliefs and practices like these have so permeated American culture that they can no longer be recognized as specifically "African" and thus are often discounted in scholarly analyses of American religious sensibilities.

It is commonly held that the distinctively African forms of religiosity found in the Caribbean and South America were developed because Africans were trying to hide their religious belief and practices from the master class. Again, as we will discuss more thoroughly later, it is more probable that these African-heritage people were trying to express their religiosity in a more African manner. Scholars tend to see what they call syncretism in the ways African-heritage people use both African and European elements in these expressions. The most obvious is the association of Catholic saints with African deities, as is common in Vodou, Santería, and Candomblé. *Syncretism* can be defined as the attempt to combine two or more different systems of belief and practice into a single system. Often the two belief systems are logically incompatible, although individual devotees seldom question the internal inconsistencies. For example, Christmas trees and Easter bunnies, which have nothing to do with the associated Christian holiday, are examples of the syncretism of European pagan rituals into Western Christianity. Even though every religious tradition engages in syncretism to some extent, charges of being syncretic are often used to suggest that the original tradition(s) have been corrupted or betrayed. However, the syncretism scholars are quick to point out that Vodou, Santería, Candomblé, and the like may not have been attempts at masking these practices. In fact, a survey of the history of these traditions suggests that these syncretic activities did not develop during times of repression. Instead we are finding that these syncretic practices developed during those periods when the people had the freedom to organize their worship according to their own needs. Similarly, in North America, slaves in situations where they had more latitude, for example those on large plantations who lived and worshipped separate from their white masters, developed distinctive ways of expressing their spirituality that drew not only on the surrounding Christian culture but also on their own ideas of appropriate worship styles. Statements by both missionaries and scholars that slaves and their descendants were "scarcely touched by Christianity" because they worshipped in a distinctively African style (see for example Stuckey 1987, 37) are ignoring the possibility that African-heritage people were active agents in the development of their religiosity and were not acting out of ignorance.

Typically West and West Central African religiosity was expressed in both public and private arenas. Secret societies made up of devotees of particular deities or initiates to specialized groups were ubiquitous throughout the regions tapped for the slave trade. That Africans in the Americas would meet in secret at night in order to engage in healing practices, celebrate rites of passage, enjoy fellowship together, or pass along elements of their culture to young people or others in their new communities should not seem at all strange. Nor should we be surprised that their Euro-American owners saw these events not as religious gatherings but as disruptions of plantation life that left their workers distracted and unproductive. Public events that we now recognize as religious in nature were often characterized by planters as "devil dances" or, as Walter Pitts characterized the black folk church that developed later, "hyperbolically ecstatic or stereotypically noisy and out of control, if not ludicrous" events (Pitts, 7, 38). Sacred drumming and dancing were important throughout West and West Central Africa and some form of drumming and dancing complete with manifestations of spirit possession seems to have continued throughout the colonial and post-Revolutionary periods.

What then can we say about the development of the distinctive religious sensibilities in American culture? The Calvinism of the European colonists was greatly softened from the earliest periods when that understanding of one's own condition, known as "conversion," became more public and consequently more certain. Whereas among the Puritans, one's experience was deeply personal and private but judged by the local elites and always held in question, by the end of the revival period, conversion had become physical and public and generally accepted as genuine by both the individuals in question and their fellow "saints." The view of God and his relationship to individuals also changed. By the time of the colonization project, God in the European mind had moved very far away from the people as his transcendence was more and more emphasized. In addition, as his justice and power were stressed, the angry God holding each sinner over the flames of hell could become a compelling image. But the slave song quoted at the beginning of this chapter presents a completely different image of God, one that continues to resonate into the twenty-first century. Satan has become a "busy old man," a force to be reckoned with certainly but much less frightening than earlier images suggested, and God, personified as Jesus, has become "my bosom friend." Very few churches in America today would tolerate the kind of imagery Edwards offered to his congregations. Instead the Africanized view of Jesus or God as a friend and companion, able and willing to help individuals along their life's paths both in this world and the next, is a much more common image.

In the twentieth century African American influences on American religion continued, particularly with the development of the Holiness and Pentecostal movements. As we shall see, these traditions again injected African religious sensibilities into American religious groups, especially through the Azusa movement out of Los Angeles. But before we look further at American religious development, let's step back and consider the religious ideas and practices the enslaved brought to these shores and consider how they changed American religiosity.

3

AFRICAN CHRISTIANITY

Kingdom of Kongo

" Although most Americans are comfortable with the idea of Muslim Africans in the slave trade period, they seem much less comfortable with Christian Africans. A literate elite dressing partially in European clothes, bearing Portuguese names, and professing Catholicism seems somehow out of place in the popular image of precolonial Africa."[1]

The Kingdom of Kongo provides a good introduction to the general argument of this book as it challenges the general understanding that all Africans in what became the United States came to Christianity via slavery. The Kongolese conversion to Catholicism in 1491 was the crowning glory of nearly fifty years of missionary efforts in Western and Central Africa. Notably, this was before the explorer Columbus first set foot on what would become known as the New World (Thornton 1988, 263). After the king of Kongo and his fellow nobility converted to Christianity in 1491, they made Catholic Christianity the state religion of Kongo. During the ensuing centuries, European missionaries as well as local priests and an active laity developed a distinctively Kongolese form of Christianity. The Kongolese people then had about two hundred years to develop their distinctive adaptation of Catholic Christianity before they began to be taken to the Americas in large numbers. Between one-third and one-half of the Africans brought to the United States by the slave trade came from the Angola/Kongo region of Central Africa. Yet, important as it is to the study of religions in America, this history is seldom recognized in texts outlining the development of America religions. Not only is this history little recognized in texts on the history of American religions, many histories of the black religious traditions provide scant acknowledgement of it. In this chapter I will review what we know of the beliefs and practices of Kongo Catholicism during the sixteenth and seventeenth centuries with an eye toward understanding how these traditions may have influenced the development of the distinctively Protestant form of Christianity that became the black church of the eighteenth century and beyond as well as how they may have influenced the development of American religious sensibilities in general.

As Robert Farris Thompson explains in his groundbreaking *Flash of the Spirit*, the term "Kongo" has changed meaning over time. Slavers in the 1500s originally applied the name solely to the Bakongo people, the primary ethnic group in the Kingdom of Kongo. Later the term was expanded to include any person brought from the west coast of Central Africa. Similarly, "Angola" once referred solely to the Ngola culture that was in what is now the northern portion of contemporary Angola. Eventually it was expanded to include the whole of the west coast of Central Africa, including Kongo. This conflation was possible since the peoples from Kongo and Angola shared fundamental beliefs and languages (Thompson 1984, 103–4).

The Kingdom of Kongo was located in the Congo River basin in West Central Africa. At its height it was about the size of California. It had been in existence for about a century and a half when the Portuguese first arrived along the Atlantic coast in 1483. By that time, the Kingdom of Kongo was already a highly developed state at the center of an extensive trading network (Hall, 114–45). Together the Portuguese and Kongolese developed a system of schools and churches that led to a high degree of literacy among the upper classes. Many in the highest levels of society spoke and read their own language of Kikongo as well as Portuguese and sometimes Latin. They also developed diplomatic relations with Portugal and independent relations with the Vatican. The Kongolese were a proud people. They saw themselves as the most noble of people. Indeed, as one of the Portuguese priests noted, there developed a widespread belief that in "all the world there is no nobility, greatness or lordship which surpasses Kongo, and that there was no part of the world more delicious, agreeable and fertile than it" (Thornton 1998, 89). Any racial claims of superiority made by Europeans were weighed against this Kongolese standard and often found wanting.

In the beginning the Portuguese trade with the Kongolese involved the exchange of copper bangles and ivory for Portuguese luxury goods and the services of technical advisers. But soon the trade expanded to include human beings. Kingdom of Kongo was a major source of slaves for the Portuguese and other European traders as early as 1502. During the earliest period the demand for slaves was low; however with the discovery and settlement of Brazil in 1630 the demand for slaves accelerated so that by 1670 as many as three thousand people a year were being sold out of the Kingdom of Kongo. At the same time that demand for workers was increasing in the Americas,

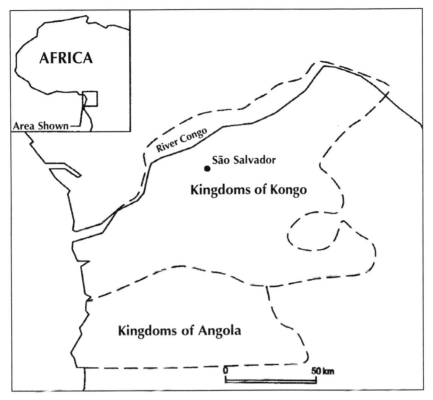

West Central African Kingdoms of Kongo and Angola

Kongo began a more than forty-four-year period of ongoing civil warfare. Warfare provided a steady stream of people into the slave trade, including soldiers and their support personnel as well as others caught on the wrong side of each battle. Trade from this area continued well into the nineteenth century with some thirty thousand being sold to the Americas during the 1820s—long after the end of legal trading in 1808. All in all, between 40 and 45 percent of the roughly eleven million Africans imported to the Americas came from this Central African region. Many people from the Kongo landed in Saint-Domingue (modern-day Haiti and the Dominican Republic), Cuba, and the British West Indies including Jamaica, as well as in South Carolina and Louisiana. In terms of the religions of America these people had significant influence on American Protestantism, Cuban Palo Monte and its related traditions, both Haitian Vodou and Louisiana Voudou, and the traditions of hoodoo throughout the southern United States (Klieman, 174–75; Hall, 155, 159–60, 163; Thornton 1998).

When the first Catholic priests arrived in Kongo in 1491 they almost immediately baptized the king as well as his principal nobles. Within a short time the Kongolese aristocracy had accepted Christianity and made it the official religion of the kingdom. By the mid-1500s the king of Kongo, Afonso I, had created a viable version of Roman Catholicism in his kingdom. The syncretic version of Catholicism developed at this time remained a part of Kongo culture throughout the kingdom's independent existence (Klieman, 713). Both modern scholars and the foreign missionaries of the seventeenth and eighteenth centuries considered Kongolese Christianity less than orthodox—the people of Kongo maintained many of their pre-Christian beliefs and practices. However, the Kongolese regarded themselves as good Christians and Kongolese Christianity was recognized as legitimate by the Vatican, the official center of Catholic Christianity. In fact, Afonso's son Henrique was sent to Europe to be educated and returned to Kongo in the early 1520s as an ordained Catholic priest. By 1596 the king's emissaries to Rome had persuaded the Pope to establish a diocese independent of the Portuguese in the capital city, São Salvador. The Portuguese sent priests, craftsmen, traders, and luxury goods to their allies in Kongo while the Kongolese supplied not only raw materials but also war captives and others to feed the growing slave trade. This trade left warfare, dislocation, famine, and disease along with the transformation or destruction of political, economic, and religious systems in its wake (Klieman, 173–76).

Between the time the first Portuguese sailors landed on the Kongolese coast in the late 1400s and the beginning of the massive trade in enslaved Africans in the 1600s, Europe underwent a massive religious revolution known today as the Protestant Reformation. Many incidents led up to what is considered the beginning of this reform movement, but when the German priest and theologian Martin Luther nailed his ninety-five theses to the door of his local church in 1517 he set off a religious conflagration that lasted for centuries. Martin Luther, John Calvin, and others attempted to reform the doctrines, rituals, and ecclesiastical structures of the Catholic church of the time. These reforms soon led to the creation of new "Protestant" churches throughout Northern Europe (with the exception of Poland) and the British Isles (with the exception of Ireland). The new denominations that were formed included the Anglicans in England, the Lutherans in Germany, and the Reformed churches in Germany, Switzerland, the Netherlands, and Scotland.

Because the Kongolese had been Christians since the early 1500s, when the traffic in human beings began, religion became a critical element in the competition among the European slave traders. As early as the 1600s the bishops of Angola (a neighboring Christian kingdom) determined that it was wrong to export Christian slaves to places in the hands of "heretics" (that is, Protestants), and the Kongolese followed a similar policy. The Dutch were preferred in this regard, as they generally took their cargo to the Spanish colonies in the Caribbean. If English traders wanted to participate in the legitimate trade, they had to certify that they were bound for Catholic destinations. Otherwise, they were limited to illegally acquiring their cargo or dealing with African traders willing to turn a blind eye to this requirement, as many were.

English shippers generally took their cargo to British colonies in the Caribbean, principally Jamaica and Barbados, where they could be sold locally or transported to other British colonies such as South Carolina, Maryland, and Virginia. Of the 5,226 Africans brought to Barbados between May of 1713 and May of 1714, some 1,500 were reexported to the northern colonies. British traders from Kongolese ports brought more than 65,000 slaves to the Americas between 1706 and 1716 and nearly 90,000 in each of the next two decades. Although there is a record of an enslaved Kongolese man who was brought to New Amsterdam (subsequently New York) as early as 1625 or 1626, the Kongolese didn't begin arriving in North America in force until around 1720. Many of these landed on the coastal lowlands of South Carolina that were just being brought under intense rice cultivation. At the same time increased demand in southern Virginia and the James River valley brought increasing numbers of enslaved Africans to these areas. Nearly 60 percent of the more than ten thousand people brought to South Carolina were from Kongo, while roughly 40 percent of the workers brought to the James River tobacco estates in the 1730s were from Kongolese areas. Demand for males to work in the rice and tobacco fields of America was balanced by the growing local demand for slave wives among the Kongolese at home in Africa. This led to a surplus of males for export and a gender imbalance within American slave communities (Broadhead, 167).

South Carolina soon became the Kongolese center of North America. The enslaved Kongolese brought not only their language and culture with them across the Atlantic but also their Catholic faith. As a consequence of the history of the Kingdom of Kongo, most of the Africans arriving in the Americas from this region had already been baptized and instructed in Christian doctrine before they left their homelands. Later, as the slave trade moved farther north along the West African coast, this was less true. Unlike the Kongolese, Africans from other areas may have been baptized before embarking from Africa or upon their arrival in America;

however they received no instruction in Christian beliefs and practices and so could not be considered to be Christians in terms of the religious beliefs and practices (Klieman, 173).

TRADITIONAL KONGOLESE RELIGION

Kongolese Catholicism incorporated many elements of the traditional Kongolese cosmology. The word for spirit or deity in the language of the Kongolese, *nzambi*, was also used as the name of the supreme god among the Kongolese people. According to Kongolese cosmology, Nzambi was approached through intermediaries such as land and sky spirits and ancestor spirits. Most of these spirits were understood to have been people who had once lived on the earth, but some were conceived of as "living, active, lucid emanations of the earth and water" (Hilton, 13–14). They were similar to human beings in that they were subject to needs and desires and might be somewhat unpredictable. Like the world of the living, the spirit world was constantly changing so that spirits that might have made one type of demand in the past might make different demands in the future. When these earth and water spirits wanted to pass into human existence, they chose parents from people who had ventured near their watery habitat. Once incarnated (born), these spirits were, according to Kongo scholar Anne Hilton, considered to be powerful sacred beings (*nkisi*) and were venerated by all (Hilton, 15).

One of the primary icons of the Kongo belief system was a circle around a Roman cross. This represented what were called the Four Moments of the Sun—that is, dawn, noon, dusk, and midnight—as well as the journey of human life from birth through adulthood, old age, and ancestorhood. This cross also represented the relationships between Nzambi (God), humanity, and the ancestors. God stood at the apex of the circle while the dead inhabited its lower regions. Humanity, existing above the horizontal line, was able to access both the Supreme Being and the world of the ancestors by way of the vertical line that crosses from one area to the other (Thompson 1984, 108–9). Religious specialists known as *nganga* were not only responsible for interactions with the spiritual world but were also healers and herbalists. The *banganga* (plural of *nganga*) were responsible for keeping the people informed as to the shifting demands of the various members of the spiritual realm (Klieman, 174–75). Among the Kongolese people the term *nkisi* was used to designate any ritual object imbued with otherworldly power that allowed it to have spiritual and material effects in this world.

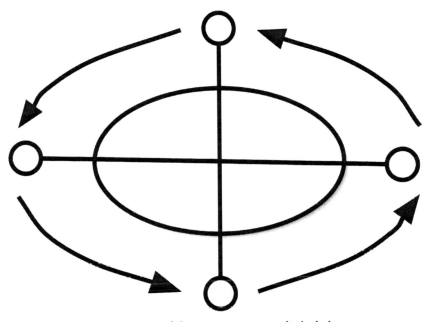

Four Moments of the Sun, Kongo cosmological view

Through ritual an nkisi spirit was inserted into a piece of sculpture or a bundle of cloth and other materials. The sculpture or bundle could then be used in a myriad of ways including healing and causing diseases, determining the guilt or innocence of accused criminals, and bringing wealth to the owner or poverty to his or her enemies. Without the animating spirit the nkisi object was merely a mundane sculpture or collection of items; without the nkisi object the animating spirit had no physical form with which to effect change in the physical world. Only when the ritual specialist (nganga) brought the spirit and object together was an nkisi empowered to act.

The nkisi object was imbued not only with the nkisi spirit but also with all the rules, regulations, songs, and other rituals required to empower it. Once an nkisi object was animated with the nkisi spirit it was considered to be a living entity with certain personality traits. People often spoke of an nkisi as being a jealous and temperamental being whose wants and desires needed to be considered if the nkisi was to perform the services for which the nkisi was constructed. However, even *minkisi* (plural of *nkisi*) that were not yet empowered or those whose power had been removed were considered semipersons that must be treated with the appropriate respect. As might be expected, this category of being, neither fully human nor just an object, challenged Europeans who encountered it, as they, particularly in the Enlightenment period, had no such category in their worldview. Thus European priests and others often denounced minkisi as merely lifeless fetishes created by simple and ignorant people.[2]

Minkisi were activated by ritual action. Often the nkisi was buried (to get it close to the dead) in a strategic place. In the case of wooden nkisi, the nganga might strike or bang the nkisi to activate it. Also shouting invectives at the nkisi might move it to action. In the late seventeenth and early eighteenth centuries, banganga began driving nails into minkisi, especially doll-like figurines, as a way of arousing them to action. The use of nailed minkisi correlated with the introduction of the icon of the Christian crucifix. Christ was considered one of the highest nkisi and his death and resurrection corresponded nicely with the Kongolese idea of moving between the worlds of the living and the dead.

Almost any item, natural or manufactured, could be transformed into an nkisi through the appropriate human activity. Thus carved objects, human figures, pots, burial mounds, churches, and even human bodies could become minkisi under the appropriate circumstances—the grave and the body buried in it were considered to be a special type of nkisi. However, it wasn't the object that defined an nkisi, but rather the ideas of containment, invocation, symbolism, and power that formed the nkisi complex. In general, minkisi were ethically neutral. That is, each nkisi could be used for good or evil based on the intentions of its owner. Power used to increase one's own status or prestige, or to inflict harm on others, was by definition evil while the same power used to benefit the community or in the interests of health and healing was considered good. All such power was considered *kindoki*. This power was believed to reside in the realm of the dead from which it could be harnessed by an nganga through the use of an nkisi for good or ill. The term *ndoki* (singular of kindoki) is often translated as *witch-craft* and considered inherently evil, but we must be careful of such characterization. The power (ndoki) of a person or nkisi was actually neutral, and the same power could be used by the nganga or owner of the nkisi for either good or evil purposes—or for good on some occasions and evil on others. The moral judgment rested not in the nkisi or the power used but in the human being controlling it.

Missionaries used these ideas to translate Christian concepts into Kikongo, the language of the people, and Christian cosmology into a version of Kongolese cosmology. So, for example, *nzambi*, the word for soul, ancestor, or other deity, was incorporated into *Nzambi a mpungu* to mean "God Almighty," while priests called themselves *nganga*, the word for religious specialists. *Nkisi* was often used in the European correspondence back home to refer to the "fetish cults" the Kongolese continued to participate in even after many generations of Christianity, but it was also used to mean "holy." Thus *nganga a nkisi nzambi a mpungu* meant "holy priest of God Almighty," while *nzo a nkisi* was a "holy house" or "church" and *mukanda nkisi* was the Holy Bible. *Loka,* to curse, conjure, or bewitch, became the term for excommunication, and the term for church, *nzo a nkisi,* could also be translated as "grave." As a matter of fact, kings and royalty were buried in the churches while the common people were buried in the nearby graveyards. Thus Kongolese churches gained a portion of their sacred quality from their association with that special kind of nkisi that is the grave. Priests were also sometimes known as *nganga nzo a nkisi,* "priest of the church/grave." In this way Christian practice and language overlapped with traditional Kongolese reverence for the dead and traditional Kongolese cosmology. In addition, the Kongolese idea that a woman could become pregnant by a spirit and that such a sacred child (incarnated water spirit) would have special powers and spiritual abilities corresponded nicely with the story of the Virgin Mary and her extraordinary son.

Because of the similarities between Kongolese beliefs and those of the Catholic church, it was easy to incorporate Catholic ideas into a Kongolese cosmology. Nzambi remained the supreme god; the ancestors and spirits remained as saints, ancestors, angels, and the like; the Four Moments of the Sun mapped nicely onto a Christian cross; and priests could take over many of the activities traditionally allocated to the banganga. Over time there developed complex diversity of indigenous and Christian ideas that Kongolese could draw upon in articulating their concept of the world. Ritual practices drew upon all of the connotations, Christian and traditional Kongolese, embedded in these ideas and symbols. Most Kongolese babies "ate salt," that is, were baptized, as soon as the priest passed through their town. For the Kongolese, the portion of the ritual where salt is placed on the baby's tongue was the significant portion of the service, since in Kongolese cosmology evil persons and spirits do not like salt. Thus baptism was believed to protect the baby from witches, neglected ancestors, and vengeful neighbors, as well as powerful nobles and slave traders (Young, 55–56). Kongolese children were given a saint's name and many also carried Portuguese-sounding surnames.

The Kongolese prided themselves in their Catholic heritage, but that does not mean that they renounced their indigenous rituals. As with many other indigenous people, the Kongolese saw no problem with engaging in what we might call *polymorphism.* That is, they engaged in several unrelated religious traditions at the same time. Throughout this period people at different social levels had different concepts of Christianity, with some nobles having a sophisticated, theological understanding while many rural people saw it as another form of ritual protection. We know from contemporary sources that the Kongolese people continually tested Christian precepts and tenets against traditional ideas. They weren't shy about critiquing those European or Christian individuals and ideas they believed fell short according to their traditional standards of conduct.

One important Kongolese concept that was kept in opposition to Christian teaching of the time was the idea that one's dead ancestors could be active participants in the world of the living, taking an interest in the health and welfare of their descendants. As we shall discuss more fully in the next chapter, Europeans of the time believed that the dead were either asleep in their graves, not to be awakened until the final judgment, or that their spirits had been judged and consigned to their eternal reward, heaven, their eternal damnation, hell, or an intermediate state of temporary punishment and purification known as purgatory. In this view, those who had died had no interaction with those who remained alive. Conversely, the Kongolese had long believed that when people died their spirits remained near where they were buried so that they could use the powers of the Other World to help their living descendants. People who attended the graves of their ancestors could depend on their help in daily life and those who neglected their ancestors might be punished by bad luck and sickness. Elaborate rituals surrounded both death and the ongoing relationship between people and their dead ancestors, and one was expected to maintain communications with one's ancestors and others with whom one could establish a relationship (Hilton, 10–12). This was in direct opposition to the Christian idea of the afterlife but would become significant when the Kongolese were taken to the Americas.

In spite of concerns expressed by the European missionaries, the people of Kongo maintained their strong relationship with their ancestors. Their all-night vigil at the graves of their ancestors was moved to coincide with the Catholic feasts of All Souls (October 31, Halloween) and All Saints (November 1) (Thornton 2002, 85), and in spite of the disapproval of the priests, the Kongolese as late as the nineteenth century continued to assemble together as families to pray the rosary, visit their ancestral grave sites, place candles on individual graves, and make major offerings to the local church as part of their All Saints' Day observances. At a time when Europeans were most usually buried in communal graves, the Kongolese maintained individual graves as sacred sites and points of contact with the revered dead. Funerals were another important part of Kongolese life. It was thought that persons who were not given the appropriate funeral rites would not be accepted as full members of the societies of the dead and consequently would not be able to aid their descendants and loved ones. Appropriate funeral rituals and ongoing communication with the revered dead, especially at their burial sites, were necessary to maintain the connection between the world of the living and that of the dead to the benefit of both.

In spite of two hundred years of Christianity, Kongo continued to be a missionary outpost. A handful of priests both European and Kongolese baptized almost all of the children and less frequently performed weddings and funerals. However, an active laity maintained Christian practice. At least once a year a teacher and group of students worked their way through all the outlying towns and villages, conducting classes to ensure that everyone learned the rudiments of Christian religion. Everyone memorized the critical tenets of the church and the most important prayers, including the sign of the cross, the Lord's Prayer, the Hail Mary, and the hymn "Salve Regina" ("Hail, Holy Queen"). All of this was included in a Kikongo-language catechism first published in 1624. This catechism covered the articles of the faith, the Ten Commandments, the nature of deadly sins and venal sins, and the sacraments of the church. It also had a lengthy section on proper Christian life. Countless travelers in Kongo commented on the degree to which these basic elements of faith and practice were known even in the most rural areas. Rural Kongolese had at least as good a grounding in their Christian faith as similarly placed rural peoples in Europe of the time, while the urban elites on both continents had a more sophisticated and learned understanding.

There weren't enough priests to establish the types of parishes found in Europe. So during the periods between priestly visits, each local community assembled on Saturdays to say the rosary, led by members of the local elite, often in chapels built by those same noblemen (Thornton 2002, 83). The people also celebrated Christmas and Easter and the larger season of Advent/Christmas/Epiphany as well as the most important holidays of Halloween/All Saints' Day (October 31 and November 1) and the day dedicated to James Major, the patron saint of the Kingdom of Kongo, on July 25.

Scholars debate the level of Christianization of the Kongolese people. John Thornton argues that the Christianity practiced in Kingdom of Kongo was recognized in Rome as orthodox and accepted by the European priests operating in the country as legitimate in spite of the "syncretism," theological translation, and adaptation they found (as cited in Young, 57–58). There was always a shortage of priests to service the vast areas of Kongo, and missionaries were constantly begging their superiors for more workers. However, even in the Americas, priests working in Catholic areas were amazed to discover that Kongolese slaves and ex-slaves maintained the foundation of Christian knowledge they had learned before their enslavement, for they still could say the prayers and recite the catechism they learned as children (Thornton 1998, 29).

ONGOING PROPHECY IN AFRICA AND THE AMERICAS

Importantly for the development of an American religious sensibility, the Kongolese brought to the Americas not only their ideas about this world and the afterworld but also a tradition of continuous revelation within a Christian environment. Americans' acceptance of closed revelation has waxed and waned over time. As a group Americans tend to be open to new religious revelations, as can be seen by the many new religious traditions that have developed here. Europeans from the early colonial and Revolutionary periods, both Protestants and Catholics, generally considered revelation closed. Both considered the Bible the ultimate authority against which any new revelation had to be evaluated (although Catholics acknowledged other sources of revelation, including sacred tradition and the word of the clergy, that Protestants generally did not accept). Those revelations that went against that biblical standard or were not considered consistent with clerical understandings of the Bible had to be rejected. Much of the literature of the centuries-long Inquisition in both Catholic and Protestant regions dealt with personal revelations that were rejected because they were not seen as conforming to clerical understandings of the Bible.

Revelation held a special place within the Kongolese worldview. It was believed that ancestors spoke to their descendants in dreams and visions and through the words of mediums and other banganga. The Kongolese considered the Bible an ancient text written at a time and place distant from their own. They saw it as less compelling than the ongoing communication with otherworldly beings such as the ancestors and other spirits maintained through traditional forms of divination and mediumship. Revelations and miracles were an important aspect of the conversion experience among the Kongolese. During the early years of the Christianizing project, individuals made the decision to become Christians because of messages from their ancestors in dreams or the words of mediums. Those who left Christian practice were often encouraged by their ancestors to return. But all revelations had to be scrutinized before they could be accepted. All the pronouncements of an nganga, either traditional priest or Catholic cleric, were evaluated not against a biblical standard but against a standard of efficacy—if such declarations provided individual or community-wide healing, or were accurate predictions about the immediate future, they were accepted as true and legitimate. If the pronouncements of an nganga were seen as self-serving or harmful to the community, they were rejected. Even pronouncements of the local Catholic clergy were measured against this standard of efficacy rather than consistency with biblical understandings. The Catholic priests might try to frame statements outside their control as the work of the devil, but it appears that the Kongolese people generally never developed a clear understanding of an absolutely evil spirit; instead they judged the pronouncements and works of spiritual beings and their human emissaries against a purely pragmatic standard. For example, priests whose pronouncements were biblically orthodox but self-serving were judged to be evil and spiritually repulsive.

During the height of the slave trade and the Kongolese civil wars that fed it, many prophets arose from within the Kongolese people. These prophets preached against the ongoing civil war and the slave trade as well as the greed, jealousy, and other misuses of ndoki found among both the Kongolese elite and their European allies. The best known of these prophets was Dona Beatriz Kimpa Vita, a twenty-year-old Kongolese woman who was possessed by the spirit of Saint Anthony.

It is said that Kimpa Vita was deathly ill, dying actually, when, in August of 1704, she had a vision. A man dressed in the simple blue hooded habit of a Capuchin monk appeared to her and said, "I am Saint Anthony, firstborn son of the Faith and of Saint Francis. I have been sent from God to your head to preach to the people. You are to move the restoration of the Kingdom of Kongo forward, and you must tell all who threaten you that dire punishments from God await them." He went on to tell her that she was not his first choice of prophets. He said that he had entered the heads of several other people previously but that he had been badly treated either by the people to whom he was trying to preach or by the local clergy, so he was trying once more with her. With that short introduction, Saint Anthony moved toward Kimpa Vita, entered her head, and merged with her. According to the later reports of this event, she felt instantly healed, strong, and in good spirits. She rose from her deathbed resolved to complete the mission of Saint Anthony to the people of Kongo (Thornton 1998, 10–11).

The Kongolese had been Catholic for six generations when Beatriz was born. Like all the Kongolese of her time, she "ate salt" (that is, was baptized) as soon as a priest passed through her town. Following local usage she was named Dona Beatriz Kimpa Vita: *Dona* is a Portuguese honorific given to all Kongolese girls (*Dom* was given to boys). It was followed by the saint's name Beatriz, the Kikongo given name Kimpa, and her father's given name of Vita. She was born into a noble although not necessarily wealthy family who traced their ancestry back to a Kongolese king. Beatriz began having the visions that established her inclination toward religion as early as eight years old. As she grew older her interests and ability in the spiritual side of life increased. She was initiated as an nganga, or spiritual medium and healer, and joined the Kimpasi society around age twelve. The Kimpasi society was a group of banganga who worked to heal communities suffering from calamities and other social problems. Kimpasi initiates were taken to a specially built compound in the forest where they "died" and were "reborn" with new, stronger connections to the spirit world. Banganga and Kimpasi initiates were possessors of their own *kindoki*, the power that gave them the ability to operate with the assistance of the Other World, the spiritual world. Although banganga often worked with individuals with problems of sickness, bad luck, or economic misfortune, Beatriz (and other members of the Kimpasi society) worked not with individuals but with communities who had suffered similar fates of illness, bad luck, or economic misfortune. By the standards of the seventeenth century the Kongolese people did not live in an impoverished culture. According to the work of John Thornton, the average life expectancy was about thirty-five years, similar to that in Europe and Asia at the same time. Infant mortality was approximately 25 percent—staggering by our standards but lower than the rate in Europe. The fertility rate was nearly 50 per 1,000, higher than Europe at the time but similar to the rates in the American colonies (Thornton 1998, 137–38). However, during Beatriz's time and for decades later misfortune was everywhere throughout the Kingdom of Kongo as several petty kings vied to unite the people under their leadership. Civil war, with all its attendant ills, including feeding the increasingly lucrative slave trade, prevailed.

Beatriz was not the first prophet to come to the Kongolese of the early 1700s. Early in 1703 a peasant woman saw a vision of the Virgin Mary, who told her that Jesus was angry with the Kongolese people and said that they should say the Hail Mary three times followed by three calls for mercy. Another man had revelatory dreams in which a small child told him God would punish the Kongolese people unless they reoccupied the deserted capital of São Salvador (and thus resolved the ongoing civil war) as quickly as possible. In 1703 or 1704 an old woman, Apolonia Mafuta, had a vision of the Virgin Mary, who after begging at the feet of Jesus to be merciful to the people, was told that he was angry at their wickedness and for not restoring the capital. Mafuta denounced various people as evil ndoki (that is, spiritually evil, greedy people, "witches") and certain objects as evil minkisi (that is, objects imbued with spiritual power and used for evil). Among the objects she denounced and threw into great bonfires were crosses and religious medals, which she claimed were being used for negative kindoki as a result of greed, jealousy, civil war, and treachery.

It was in this religiously charged environment that Beatriz had her vision, was possessed by the spirit of Saint Anthony, and began preaching against greed, jealousy, and other misuses of kindoki. While the Capuchin missionaries were generally considered to be nganga who used their own style of nkisi to protect against witches, Beatriz and her followers believed them to be witches who promoted themselves to the detriment of the people (Hilton, 19). On her way to meet the legitimate but beleaguered King Pedro, she attempted to tear down the large cross standing in the plaza of the local church. She rebuked the king for not reoccupying São Salvador and not bringing the civil wars to a close. She also denounced the local priest as a jealous and envious person who refused to recognize any Kongolese saints. The king accepted her rebukes without taking any further action.

Unable to move the king, Beatriz continued her preaching and teaching. Her message emphasized the importance of Saint Anthony, Jesus's anger with the Kongolese people, and his impending punishment. She encouraged the people to pray and call for mercy, but she also encouraged the people to be happy. She said that good things would come to devotees of Saint Anthony and that soon they would have their own saints just as the Europeans did. The Catholic priests claimed a racial superiority based on the fact that the church originated outside of Kongo and that its earliest leaders and most important saints were Europeans. Beatriz claimed that God had revealed a truer version of church history to her. Instead of the story told by the Capuchins, the truth was that Jesus was born in the royal city of São Salvador and was baptized in the northern province of Nsundi and that Mary, Jesus's mother, was actually a slave of the Marquis Nximba Mpangi when he was born, making both Mary and Jesus actually Kongolese. According to Beatriz, Saint Francis, the founder of the Capuchins' order, was also Kongolese, and of course Saint Anthony was now present in her head.

Beatriz also proclaimed new, truer versions of the Hail Mary and Salve Regina prayers. Her revision of the Salve Regina became known as the Salve Antoniana because it reflected the essence of Saint Anthony's reformist teachings. Most importantly, these teachings repudiated the power of the sacraments, maintaining that the intention of the believer was more important than the performance of the sacraments, changing the theology from a

European to a Kongolese understanding. In addition, the prayer elevated Saint Anthony above the other saints, above the Virgin Mary, making him "a second God." The prayer generally ended with the people shouting "Tari, Tari" ("Mercy, Mercy").

Although interrogated by the local priest on suspicion of heresy, Beatriz remained under the protection of King Pedro and was allowed to continue to preach and teach. To the king and his counselors her behavior and appearance were consistent with one who had died and been reborn as a person possessed by an Other Worldly entity. The local priest also believed that she was possessed, not, however, by a saint but by the devil or one of his demons, making her a witch in the European understanding of that term.[3]

Having determined that Beatriz was of the devil, the priest, Father Bernardo, planned to denounce her from the pulpit in an effort to counteract her increasing popularity. He planned on condemning her as controlled not by Saint Anthony but by demonic forces and on berating his audience for following and supporting her. However, before Father Bernardo could preach against her, Beatriz left the town and carried her message to a wider area. She also began to heal the sick and cure infertility, the bane of eighteenth-century Kongolese women. Women who sought treatment for infertility began to tie small ropes and threads on Beatriz's hands and feet as a sign of their faith in her power. This paralleled the Kongolese custom of tying or binding an nkisi to ensure that its power is held in and its healing promises met.

In her travels Beatriz visited other petty kings in an effort to gain the support for her mission and the reunification of the country. Although the royalty were generally uninterested in her message, she had great appeal among the common people, who felt abandoned and exploited in the uncertainty of the times. Throughout the Kingdom of Kongo people began singing the Salve Antoniana and praying the Hail Mary followed by cries for mercy. Beatriz moved her base of operations to São Salvador, reoccupying the city with her followers. She began to commission Little Anthonys to assist in her work and act as missionaries throughout the country. The Little Anthonys were also possessed by the saint although they were subordinate to Beatriz. Others also manifested saintly possession. Another Saint Anthony, as well as a Saint John, Saint Ursula, Saint Lucy, and Saint Isabel, appeared. The people started making their own nkisi, sacred objects, in the form of little cast metal statues of Saint Anthony that were meant to replace the other symbols of Catholic worship that Beatriz declared were objects of misdirected kindoki. (Scholars think that the production of these types of religious objects in Kongo dates from this period.) Within a few months

Beatriz and her Little Anthonys won the support of large masses of the common people.

Such spiritual power also gave Beatriz political power, which she tried to use to reunite the country. She wanted to be able to crown a single king of Kongo, chosen by an angel. She also wanted to overturn the Capuchins' continual denial of Kongolese saints. Toward that end she elaborated a new creation story, one in which the Europeans were created from a white stone called *fuma* while the Kongolese were the product of an *nsanda*, a tree whose bark could be pounded and woven into black cloth. The fuma stone connected the Europeans with the world of the ancestors (which was associated with the color white), water, and great spiritual power. The black nsanda bark associated the Kongolese with the world of the living (which was associated with the color black), childbirth, and worldly wealth. Beatriz and a select group of her male followers made themselves crowns of nsanda cloth. These men were called her angels.

Early in 1706 Beatriz proclaimed that she must visit heaven frequently, so she would die every Friday, go to heaven, dine with God, plead the case of the people and restoration of the Kingdom of Kongo, and be reborn each Monday. At about the same time, she formed a close relationship with a man named João Barro, who became her principal guardian angel. Twice she became pregnant with his child, but each time she was able to abort it with local medicine. However, the third time she became pregnant the medicine failed. This failure began the cascade of events that would lead to the failure of her mission.

Although she tried to keep her pregnancy secret, as her neared the end of her term she cut down on her public appearances and took longer sojourns to heaven. When she could no longer hide her pregnancy, she left São Salvador and returned to the valley of her family with the prophetess Apollonia Mafuta, Barro, and a young serving girl. She gave birth to her son, whom she named Antonio in honor of the saint who possessed her body. Unfortunately agents of King Pedro who were trying to clean up the Antonian movement from that area discovered her. She, Barro, and Mafuta were first questioned by Father Bernardo and then by the king. In her shame at not maintaining the chastity she required of her Little Anthonys, she confessed to her great sin of unchastity (but not to any heresy regarding her possession by Saint Anthony). The king's royal council sentenced Kimpa Vita, Apollonia Mafuta, and João Barro to death by burning. Two days later, on July 2, 1706, she and Barro were executed (Mafuta was deemed insane and spared from the flames. Kimpa Vita's infant son also escaped). Dona Beatriz Kimpa Vita was dead; however, for many years after her death thousands of her "Little Anthonys" continued her movement.

This is an important story not only in the history of Christianity in Kongo but also in the story of religion in America. In the decades following Beatriz's death, thousands of people from this area were enslaved and taken to European colonies in North and South America. As events unfolded, Antonians, followers of Beatriz as Saint Anthony, were more often on the losing side of the conflicts that eventually placed King Pedro on the Kongolese throne. Thus it is probable that many of the Kongolese who were caught up in the slave trade during this period were her followers—and even those who were not Antonians would have been Catholic Christians in a more orthodox style. Kongolese people began arriving in large numbers in North America in 1720, most to the lowlands of South Carolina, and soon South Carolina was the Kongolese center of North America—only Brazil had a greater percentage of Kongolese people. These people brought their language, their culture, and their Catholic faith with them across the Atlantic. They influenced the development of the ring shout, baptismal ceremonies, the construction of burial mounds, and quilt making. They also brought the attitudes that fueled Beatriz's movement, including a belief in the ndoki of those whose actions were detrimental to individuals or the community as a whole.

In his article "African Dimensions of the Stono Rebellion," John Thornton argues that the Stono Rebellion of 1739, one of the largest and most costly such uprisings in the United States, was shaped by the African background of its participants, especially those from the Kingdom of Kongo (Thornton 1991). Eyewitness accounts suggest that the enslaved rebels were Catholics who were enticed by the Spanish authorities in nearby Florida, then under Spanish control, to leave South Carolina to enjoy not only physical but also religious freedom in the area around Saint Augustine. The Spanish authorities had been accepting runaways from Georgia and South Carolina, giving them not only protection but also freedom since the late 1600s (Young, 68–70). Thornton suggests that these Kongolese slaves, who he says were "proud of their Christian and Catholic heritage, which they believed made them a distinctive people," would have found such an offer appealing. In addition, because of the protracted civil wars in Kongo, many of the enslaved would have been former soldiers trained in military discipline and the use of firearms rather than simple villagers without such training (Thornton 1991, 1103). In addition, Mark Smith suggests that the date of the rebellion, Sunday, September 9, was chosen because of its proximity to the Catholic feast of the nativity of the Virgin Mary on September 8

(Smith, 114–15). The rebels, perhaps as many as a hundred strong, fought well, reportedly capturing a supply of guns and using them to their advantage (Thornton 1991, 1109). They also exhibited other evidence of military training, such as forming themselves into units under banners similar to those African armies flew, using drums to encourage others to join them, dancing in preparation for attacks, and using African (as opposed to European) styles of engagement (Thornton 1991, 1111–13). Although the rebellion was short-lived and unsuccessful, it was the largest such uprising in the British mainland colonies.

CONCLUSION

The British Anglican colonists of the southern colonies would not have recognized the religiosity of their Kongolese bondspeople, since it was doubly removed from their own religiosity. According to the beliefs of the time, Catholicism was little better than heathenism. While there was little effort to convert the enslaved to Anglican Protestantism, there also was little effort to sustain or encourage the religiosity they brought with them. But cosmological and religious ideas are hard to expunge. As we shall see, ideas about the relationship among human beings, God and other spiritual beings, and the esteemed dead continued in the Americas and eventually many of these ideas crossed the racial boundary and found their way into the views of non–African-heritage peoples. The idea that religion should serve the well-being of common people, which would have resonated with medieval Christians, was lost during the Reformation but, at least in North America, was recovered in later centuries.

The peoples of Kongo and Angola were not the only Africans who attempted to maintain cordial relationships with their ancestors and other honored dead. All along the western and west central coasts of Africa, reverence for the dead and rituals for the newly or long-term dead were common. According to the general theory of interaction between the master and slave classes of North America, the enslaved should have given up these ideas and rituals and moved toward a more European-style attitude toward death, dying, and the afterworld. However, that is not what happened. Instead our contemporary view is more analogous to that of our African than our European forebears.

4

THE DEAD ARE NOT DEAD

Those who are dead are never gone:
they are there in the thickening shadow.
The dead are not under the earth:
they are in the tree that rustles,
they are in the wood that groans,
they are in the water that runs,
they are in the water that sleeps,
they are in the hut, they are in the crowd,
the dead are not dead.[1]

Several important books have been published detailing the influences of Kongolese religious ideas on the religious sensibilities of the southern United States. However, there has been little work that has placed these influences into the larger context of the developing American religious sensibility. The Kongolese and their descendants provided deep and widespread influences, especially during the two-hundred-year period between the arrival of the first Africans and the eve of the Civil War. An important change to American religious sensibilities can be found in American attitudes toward the death, dying, and the afterlife. Americans changed the way they treat the dead as well as their ideas about connections between the living and those who have died. By the time of the Civil War, American and British ideas and practices around the dead were significantly different. Many threads came together to trigger these changes but generally unrecognized is the way American sensibilities around death, dying, and burial became more like those found in West and West Central Africa.

CREATING AN AMERICAN SENSIBILITY ABOUT THE DEAD

Philippe Ariès has written the definitive history of death, dying, and burial practices in European societies (Ariès 1981). However, almost ten years before he wrote this book, *Hour of Our Death*, he published an article entitled "The Reversal of Death: Changes in Attitudes toward Death in Western Societies" (Ariès 1974). In it he described contemporary American funeral practices as "childish and ridiculous" in comparison to those of the British and French. He suggested that these differences probably stemmed "from very deeply rooted characteristics" (156). What he found most ridiculous was the American custom of elaborate funerals with an embalmed body made to appear as lifelike as possible and interment in well-maintained cemeteries designed to look like rolling parkland. He thought the British custom of making "the body disappear, in a respectable way of course, but quickly and completely, thanks to cremation" was more efficient (154, based on the research of Geoffrey Gorer [Gorer]). He said that American funeral customs are based on a "denial of the absolute finality of death and the repugnance of physical destruction without ritual and solemnity" (154). In trying to explain this difference between Americans and their British cousins, he mentions similar customs in some Mediterranean areas and the solemnity afforded the king of France as well as "archaic ceremonies of mourning" found in non-Western "traditional" societies. While his observation is interesting, his rationales are weak. During the earliest British immigration, English Catholics and Protestants were killing each other in an effort to make one or the other tradition the establishment religion, and most early British settlers carried extreme anti-Catholic feelings with them across the Atlantic. It is doubtful, then, that American funeral customs would have developed from some sort of appropriation of Italian or French customs. To what then can we attribute this change? After looking at the funeral customs and ideas of the afterlife of the earliest American settlers, we will look at the ways Kongolese customs may have led to what Ariès called "this peculiarity of American society" (154).

DEATH IN EARLY AMERICA

During the colonial and early Revolutionary periods English Protestant religious ideas made death a forbidding prospect. Although God knew the ultimate resolution of each individual's soul—in fact had already predetermined it—the individual lived and left life in a state of uncertainty. Even individuals who had the expected conversion experience that granted them membership in the local congregation continued to doubt their experience was legitimate and their salvation assured (Wills, 54–56). Protestant theology, in rejecting Catholic ideas of purgatory and the idea of indulgences and other types of prayers and ceremonies for the dead, maintained that no ritual help or assurance could be given concerning the fate of oneself or one's beloved relatives. God could save the worst sinner while good acts did not guarantee the salvation of anyone's soul. One's choice to live a life of repentance, hope, love, and the fear of God was seen as a *possible* manifestation of one's appointment among the elect. However, living such a life could not change one's status as included or excluded from among those destined for an eternal reward—and exclusion meant perpetual separation from God. The possibility of an eternity in hell was a perennial theme of English Protestant sermonizing. And while one's friends and ancestors might have achieved a heavenly reward, they were thought to be completely absent. According to Christian understanding of the time, the dead played no part in the continuing lives of the living.

Throughout the European medieval period individuals were buried in common graves under the church floor (the very rich), along the outer wall of the church (the well-to-do), or in the adjacent cemetery (everyone else). Graves were rarely marked and even when wealthy families began including memorials in their burial practices, these plaques or monuments were seldom in the same location as the body. Families might choose to be buried in the same location, for example, "near the door," "beneath the Calvary cross." However, except for the exceptional few, such as famous saints, clerics, or royalty, personal, marked graves were unknown. Unmarked graves and disorderly (according to our contemporary standards) cemeteries were also characteristic of early colonial burial grounds. In the seventeenth and eighteenth centuries, laws had to be passed requiring families and friends to ensure that bodies made it to the graveyard (instead of being discarded along the way) and were buried at a depth that ensured no bones or other body parts could work their way back to the surface (Stannard, 129, 157–60). As late as 1835, some American communities were still burying their dead in common pits in cemeteries near the church building (McDannell, 103), and prior to the mid-1600s it appears that Puritans seldom marked the graves of their deceased at all (Stannard, 116).

During much of the medieval period, it was believed that the dead slept awaiting resurrection of the body and their final judgment. This sleep was only troubled by the individual's past impiety or the stupidity or treachery of his or her survivors. In general, the beloved dead were only permitted to return on certain days such as carnivals (Ariès 1981, 604–5). In the later medieval period these ideas changed and survivors began to believe that the body and soul separated at death so that the soul might begin its immortal existence without waiting for the resurrected body. Judgment was immediate and the souls of the dead were taken at once to their heavenly reward, sent to their eternal punishment, or, in Catholic countries, confined for temporary purification in purgatory. The dead continued to be separated from the living, having moved beyond mundane concerns. Throughout the medieval period and into the early modern period, the deathbed, not the grave, was the most important site for ritual activity. Funeral services and burials were secondary and often the surviving family and friends did not even attend. During the early 1600s, during the reign of Queen Elizabeth, the British Puritans gained a measure of public acceptance and political influence. During this time they promoted an approach to funerals that attempted to eliminate any ceremony and ritual by removing the care and handling of the dead from the religious to the civil sphere (Stannard, 108–9).

In New England the Puritans brought these ideas about death and burial with them. Although they were not as zealous about funeral practices as those who remained behind in England, for at least the first couple of decades there is little evidence of any funeral ceremonies. No tombstones, funeral sermons, other writings, or journal entries suggest any special treatment of corpses or any funeral or burial ceremonies. Instead, as had been true on the continent for generations, the deathbed was more important than any postmortem activities, and funerals as we understand them were nonexistent. Diaries and other writings detail deathbed conversations and the details of individuals' final moments. Afterward, the dead were washed and dressed by family members, placed in a woolen shroud or simple coffin, and carried by friends, family members, or common laborers to the graveyard, where they were interred. Graves continued to be communal, were generally not more than a couple feet deep, and went unmarked. Graveyards were dismal neglected places, there were few markers, and often one would see bones and remains poking out of the ground.

By the 1700s, however, the Puritans had developed extensive and expensive funeral rituals. While the deathbed continued to be an important site for those dying, funerals focused on the loss to the community the death entailed. Bodies were washed and laid out either in the home or at the church where the deceased had been a member. Invitations to the funeral in the form of gloves were sent to family and friends, and the community was notified of the death by the ringing of church bells. After the funeral service those in attendance moved in procession to the burial ground. The upper classes were generally buried in family tombs while those with fewer resources were still buried in communal gravesites. After the interment, the mourners, wearing their funeral gloves, scarves, and other mourning clothes, returned to the church or family home for a funeral feast. Rings decorated with death's-heads, skeletons, coffins, and such reminders were distributed to those in attendance. Such funerals were expensive. Among the upper classes funeral costs might consume as much as 20 percent of the deceased's estate. Of course, those with fewer resources had simpler funerals (Stannard, 111–13).

Puritan theology left no room for any connection between the living and the dead, who received their predestined reward or punishment immediately upon death. The prayers, sermons, and other funeral ceremonies concentrated on the well-being of the survivors rather than providing any comfort or solace for the one who had died (Stannard, 110). Sermons began to eulogize the deceased, while prayers focused on healing the rift left in the community by the loss of one of its members. Prior to the mid-seventeenth century there is little evidence that New England Puritans even bothered to mark the gravesites of their dead, although there may have been some simple wooden crosses at the burial grounds. After the 1650s, however, carved tombstones began to populate burial grounds (Stannard, 116–17).

It was only during the early modern period, with the rise of Romanticism in the second half of the eighteenth century, that Europeans and Euro-Americans began to think of the dead as having any interest in the affairs of the living. During this period, people began to anticipate reuniting with their families and friends in the afterlife. An interest in the afterlife of the individual, both body and soul, gave rise in the United States to private cemeteries with individually marked graves. The Spiritualist tradition that also developed in the mid-1800s enabled the living to communicate directly with those who had gone before, tying the living and dead more closely together. We'll consider the rise of Spiritualism as well as the movement toward private cemeteries and the contemporary propensity to create memorial displays at the sites of deadly tragedies after we look at the ideas about death, dying, and the afterlife brought by the enslaved to the Americas.

LIFE, DEATH, AND THE AFTERLIFE:
THE AFRICAN VIEWPOINT

African ideas about death and the afterlife provide a positive counterpoint to the dreary viewpoint of European Americans. Most West and West Central African societies had individual gravesites and complex funeral rituals. Because bodies generally had to be buried quickly, before family and friends could assemble and prepare the appropriate materials, a simple first burial was often followed by a much more extravagant second funeral. This second celebration might take place days, weeks, months, or even years after the original interment as families gathered together the necessary resources for an appropriate commemoration. The actual burial site was generally within the family compound, perhaps even under the floor of the family shrine or the room of the most prominent man. Offerings were made at the gravesite, and it was expected that the dead would continue to be concerned about the ongoing life of the family. As we saw in the description of Kongolese society, the living members of the family were expected to maintain connection with the ancestral dead by a series of ongoing offerings and rituals. The dead enveloped in the nkisi (that is, the grave) could return and speak to their descendants and others through the mechanisms of possession trance, dreams, and the like. Those dead who were without descendants or whose descendants were inattentive became "ghosts," or as they were known in Kikongo, *zumbi*, who wandered aimlessly, haunting the living and drawing others into the world of the dead (Frey and Wood). We'll come back to the zumbi, or zombies, as they came to be known in Haiti and the American imagination, in chapter 8.

Recent archeological evidence suggests that throughout colonial America the enslaved continued to follow their own burial customs rather than adopting those of the master class (Butler 2008, 93).[2] This wasn't always easy. Slave funerals were an ongoing concern throughout the Americas.[3] On the one hand, funerals served as a gathering of the enslaved and might provide a venue for talk of insurrection. And in fact planning for many uprisings *did* begin during funerals. On the other hand, funerals were important to the enslaved, and even the most hardened masters seemed to allow some sort of funeral ritual. Neighbors often allowed their slaves, especially family members or members of the same African "nation" as the deceased, to attend such events. While members of the master class might attend the funeral of a beloved domestic or well-regarded field hand, generally funerals were all-black affairs, often held at night or on Sundays in order to provide a proper funeral according to the customs of the departed and of the mourners. When the conditions required swift interment, as was as common throughout slave areas as it was in Africa, the African idea of a second funeral at a more convenient time provided a rationale for subsequent memorial events. First and second funerals allowed enslaved Africans, including the Kongolese and their American-born offspring, to maintain many of their cosmological and religious views.

The moment of death itself does not seem to have been very significant for the enslaved. More important was the subsequent handling of the body, its interment, and the embellishment of the gravesite. At a time when legislation had to be passed in New York and Boston requiring that corpses be carried to the gravesite and actually interred, the enslaved were extremely offended by the idea that bodies should be left unburied and developed elaborate rituals to ensure the proper burial of their dead (Ariès 1981, 350; Stannard, 129; Roediger, 167). Usually women washed the body, encasing it in a white cloth shroud, and either placed it directly into the coffin or on a "cooling board," a table covered with a white sheet. One or more people kept watch over the cooling body, protecting it from the desecration of rats or other animals and honoring the dead by their presence. After the other members of the community (and often surrounding communities) returned from the fields, a "settin' up" or wake was held in the home of the deceased. Singing, chanting, praying, clapping, and even the embrace of the corpse allowed each member of the community to make the appropriate leave-taking. Around midnight the mourners formed a procession, carrying the body to the gravesite. Mourners moved slowly and deliberately, taking care to avoid any mishaps along the way. Singing, if allowed, was of slow-paced hymns appropriate for the pace of the mourners. Graves were dug along an east–west axis so the body would not be "crossways in the world," and bodies were interred facing east so that they would be facing the sunrise in that "Great Getting Up Morning," the rebirth suggested by Kongolese cosmology, or a posthumous return to their African homeland (Roediger, 177–78).

Preaching at the gravesite might be done by the master, but more generally local or itinerant preachers, members of the community, or even older women stepped forward to provide appropriate prayers, Bible quotations, and other funeral orations. Unlike the sermons preached at white funerals, which focused on the survivors, sermons at black funerals focused on the future resurrection of the dead and their expected reunion with family and friends. As an example David Roediger quotes the preacher at the funeral of "Sister Dicey" who said, "But on that Great Getting Up Morning, when the trumpet of God shall sound . . . we will meet you in the skies and join the hosts of saints who will go marching in" (Roediger, 171). Although the Kongolese idea of reincarnation seems to have been lost here, there was no question that all would be reunited "in the sky." The response of the mourners was varied. Some maintained stoic reserve, but more generally crying, shouting, and singing characterized these funerals. Often the combined grief and religious ecstasy was so great that mourners had to be carried away from the burial by their friends. Beads, bracelets and other jewelry, wreaths, and seeds were often interred with the body (Butler 2008, 103). After the body was lowered into the grave, each mourner tossed a handful of dirt onto the coffin in a final farewell gesture. Often food and personal effects of the deceased or items needed in the afterlife were interred along with the body or used as grave ornamentation later. Fowls might even be sacrificed at the gravesite, in line with African practices of veneration of the dead. The return from the gravesite was more cheerful and faster paced, almost festive. This festive air continued at the subsequent funeral feast that continued into the early morning hours. Generally there was a second funeral arranged sometime after the burial when family and friends could provide the proper respect to the deceased (Roediger, 173–74).

All of the ritual and celebration attending the preparation for the funeral, the burial, the festivities afterward, and the second funeral indicate the ways that African ideas about dying and the dead were continued even under the harsh regimes of slavery (Roediger, 174). While white corpses might be buried in nondescript or even unmarked graves, or later in park-like vistas of simple grass plots, slave gravesites (and later those of freed African Americans) were heavily decorated with wood sculptures, broken crockery, and personal effects. According to Robert Farris Thompson, the preeminent scholar of Kongolese culture, "Nowhere is Kongo-Angola influence in the New World more pronounced, more profound, than in black traditional cemeteries throughout the South of the United States." He suggests that these American graves reinstate the notion of the grave as an especially strong nkisi charged with the power of the human soul as well as being a spirit-embodying and spirit-directing object (Thompson 1984, 132). The last objects used by the deceased were often placed atop the grave, both to honor the dead and to keep the spirit of the deceased from following the mourners back to its previous home. White objects were invocative of the realm of the dead, while seashells were believed to both encompass the spirit's immortal presence, symbolizing the watery divide between the realms of the living and the dead, and invoke the Middle Passage, which brought the original Africans to the Americas. Trees planted on the gravesite, lamps, bottles, pipes, cars, airplanes, inverted containers, and crockery cleverly pierced or broken placated the dead and prevented them from wandering while helping them make the journey from the upper world of the living to the lower world of the dead (Thompson 1984, 132–42).

AMERICAN SENSIBILITIES
AROUND DEATH, DYING, AND BURIAL

As Ariès suggests, both burial customs and ideas about the relationship between the living and the dead are significantly different on the two sides of
the Atlantic. As late as 1835 Euro-Americans were still burying their dead
in disorderly and often unmarked graves. In that year John Jay Smith Jr. a
Philadelphia Quaker, distraught at not being able to identify the gravesite of
his young daughter who had died in the scarlet fever epidemic, began making plans for a new form of burial grounds, what would be called the lawn
cemetery (McDannell, 103). Colleen McDannell describes Smith's anguish
at the loss of his daughter's gravesite, the general disrespect afforded the
Philadelphia dead, and his subsequent creation of Laurel Hill, one of the first
rural cemeteries. She says, "John Jay Smith's disgust at Quaker burial practices reminds us that by 1835 traditional Christian burial customs were no
longer accepted by urban Protestants. What unnerved Smith was the idea
that individual gravesites could not be recognized and that dead bones were
being dug up. Smith rejected the long-standing Christian attitude that "normal" dead bodies should not be accorded special treatment" (105).

Both Europeans and Americans endured the epidemics of this period
and both participated in the Romantic movement that both Aries and Mc-
Dannell credit with the change in American attitudes toward the dead and
their final resting place. However, it was only in America that burial customs
and attitudes toward the dead evolved into the elaborate system we find
today. We can follow Aries's suggestion to look to the "archaic ceremonies
of mourning" found in non-Western "traditional" societies (Ariès 1974,
154), particularly those already present on American soil, for the models of
this evolution. In general, scholars only look at the ways African culture has
taken on aspects of the European culture it encountered in the Americas,
but in this instance it seems as though Euro-American beliefs and practices
have become more like those of Africa. It's not clear how such a change
could have happened. It's unlikely that Smith looked to the burial practices
of those blacks in his city for a model of a more satisfying way of interacting
with the bodies and spirits of deceased loved ones. Yet, the space that he
and his friends designed was closer to the design of a slave cemetery than
to any existing European models, and today Americans in general feel more
sympathy and identification with the description of the slave funeral than
those of the early colonists, whose ideas should have had a stronger impact
on American religious development. And our attitudes toward the place
of the beloved dead are more similar to the African than the European

viewpoint. Many of us also think that the funeral for and burial of our dead are important. In fact, we've developed a whole industry to help us treat our dead in a competent, dignified, and caring manner.

Not only have our burial customs changed, so have our attitudes toward those who have died. During the nineteenth century and the development of the rural cemeteries with their parklike environments, social custom dictated that survivors would maintain the gravesites of their family members. Soon individual gravesites began to be treated like shrines, complete with flowers, plants, fencing, and personalized grave markers. Such decorations assured the living that their dead would never be forgotten and tied the living and the dead together in a way not seen before in European or Euro-American history (McDannell, 114). During the first decades of slavery in America, funerals were one of the few occasions during which the enslaved could join together to continue their own cultural practices. By the time of the Second Great Awakening around the turn of the nineteenth century, however, blacks not only continued their own cultural practices, they began to share some of their religious sensibilities with their white neighbors. Many Kongolese ideas about the dead and spiritual communications migrated across the racial barrier during that period. New religious traditions that rejected the strict doctrine of predestination and honored visions and trances developed during this period. Africans who were already familiar with religious trances and visions were able to help their white coreligionists move into this religious space. For a short period during this time, blacks and whites worshipped together. When they separated, blacks continued these beliefs and practices in their own congregations, while whites took what they had learned about death and burial into the mainstream American religious beliefs and practices, often forgetting the sources of these ideas and behaviors. Even today many of the ideas brought to the Americas by the Kongolese and other Africans continue to influence American religious life, including a belief in the possible continued communication with those who have died and a positive valorization of those communications among both religious and nonreligious Americans.

SPIRITUALISM

In several popular television shows and movies individuals are able to see and communicate with people who have died. In the case of the television drama shows such as *Medium* and *Ghost Whisperer*, the dead have unfinished business that needs to be resolved before they can fully quit the earth and move on to their afterlife. In other shows, for example, John Edwards's *Crossing Over* and James Van Praagh's *Beyond*, audiences come to see performing mediums bring messages from their friends and relatives who have passed over. The American Spiritualist movement provides the theoretical foundation for these types of productions. Spiritualists believe that they can pierce the veil between the spiritual and material worlds in order to allow their dead relatives and important public figures to speak through them. Even though Spiritualism has receded in popularity among religious traditions, the idea that humans can summon nonphysical beings, including not only one's own beloved family and friends but also famous people; great religious figures, especially endowed gurus and teachers, angels, and saints; and mythological beings continues to have an allure for twenty-first-century Americans. Within Christian communities angel summoning and the whole phenomenon of connecting, working, and healing with angels continue this tradition. The contemporary obsession with vampires and zombies—the undead—should also be considered part of this phenomenon. African Americans are not generally considered a part of this tradition, since most scholars tend to focus their attention on mainstream black church traditions and ignore anything that contradicts the image of African Americans as participating only in a very narrowly defined form of Christian religiosity. However, as we shall see, African Americans both were influential during the developmental stages of this tradition and maintain their own tradition of "speaking with the dead" into the twenty-first century.

The American Spiritualist tradition is generally considered to have started in 1848 with a pair of young farm girls who reportedly communicated with the spirit of a murdered peddler. However, the idea that there was an invisible, spiritual world that could be contacted by the living is much older. For European colonists and their descendants, however, the invisible entities one might encounter, such as those contacted by Tituba and the other young girls caught up in what became known as the Salem witch trials of 1692, were more likely to be demonic than beneficial. Nonetheless, the American Spiritualist tradition both radically changed American perceptions about the dead and the invisible world they inhabit and greatly expanded the types of beings one might encounter from that world. Significantly, this movement was born in the same part of the country as the early abolitionist and suffragist movements, and these three movements may have influenced each other. Although nearly forgotten today and ignored by many accounts of religion in America, during its heyday Spiritualism attracted hundreds of thousands of people, who consulted the great mediums of the time. It was reported that there were three hundred Spiritualist clubs in Philadelphia in 1854. Robert Cox has estimated that nearly one-third of the American population, as many as eleven million people, was involved in Spiritualism by 1867 (R. Cox, 237n2). Among the influential people of the time who consulted mediums or were sympathetic to their ideas were Ralph Waldo Emerson, Henry Wadsworth Longfellow, and Mary Todd Lincoln, the wife of president Abraham Lincoln.

There was also a vibrant free black community in Philadelphia at that time with its own churches, including Saint Thomas's African Episcopal and Richard Allen's Bethel African Methodist Episcopal, schools, and benevolent and literary societies. This was one of the largest groups of free Africans in the country, with the entire range of individuals from the prosperous to members of the lowest classes, and including a strong black middle class (Winch, 84, 83). They bought and managed their own black cemetery and were active participants in the Pennsylvania Abolition Society. It is not too far-fetched to suggest that black Philadelphians joined their white neighbors in this new religious movement.

The night of March 31, the Fox family of Hydesville, New York, was awakened to a series of loud rapping noises that they interpreted as the work of a spirit presence. By developing a code in which raps could signify "yes," "no," or a letter of the alphabet, the Fox children were able to "talk" to the spirit, who they named Mr. Splitfoot. Old Splitfoot was one of the many euphemistic names commonly used for the devil and may indicate that the girls originally thought that they were conversing with a demonic being. However, they quickly determined that this invisible entity was the spirit of a peddler who had been murdered and buried in the cellar by previous owners of their house. Soon the girls, Catherine (also known as Kate) and Margaret (or Maggie), were taken into the home of friends in Rochester, New York, where they began communicating with the spirits of the dead relatives of their hosts and their friends. From the first night when neighbors attempted to determine the source of the noises, the Fox sisters were able to convince many people of the genuineness of the phenomena that followed them from Hydesville to Rochester and later around the country. Many others were not convinced, but no one was ever able to prove fraud on their part (Kucich, 5).[4] From the beginning the spirits who spoke to the Fox sisters and the other mediums that quickly followed them challenged the worldview of their contemporaries. While disquieted spirits like the murdered peddler who served as their first contact with the spirit world might be thought to hang around their death or burial sites, it was generally understood that once separated from the body one's spirit entered into the realm of heaven or hell without maintaining any connection to the world of the living. However, this new form of communication with the spirits of the departed not only seemed to "prove" that the individual consciousness continued to exist after death but also provided a new view of what the continued existence was like.

The Fox sisters lived in an area of upstate New York that has become known as the Burned-Over District because of the great number of religious reform movements that swept through there in the early to mid-1800s. These movements include the Second Great Awakening revivalist movement, the Millerist movement that became the Seventh Day Adventist Church, Mormonism, Quakerism, Shakerism, and several early precursors of modern Pentecostalism. This area was also known for its social radicalism, including movements promoting women's suffrage and abolition. The Seneca Falls Convention, the first women's rights meeting, was held in this area in 1848, and Frederick Douglass, the former slave and abolitionist lecturer, established his newspaper, the *North Star*, in Rochester. This environment was fertile ground for the idea that direct (rather than mediated) communication with God, angels, and other spiritual beings was possible and the notion that God would not behave harshly toward his children. Spiritualism offered a third way between the harshness of Calvinism, which proclaimed that only a few were predestined to be saved, and the fatalism of modern atheism, which postulated that death extinguished individual consciousness.

Rochester also had a thriving free African American community as well as a large group of sympathetic white abolitionists (Kucich, 6). African Americans were generally not converted to Christianity in great numbers until the late eighteenth century, with the coming of the Second Great Awakening. Before that time, they often gathered together to celebrate or worship in their own way. There are many intriguing hints that the African veneration of the dead continued among northern blacks. For example, the Pinkster Festival popular in eighteenth-century Albany, New York, gave African Americans the opportunity to celebrate a "carnivalesque inversion of the social order." It also appeared that participants invoked the spirits of the dead, who spoke through designated mediums (Sweet, 74–76; Stuckey 1999, 171–73).

There were free blacks in the American north who were Christians and who organized their own congregations earlier than the general conversion of Africans during the Second Great Awakening. African-based churches (such as the Union Church of Africans, which was founded in 1813 in northern Delaware and was the first church in the United States to be both organized by and wholly under the care of black people) were "intensely conscious of their African heritage and celebrated it in the name of their church and in their daily religious practices." Like the Kongolese people who may have been their ancestors, members of these congregations saw themselves as good Christians who practiced their own particular strain of Christianity (Riordan, 223). Based on commonalities among African cultural groups, such as beliefs in nature spirits, the continued regard of dead ancestors, divination, and a tradition of communicating with invisible beings through the possession trance, within these congregations the type of speaking with the dead developed among Spiritualists would not have seemed strange at all (Kucich, 28–29).

Two important European sources for the modern Spiritualist movement are the works of Emanuel Swedenborg and Franz Mesmer. Swedenborg (1688–1772) was a Swedish philosopher and mystic who wrote extensively about his conversations with God, Jesus, spirits, and angels while in a trance state. According to Swedenborg, there was not a single heaven and a single hell but rather a series of spheres through which a spirit progressed after death. Toward the end of his life, small reading groups formed to study his writings. These developed into a religio-philosophical system known as Swedenborgianism. Many famous people on both sides of the Atlantic were influenced by Swedenborg's writings, including the family of Henry James, the father of the novelist Henry James and the philosopher William James. On the other hand, Mesmer (1734–1815) did not contribute any religious beliefs to the early Spiritualists. However, his technique, mesmerism, now commonly known as hypnotism, provided a way to induce the trances many mediums used to contact spiritual beings. Mesmer thought that there was a magnetic fluid or ethereal medium residing in the bodies of animals and humans that enabled him, and others using his techniques, to hypnotize them.

In the United States a generation after Swedenborg, Andrew Jackson Davis (1826–1910) claimed to experience visions of Swedenborg while in a mesmeric trance. Although his chief clairvoyant gift was the diagnosis of disease, he was also very influential in the elaboration and clarification of Swedenborg's ideas about the afterlife. Known as the Poughkeepsie Seer, Davis developed what he called a "harmonial philosophy" in which like attracted like; those who had died continued their attachment to those they left behind, often not even realizing that they had died; and spirits maintained their mortal flaws after death, so that mischievous or evil people became mischievous or evil spirits. However, according to this philosophy, the longer a spirit was dead the more it progressed, rising toward the highest heavenly sphere. Based on his visions Davis described the afterlife, which he called Summerland, as a series of spheres where spirits were drawn together based on their commonality of interests, emotional connection, or moral condition. By seeking spiritual knowledge and working with those from the higher spheres, spirits could advance through the spheres, perfecting themselves and eventually approaching the sphere of the Deity.

But learned and educated men were not at the heart of the Spiritualist movement. Instead it was uneducated young girls who formed the bulk of mediums that brought messages from the "other side" to audiences around the country. There were also African American mediums who were able to attract audiences within both the black and white communities, including the black Shaker Spiritualist Rebecca Cox Jackson and the flamboyant Spiritualist and trance medium Paschal Beverly Randolph, a New Yorker of mixed race.

Rebecca Cox Jackson (1795–1871) was a free black from Philadelphia who brought manifestations of spirit communications to her Quaker community in Watervliet, New York, and later took part in Spiritual circles in Philadelphia. Even before she became a Spiritualist Jackson experienced dreams and voices. Her spiritual journey began in the African Methodist Episcopal Church, where she experienced her conversion in 1830 and later was sanctified before finding a spiritual home among the Quakers. It was among the Quakers that she first began to experience spiritual messages from Quaker elders who had passed on, Holy Mother Wisdom, Native Americans, East Indians, and Mother Ann Lee herself (Albanese, 238–39). Religion scholar Catherine Albanese asks whether Jackson's Spiritualism was shaped by her African American culture and suggests that her race was only one factor in her Spiritualism (Albanese, 140).

Randolph was a prominent occult theorist, Spiritualist, and trance speaker who wrote extensively on Spiritualist subjects before moving on to Rosicrucianism, occultism, and "sex magic" (Cox 2003, 166–67). After a varied career, by 1852 Randolph was listed in the *Utica City Directory* as a clairvoyant physician and psycho-phrenologist with the title of "Doctor" preceding his name. He was heavily influenced by the great lights of the Spiritualist tradition, including Andrew Jackson Davis and John Murray Spear. However, in 1858 he renounced Spiritualism, feeling that he had been possessed by a demonic power (Albanese, 244–45).

Black mediums shared with their white counterparts the stereotype of being more "intuitive, inspirational, religious and altogether mediumistic," and religion scholars suggest a close connection between African American communities and the Spiritualist movement (Braude, 29; Levin and Gleig, 266–67). Ann Braude has even said that the Spiritualist movement served as a bridge between European spiritual ideas and African

American folk practices. She suggests that Spiritualism found a natural resonance among African Americans in the south, who maintained many of their beliefs about the relationship between the living and the dead, including the idea that invisible beings were not necessarily ill-intended or dangerous (Braude, 28–29). As we have seen, until this time Europeans and Euro-Americans generally placed the spirits of the dead beyond the reach of the living. Once dead, one's spirit was considered to have moved on to whatever eternal fate for which one was predestined. The living were unable to effect any change in their loved ones' conditions and the dead maintained no concern or relationship with those they left behind. Especially in the south, Spiritualism was seen as completely compatible with Christianity. Braude suggests that this may have been due to the influence of blacks, who did not find spirit communication at odds with Christian beliefs, within southern Spiritualist communities (Braude, 30).

As we will discuss in more detail in chapter 6, the prominent religion at the time of the Fox sisters' visions was a strict form of Calvinism. Christian doctrine stressed that humanity was morally and spiritually bankrupt, unable to follow God's commandments or escape his condemnation. All people were entirely at the mercy of God, who chose who was to be saved and who condemned. Although one must believe in the Gospel to be saved, no act of faith or virtuous action on the part of an individual could change one's predestined end. In time, many turned away from religion altogether, preferring atheism and the assurances of science. But atheism didn't provide much comfort in times of spiritual need. Spiritualism, on the other hand, proposed that one could work toward one's eventual salvation not only while alive but also after death. Although Swedenborg originally proposed both heavenly and hellish spheres, later Spiritualist thinkers proposed a more benign cosmology wherein everyone could eventually advance to the highest spiritual sphere.

In spite of the fact that Christianity has always proclaimed that souls continued to live on after physical death, the hope of an eventual reunion in heaven provided little comfort to those who lost their friends and family members prematurely. The cholera epidemic that swept through the country in 1849 took many, especially children, from their families. Thousands died in New York and throughout the country, including approximately one-tenth of the population of Saint Louis and over three thousand in New Orleans. Spiritualism provided a comfort to families of these and others who died prematurely. Both Horace and Mary Greeley and Abraham and Mary Lincoln repeatedly went to Spiritualist séances in order to contact their young sons who had died in childhood. Later the Civil War would provoke another upsurge in Spiritualist séances as families tried to connect with those who died in battle and were buried far from home.

The early nineteenth century was also a time of westward expansion. The adventuresome could pull up stakes and move to the western frontier, where they could reinvent themselves according to whatever vision they possessed. It was a time of great possibilities. Anyone who wanted to could make something of himself regardless of his, or his family's, previous situation, including in some cases the previous state of enslavement. This was also the time of the great American reform movements of abolition and suffrage. Not satisfied with the status quo, Americans were working together to change conditions for the most downtrodden of their members. Spiritualism resonated with these cultural movements. It suggested that one could have direct access to the spiritual world without the mediation of ministers or church hierarchy. And the spirits were generally progressive, supporting the important social movements of the day.

Spiritualists did not define their faith according to any prescribed set of ceremonies or specific creeds. Instead they followed a doctrine of individual liberty and responsibility that encouraged everyone to seek the light needed as a guide for his or her own spiritual development. Because there was no central authority, Spiritualists (and their spirit guides) often disagreed on even the most important ideas about their tradition. They did however generally hold to some common ideas, including the existence of a Divine Spirit, the "universal brotherhood" of humankind, the unceasing progression of the soul after death, and a belief that hell is a condition of the mind rather than a physical place. These ideas led Spiritualists to see the world as an organic, interconnected whole. The most fundamental belief of the Spiritualist movement was that death was not an ending but merely a change of state, that a spiritual essence survives a person's death and that that essence can communicate with the living. Based on the visions of Andrew Jackson Davis, many Spiritualists called the afterlife Summerland, a series of spheres where people worked toward the spiritual aspirations that would bring them into harmonial relations with one another. Based on the ideas of Swedenborg and Davis, Spiritualists believed that when the body dies, the spirit, which is composed of a sort of subtle matter, withdraws. The spirit may remain near the earth plane for a longer or shorter period of time before advancing to the higher planes until it finally reaches the sphere of pure spirit. There was no hell in the cosmology of most Spiritualists. Rather those who were evil or malicious on the earth plane would simply take a longer time to advance through the spheres toward pure spiritual being.

In many ways the Summerland of Spiritualism was similar to the afterlife envisioned by the Kongolese. In both cases, the afterlife was not that much different from the world of the living. According to the reports of spirits contacted by Spiritualist mediums, the Summerland resembled a beautiful Victorian community where spirits dwelled together with their friends and relatives, attending lectures, concerts, and artistic exhibits, and worked together for the benefit of both those in spirit and those still in their bodies. Husbands and wives, parents and children, friends, and others with mutual affinities could find each other in the Summerland and were able to enjoy each other's company. Even family pets could find their way into the Summerland as important members of the family circle. Sympathy, the mutually shared condition of emotional feelings between two or more persons, was thought to be the driving force that brought people together both in body and in spirit. Just as an injury in one part of the body can be felt in another through the workings of the sympathetic nervous system, so too sympathetic individuals are drawn together to work on mutually pleasurable projects. Sympathetic relationships between people draw together communities that can overcome all barriers, even the barrier between the living and the dead.

As another echo of Kongolese cosmology, another central tenet of Spiritualism is the belief that those who have died, who are "in spirit," can communicate with the living through the agency of mediums, sensitive individuals who can hear, see, or feel spirits or cause spirits to interact with the physical world. The Fox sisters and many early mediums relied on physical mediumship, where the spirits communicated by rapping sounds, apparitions, levitation, and other physical manifestations of their presence. Although not all such manifestations have been explained, many mediums were exposed as frauds who produced these manifestations themselves or with the help of accomplices. Later mediums and most of today's mediums, often called channels, rely instead on mental mediumship, including clairvoyance (clear seeing), clairaudience (clear hearing), clairsentience (clear feeling), crystal gazing, divination, dowsing, and the like. Just as West and West Central Africans communicated with their honored dead through trance possession, trances and trance speaking were used by both physical and mental mediums to transmit the words of spiritual beings directly to their human audiences.

Spiritualist performances in public venues quickly evolved. Many included a lecture or sermon outlining Spiritualist principles and adding a veneer of scientific authority to the proceedings. While many of these lecturers were men, the stars of the shows were the mediums that offered spirit messages to those in attendance. These mediums were generally women who, it was assumed, did not have the training or intellectual prowess to speak for themselves but proved to be perfect conduits for the words of the spirits. Soon Spiritualists organized summer camps throughout the East Coast and down to Florida. At these camps visitors could receive readings and take classes to develop their own spiritual abilities. Some of the most successful of these camps, including those in Lily Dale, New York, Cassadaga, Florida, and Chesterfield, Indiana, are still open today (T. Leonard, 29).

In 1888 Spiritualism was dealt a heavy blow when Margaret (Maggie) Fox claimed that she and her sister were frauds who manipulated their toes to produce the first rapping. She proclaimed Spiritualism as evil and mediums like herself as charlatans. Less than a year later Maggie recanted her claims against Spiritualism, and observers were left to wonder which of her statements held the truth. However, by that time thousands of people had already had their own experiences of talking to the other side. Critics claimed that Maggie's confession fatally damaged Spiritualism's public image, while true Spiritualists continued to support the movement. Spiritualism provided a welcome alternative to the Calvinist religion of the time and provided comfort, especially in times of war and epidemics when death cut wide swaths across the population. Although there are few contemporary Spiritualist congregations across the country today, the movement has given us many theological ideas that continue to permeate American society, including the ideas that all souls are redeemable; that heaven and hell are psychological concepts, rather than physical locations; and that the beloved dead still maintain an interest in their living friends and descendants (T. Leonard, 30–31).

CONCLUSION

Both the new burial practices that developed during this same time and Spiritualism depended on a new vision of the relationship between the living and the dead. The relationship that developed was a complete reversal of the previous Calvinist metaphysical view, in which the dead are gone and neither maintain an interest in the living nor are interested in any form of communication with living friends and relatives. While both the history of changes in burial practices and Spiritualism seem to be the history of white culture changes, they are both based on a metaphysical foundation that is more African than European in its form. Tellingly, these practices developed in the northern states where strong free African American communities had been in existence for generations and where African American funerals and celebrations like the Pinkster festivals were celebrated on the streets of the cities. White Americans would not have been unfamiliar with African Americans' approaches to death, dying, and the afterlife, so it's not unreasonable that these ideas might have become part of these new American attitudes. Why did white Americans become more concerned about the final resting places of their dead and the rituals surrounding funerals and burials? For several hundred years, communal unmarked graves were the commonly accepted form of burial. Then, suddenly, such burials and the graveyards were no longer acceptable.

What psychological changes allowed early Spiritualists to assume that the entities that spoke to and through them were either the beloved dead, famous people, or highly evolved spiritual entities when the history of possession and similar phenomena in European contexts almost always assumed such communications were demonic? Little more than 150 years after the infamous Salem witch trials, people were invoking spiritual entities, asking their opinions, and following their advice. The Fox sisters named the first spirit they encountered Mr. Splitfoot, assuming a demonic source. Yet very quickly they revised their opinion, being told, and believing, that they were speaking instead to the spirit of a person—an unhappy and disreputable person, but a person nonetheless. What allowed them, their neighbors, and audiences to make that mental leap? Is it possible that African American ideas about life, death, and the afterlife influenced even their racist neighbors? All Spiritualist mediums brought their own life experience into the séance room with them, so we have to assume that the African Americans who participated in Spiritualist circles also shared their cosmological and metaphysical views with those sitting beside them. While we cannot see exactly how these changes came about, it is true that at the end of this period all Americans were more African in their approach to both their treatment of the dead and their willingness to communicate with the dead and other spiritual entities.

5

CHILDREN OF ODUDUWA

The Oyo Empire

"Who among the gods can accompany his devotee on a distant journey over the seas without turning back? It is Ori, it is Ori alone who can accompany his devotee on a distant journey over the seas without turning back" (traditional saying from Ifa texts).[1]

The Yoruba-speaking people of West Africa, who made up the Oyo Empire and its client states, were latecomers to the slave trade, not contributing significant numbers in either the Caribbean or the United States until the late eighteenth to early nineteenth centuries. Although only about 9 percent of the Africans brought to the Americas were from Yoruba-speaking areas, and the majority of those were delivered to Saint-Domingue (Haiti), Cuba, and Bahia (Olupona and Rey, 22n1), we do find Yoruba enclaves in certain areas of the United States. South Carolina and Louisiana stand out prominently among these, and Yoruba ideas have infiltrated into American religious sensibilities, not only from these areas but also from the islands of the Caribbean, especially Haiti and Cuba. Unlike in the Kongo and Fon areas, there was little Christian missionary activity in the area populated by what we today call the Yoruba people until after the close of the slave trade, so they had little introduction to Christianity before their entry into the Americas. On the other hand, as Jacob Olupona and Terry Rey suggest, the religious culture of the Yoruba people has spread throughout the world, forming a "taproot of African diasporic life" (Olupona and Rey, 4), and it continues to influence American religious sensibility.

There is no accurate census of people who participate in or who are familiar with the religious system we place under the umbrella of Yoruba religion today. However, almost twenty-five years ago Sandra Barnes estimated that "more than 70 million African and New World people participate in, or are closely familiar with, religious systems that include Ogun [one of the many Yoruba deities], and this number is increasing rather than declining" (Barnes, 1). This estimate places the Yoruba tradition ahead of many of the smaller so-called world religions, including Judaism, Sikhism, Jainism, and Zoroastrianism (Olupona and Rey, 8). In addition it is important to note that the Yoruba religious culture described in this chapter has attracted many members who do not share Yoruba racial or ethnic heritage. In fact, as Olupona and Rey suggest, it has not only taken root in its African homeland and among all types of peoples in the Americas but has also spread to Europe and even Asia (8).

HISTORY

The people we identify today as the Yoruba were not the first to inhabit the area of southwestern Nigeria we commonly associate with them today. Scholars suggest an earlier people, represented by the Nok terra-cotta heads discovered in northern Nigeria, populated the area from around 900 BCE to 200 CE or earlier. Although the ethnic group we call the Yoruba today did not see themselves as a single entity until the nineteenth century, people who spoke variants of the Yoruba language and who saw the world through the lens of Yoruba cosmology populated this area of what is now southwestern Nigeria and eastern Benin by the end of the first millennium CE. There is little archeological evidence to help determine where these people came from. It is clear, however, that by 950 CE they had a highly developed artistic and ritual center in Ile-Ife, the city-state that became the spiritual and cultural center of Yoruba culture (Bascom, 8). There are many archeological indications that during these earliest periods there were already complex city-states, headed by sacred rulers, councils of elders, and chiefs. These areas have one of the oldest and finest artistic traditions in Africa, and by 1100 CE there was a well-defined artistic tradition that produced highly naturalist sculpture in terra-cotta and stone, followed by works in copper, brass, and bronze (Drewal et al., 13).

While Ile-Ife was the artistic and ritual center of this cultural group, the city of Oyo became its political center, and its citizens are often known as the Yoruba proper. Soon the kings of Oyo expanded Oyo's reach, bringing neighboring cities and towns under its authority, forming the Oyo Empire while allowing the citizens of each client city to maintain their identification with their own town. As with many ethnic groups, when these peoples were brought together under slavery, colonialism, or moder-

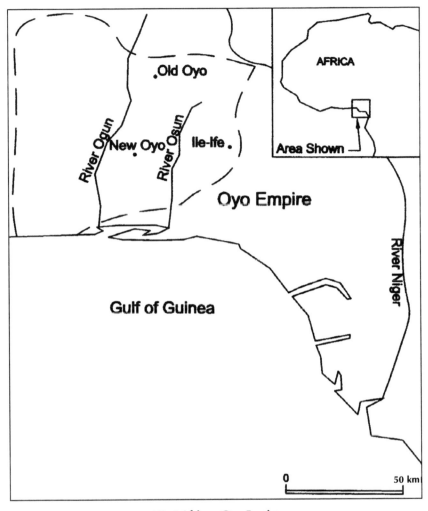

West African Oyo Empire

nity, their local differences became less important, and they became categorized into a single entity known as the Yoruba.[2]

The mythological records suggest that Ile-Ife (the city of Ife) was established when the God of whiteness, Obatala, on the command of the great God, Olodumare, climbed down a golden chain from the sky and scattered soil on the water that covered the earth, then dropped a five-toed chicken onto that soil to scatter it further. Once the new ground was tested for firmness, Obatala stepped onto the earth and established a sacred grove at that site. Later a group of deities, known as the *Orisha*,[3] led by

Obatala, descended onto the earth and established the first towns, farms, and sacred sites, working together to civilize the newly created earth. Later still, again at the command of Olodumare, Obatala formed the bodies of human beings so that Olodumare could breathe the breath of life into them. These became the people that would populate the earth so the deities could return to their home in the sky or, some say, under the earth. Other myths say that a different Orisha, Oduduwa, climbed down the golden chain and scattered the soil upon the waters to form firm earth. It is Oduduwa who is named as the first king of the Yoruba people in all traditional histories, and it is his sixteen sons who are said to have established all the great cities of Yorubaland. Even today the Yoruba people are known as "the children of Oduduwa."

Over their nine-century history the Yoruba people developed a series of kingdoms, one of the earliest of which was based in the city of Oyo near the Niger River. The Oyo Empire that developed between 1600 and 1830, supported by its fearsome cavalry, became the most important political power in the area. It maintained ties with both Ile-Ife and the Kingdom of Dahomey and developed the trading empire that first established ties with the Europeans plying Africa's western coast (Drewal et al., 13). There is little recorded history of the Yoruba before 1698, when cavalry from the city of Oyo, by then the center of the empire, invaded the Kingdom of Allada in southern Dahomey. By this time Yoruba slaves, prisoners of the ongoing civil wars within the empire, were already being exported out of the Kingdom of Dahomey through the port at Whydah. In fact, by the 1630s the Yoruba language had become the lingua franca along what was called the Lower Guinea coast from the Volta River to Benin, and Yoruba culture and religious traditions were widely known and practiced throughout this area even though it was outside Yoruba political domination (Thornton 1992, 190). Around 1727 the Kingdom of Dahomey began paying tribute to the Kingdom of Oyo and relations continued between the two realms for almost a century until 1827. Off and on throughout this period conflict between these two great kingdoms funneled people into the West African slave trade, and after 1827 increasing conflicts within the Oyo Empire and between it and its neighbors greatly increased the number of Yoruba-speaking slaves exported to the Americas (Bascom, 12–15).

While wars raged throughout Yorubaland and Dahomey, the Haitian Revolution (1791–1804) changed the political face of the Caribbean. Haiti was once the largest sugar producer in the Americas. But after the revolution both planters and their European buyers turned their collective backs on the island. Cuba, until then little more than a reprovisioning stop for ships entering and leaving the Caribbean, soon took up the mantle of sugar production, consequently increasing its import of slaves from a trickle to a deluge. Not only did the gross number of Africans increase as the number and size of the sugar plantations grew, but the ethnic makeup of those coming from Africa also changed. Whereas between 1760 and 1820 almost half of those imported into Cuba were classified as Kongolese or Carabali, while the Yoruba represented less than 10 percent, between 1850 and 1870 almost 35 percent of the enslaved entering Cuba were classified as Yoruba and no other ethnic group contributed as much as 20 percent to the total numbers during this period (Brandon, 58).

As with others of the enslaved, the Yoruba brought to the island their music, religion, and culture. Primarily in the capital city of Havana, but also throughout the island, freed and enslaved children of Oduduwa set up enclaves of their culture in the *cabildos* and confraternities. Because the Cuban authorities preferred that Africans be separated according to their ethnic heritage, most of these organizations were bastions of a single African culture. Thus through singing and dancing, the celebration of holidays, and public and private rituals, the Yoruba-speaking people were able to reconstitute large portions of their indigenous culture. After Cuba gained its freedom from Spain, many of these cabildos were put under tighter scrutiny, and it appears the religion that developed there, known today as Santería or Lukumi, moved into the homes of its practitioners, where it continued to develop and evolve (Brandon, 71–72).

Because of its proximity to the Florida mainland, Cuba has had a relationship with the developing United States from before its beginning as an independent nation. However, it wasn't until the Cuban Revolution of 1959 that significant numbers of Cubans migrated to the United States. Together with a second wave of refugees who left Cuba from the port of Mariel in 1980, Cubans, devotees of the Yoruba Orisha, have made a significant impact on American religion in the twentieth and twenty-first centuries. Today it is estimated that there are more Orisha devotees in the United States than in Cuba, and with the publication of Stephen Prothero's *God Is Not One*, their religion is beginning to take its rightful place among the "religions that run the world" (Prothero, quote from book cover).

COSMOLOGY

According to Yoruba cosmology, everything is encased within the calabash of existence. Sometimes called a bottle gourd, a calabash is a type of fruit

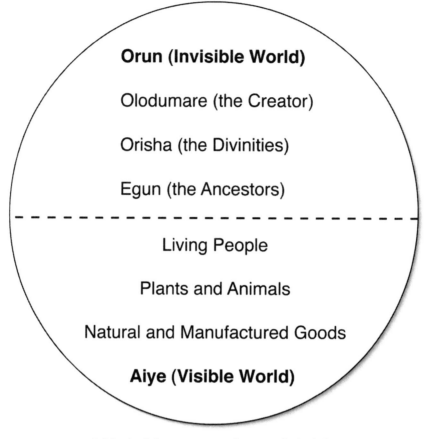

Orun (Invisible World)

Olodumare (the Creator)

Orisha (the Divinities)

Egun (the Ancestors)

Living People

Plants and Animals

Natural and Manufactured Goods

Aiye (Visible World)

Calabash of the cosmos, Yoruba cosmological view

that grows in tropical regions. When it is dried, the outer skin of the calabash turns into a hard case that can be used as a container, serving bowl, or
water jug. Calabashes grow in many different shapes, one of which is a
globe. The calabash of existence is imagined to be such a globe, containing
everything, including people, plants, animals, and all natural and manufactured goods as well as the great God Olodumare, all the lesser deities, called
the Orisha, and the ancestors. The visible and invisible worlds, known respectively as *aiye* and *orun*, are not separate worlds but merely two different
planes of the one world of all existence enclosed by this calabash. People
easily move between the visible world and invisible world as they are born,
live, die, and are reborn. When the Yoruba people saw the face or mannerism
of a grandparent in a child they said that the elder had been reborn to enjoy

the pleasures of the visible world again. Rebirth for the Yoruba was a positive experience. Instead of being a punishment for the sins of one's previous life or the penalty for not having learned certain spiritual lessons, rebirth was seen as the reward for having been a good person, for having helped the family prosper, and for having made the world a better place. All but the worst individuals were reborn, returning to the visible world over and over again to enjoy life among family and friends.

The Orisha, the deities of the Yoruba pantheon, also have the power to interact with both the visible and invisible worlds, sometimes even taking on human bodies. In mythological times, the Orisha lived in the visible world and interacted with human beings directly while still being able to journey to the invisible world at will. Later they all retired to orun but were still able to communicate and work with their devotees. In the mythology the number of Orisha is said to be 101 or 201 or 1001, that is, as many as you can know plus one more—an innumerable number. Some of these deities were worshipped throughout Yorubaland, but others were of only local significance. Each town was under the protection of one or more locally important Orisha, often the deities of the ruler and his family. Similarly each extended family worshipped some small group of Orisha, generally those associated with the father or his lineage in general. Some deities, such as Ogun the blacksmith Orisha, were associated with certain professions and worshipped by all those engaged in that work. Women, who generally married out of their own extended family, might or might not bring their deities with them when they settled into their husbands' compounds and might or might not participate in the worship of their husband's Orisha. Children might worship the gods of their father, their mother, or other deities as well as or instead of those of their parents. If a woman was unable to have children in spite of prayers and sacrifices at the shrine of her own or her husband's Orisha, she might visit a diviner who would direct her to the shrine of another deity. If a child was born after the appropriate rituals, he or she was said to "belong" to that deity and would be brought up in its worship, even if no one else in the family worshipped that Orisha. Adults might acquire the worship of additional deities as their life circumstances changed, as they took up a certain profession, or when they made offerings to a new Orisha in order to improve an unfortunate turn of events. An individual might worship his deity or deities in his or her own compound but more generally all the worshippers of a deity or group of related deities would join together into a cult group or worship community for ceremonies and festivals. People often traveled to other towns in order to participate in the festivals of their own Orisha or those of others. Although there were community cults, particularly those associated with the ruler and his family, each individual's worship was his or hers alone and no one was persecuted because he or she did or did not worship a particular Orisha (Bascom, 77–78).

This organization meant the Yoruba people had a great many religious specialists like priests and diviners and that many more people were experienced in the daily ritual requirements of the Orisha they worshipped. Large community-wide rituals were led by the priests associated with the king or local ruler, and popular worship groups might have groups of male and female priests who were primarily responsible for the rituals of that group. The senior men and women of a compound or family were responsible for making certain offerings to lineage ancestors and the Orisha of the clan, and the father of a nuclear family was responsible for honoring his own ancestors. Members of certain occupations and some secret societies also were responsible for the worship of the Orisha associated with that occupation or society. In addition, individuals who had been initiated into the worship of an Orisha were taught how to perform the appropriate daily rituals for that Orisha. Such individuals might also be able to introduce and perhaps even initiate others into the worship of their Orisha. Thus the men and women who brought outside Orisha into their quarters were considered capable of providing at least some level of worship activities to those Orisha whether or not there was a larger worship community in the local town or one nearby.

Although there are innumerable Orisha, there are about thirteen that were generally known and widely worshipped (Bascom, 78–92). These include Olodumare (also known as Olorun or Olofi), who is the high or great God who lives in the sky and is the father, creator, or ruler of all the lesser Orisha. Christian missionaries syncretized Olorun with the Christian God and the Islamic Allah. In general Olodumare is not the object of any cult or ritual. It is Olodumare who establishes each individual's destiny for this lifetime (78–79). Eshu, who is also known as Elegba or Elegbara, as well as Legba among the Fon, is the trickster deity as well as the messenger among the Orisha and between the Orisha and human beings. Most towns and individual compounds had an image of Eshu at the entrance, as this is the deity who opens and closes the doors to blessing and opportunities. As the trickster he delights in mischief-making, although often in an effort to test an individual's resolve or devotion. Christians and Muslims often conflated Eshu with the biblical Satan, although that is a misrepresentation of his role as divine messenger and enforcer of the will of Olodumare and the other Orisha. Regardless of what other Orisha an individual might worship, everyone made frequent offerings to Eshu so that he might not trouble them and so that he would open the lines of communication to the other Orisha (79–80). Ifa, also known as Orunmila in Yorubaland or Fa among the Fon, is the Orisha of the divination system also known as Ifa. Orunmila had his own independent priesthood, known as the *babalawo* (fathers of the mystery), whose primary role was to provide divination to the community as well as to assist individuals in making the offerings and performing the rituals called for by divination. Ifa and Eshu work together to help people manifest their best destiny by softening a difficult one or strengthening an auspicious one (80). In many ways Olodumare, Eshu, and Ifa were the most important of the Yoruba Orisha. They were known across Yorubaland and were worshipped by all people from the highest king to the lowliest slave.

Orishala (also known as Oshala or Obatala) and Shango are the archetypical old king and young king of the Yoruba pantheon. Orishala, whose name means "the great Orisha," is the creator deity who fashioned not only the world but also human beings. As Obatala (the King of the White Cloth) this Orisha is the most important of the white (cool) deities. He was often imagined as the wise old man who brought the coolness of old age to his interactions with humanity (81–82). Shango, on the other hand, is the impetuous young king and the deity of thunder. The Orisha Shango is said to have been an early king of the Oyo who was a great magician and who developed the cavalry used so effectively by the warriors of Oyo. It was said that Shango's mother was a member of the neighboring Nupe tribal group (84–87). Ogun (Gu among the Fon and Ogou in Haiti), the Orisha of iron, was one of the best known of the Orisha. He was the patron not only of blacksmiths but also of all those who use the results of the blacksmith's arts, including farmers, soldiers, hunters, barbers, carvers, and, in modern times, truck drivers and railroad workers. Whereas Eshu opens the door between the two realms, it is Ogun, using his trademark machete, who clears the path between them. Even today many oaths are sworn on a piece of iron, as it is said that Ogun is more prompt in punishing oath breakers than either Allah or the Christian God (82–83).

Shopona, the God of smallpox and other similar diseases, is one of the most ambivalent Orisha in this pantheon. In modern times the Nigerian government has banned his worship because it was believed that his priests spread the disease in order to obtain the property of its victims. However, the priests themselves told Bascom in the 1960s that their role was to try to prevent the disease and help those afflicted to recover. In some stories it is said that when Shopona was exiled from Yorubaland he went to Dahomey and was crowned as a king there. Even after the cult was banned in Nigeria, it continued to be practiced in neighboring Dahomey. West Africans were familiar with a type of inoculation against smallpox, and based on information from some enslaved Africans in the early 1700s Cotton Mather convinced the people of Boston to accept inoculation and avoid a smallpox epidemic (Wells, 59; Farmer). Because Shopona and the disease he is associated with were so widely feared, people avoided saying his name, using instead any one of a variety of nicknames, including Baba (father), Oluwa (lord), Babaluaiye (father, lord of the world), Obaluaiye (king, lord of the world), and the like (91–92). In the New World, his name was generally dropped completely in favor of one of these nicknames. Although smallpox has been completely eradicated worldwide, Shopona hasn't lost his place in the Yoruba pantheon but has become associated with other virulent diseases, including HIV/AIDS.

Most of the female Orisha were associated with the major rivers in Yorubaland, including Oya, who was associated with the Niger River, Yemoja, who was associated with the Ogun River, and Oshun, who was associated with the river that bears her name. Oya, Oshun, and another river Orisha, Obba, were all wives of the great king Shango. Like her husband, Oya is a warrior. She often manifests as the strong wind that precedes storms, so it was said that she led Shango, the king of thunder and lightning, into battle. She is also the owner of the marketplace and is the patron of the market women who ply their trade there. Oshun is often called the Yoruba Venus. She is the beautiful young woman who takes meticulous care of her appearance and is said to have brought "civilization" to the Yoruba people. In the mythology she had liaisons with many of the male Orisha, including Shango, Ogun, Shopona, and Ifa, but throughout she remained her own person. Whereas Oshun is associated with all the charms of young women, Yemoja stands as the great mother in the Yoruba pantheon. She was also said to have come from the Nupe people and was sometimes named as the mother of Shango, as well as many of the other Orisha. Not all of the water deities are female, however. Erinle (also known as Eyinle or Enle) is a hunter deity associated with a small river. It was said that he tried to seduce Obba, the wife of Shango, and that, in turn, he was seduced by Yemoja. As a denizen of the forest, he is one of several Orisha associated with healing herbs and practices (87–91).

When African people were enslaved from whatever area, there was little effort made to balance the types of people taken across the Atlantic, so the social and religious hierarchy they were familiar with couldn't easily be replicated in their new environment. However, because among the Yoruba and others much of the religious and political power was diffused throughout the culture, there was the possibility of re-creating a portion of their societies in their new surroundings. Even in the absence of others of their clan, family, worship community, or even language group, individuals could continue the worship of their own deities and pass at least remnants of that worship on to their children. Thus when Africans arrived in Cuba, Haiti, and even portions of the United States, they were able to form communities in the cities and on the plantations. They were also able to share the worship of their deities and in many ways reconstitute portions of the religious systems of their homelands. This is most obvious in Cuba and Haiti, where the religious ceremonies of the Yoruba and Fon were used to construct the religions known today as Santería, or Lukumi, and Vodou, but we also find elements of these African traditions in the United States. We will discuss the largest of these traditions, Santería, in chapter 9.

The Yoruba people saw this earth as basically good, not as a vale of tears or abode of suffering but as the marketplace where one could make his or her fortune and reputation. These ideas are embedded in two proverbs. One says that orun, the invisible world, is home, while aiye, the visible world, is the marketplace. Home in this context is the afterworld, where one went to eat, sleep, and recharge, while the marketplace, this world, was the center of all activity. A second proverb says, "Life in heaven cannot be pleasant, otherwise people would not live so long and come back so quickly." People might live fifty, sixty, seventy, or more years, yet after death they were believed to be reborn quickly, often as the next child born into the extended family.

The Yoruba people believed that each person was born with an individual destiny, called *ori*, for this lifetime. This destiny, which was chosen or given to the individual before birth as part of an agreement with Olodumare, determined the basic outlines of one's life, including the time and place of birth and one's aptitudes and abilities, as well as one's intelligence, competence, personal limitations, and capacity to defend oneself, and the time of one's natural death. Although some destinies were soft and easy, others were hard and difficult. Among the Yoruba one of the functions of what we call religion was working with the Orisha and the ancestors to soften a difficult destiny or strengthen a good one so that the individual could live the best, most productive life possible within the limitations of his or her individual destiny. When one was having problems, sickness, or bad luck, the diviner as the mouthpiece of the Orisha would make suggestions of how one could get back on the path of one's best destiny. One's destiny, one's ori, was also considered to be an individual deity. While everyone might share in the worship of all of the other deities, even the lineage ancestors, one's ori was unique to oneself. It was said that before any Orisha or ancestor could help an individual, permission had to be obtained from his or her ori to ensure that such help was in the best interest of the individual. There were also divination verses that said specifically that it was one's ori that accompanied one from birth throughout life. Another being, human or spiritual, might desert you, but your ori remains always available to help make your life better. No matter where you might roam, even if you were carried across the great ocean, in the belly of a slave ship for example, your ori would be there to help and comfort you during the worst of times (Abimbola, 132–49).

Divination and possession trance are the ritual activities that make it possible for the devotees of the Orisha to speak to them directly and to learn the actions that will manifest the best portion of their destinies. Through drumming and dancing the Orisha were called into the presence of the worship community where they would take over the consciousness and body of one of those present and become incarnate through them. Rituals might be performed by a small group of devotees at a personal shrine or might be citywide events that involve a large shrine in the wilderness surrounding the village, at the river, or at a prominent location near the king's palace or the central marketplace. The priests and initiated followers of the Orisha being honored performed special rituals out of the sight of the rest of the community, but public drumming and dancing including one or more of the priests being possessed by the honored Orisha were generally part of the ceremony. In many cases the whole city as well as visitors from neighboring cities would turn out for the public portions of these rituals. One need not be a worshipper of the honored Orisha to participate. The possessed priest or priests would speak to the assembled crowd or to individuals. When speaking to the assembly, the message generally concerned the community as a whole or the actions of its leaders. Private consultations with individuals or small groups generally only concerned that individual or group. Through such ceremonies not only did the people worship their deities but the deities were also empowered, through the mechanism of possession, to speak directly to the people.

Divination provided a more intimate setting for communication with the Orisha and the ancestors. Although divination might be performed for the community as a whole or for the king and his council, it often provided a direct link that allowed an ordinary individual or family group to communicate directly with deities or deified ancestors. Priests and initiates often began their day by doing a simple divination to speak to the Orisha at their personal shrines. However, those who had established themselves as professional diviners made themselves available to anyone who wanted to determine his or her life's path or ask a question when his or her life seemed to be going badly. These professional diviners tended to be the *babalawo* who had been initiated into the priesthood of the Orisha of divination, Orunmila. Regardless of which Orisha or set of Orisha one might worship, everyone turned to the priests of Orunmila in times of personal troubles or significant life events. There were other forms of divination practiced among the Yoruba people and their cousin-neighbors, but Ifa (Fa among the Fon), the divination taught by Orunmila to his first priest and followers, was, and is, the most well-known and respected.

Divination was not merely a form of fortune-telling among the Yoruba. Instead it was a method to discover the outlines of one's personal destiny and, if necessary, to soften or strengthen it. One of the best-known examples of divination and destiny in the Western world is the story of Oedipus the king. Originating in fifth-century-BCE Greece, the myth of Oedipus tells how Oedipus's parents learned through divination that the child would one day kill his father and marry his mother. Determined to forestall such a horrid destiny, the king ordered that his young son be killed. Events conspired against the will of the king, and the child, instead of dying, was raised in a neighboring kingdom. When as an adult Oedipus himself, who thought that the king and queen who raised him were his father and mother, went for divination and learned of his destiny, he left the kingdom of his adopted parents and ended up in that of his birth parents, where he manifested the destiny laid out for him. This is an example of what might be called fixed destiny—no matter what actions were taken by the young Oedipus or his parents, there was no way he could have avoided the life foretold for him.

The Yoruba people believed in a more malleable type of destiny, one that could be modified within certain parameters. From a Yoruba point of view what was missing from the story of Oedipus was an effective way of avoiding such a horrible destiny. Always included as part of Yoruba divination was the remedy for avoiding the worst aspects of a difficult destiny. Generally this remedy was an offering to one or more deities who agreed to come to the aid of the inquirer. These offerings, under the umbrella of "sacrifice," could persuade a deity or ancestor to protect the inquirer from the worst aspects of a difficult destiny or help to bring out the best of a good one. What must be sacrificed might be any natural or manufactured item that appealed to the otherworldly being, including food, cloth, money, manufactured items, changes in behavior, or in some cases the lives of different animals. Like human beings, different Orisha favored different foods, fruits, colors, and animals, and it was part of the responsibility of the diviner to determine just what would provide relief in each particular case. Often in the divination texts those items the inquirer was asked to sacrifice were exactly what he or she would need at some future moment to avoid the worst part of the proposed future. In those cases, the inquirer would be asked to leave certain items at the foot of a particular tree. Later it would be found that the items left in that location were exactly what was needed when the moment of destiny arrived.

YORUBA SACRED SPACES

In describing the altar-making traditions in Africa and the New World, Robert Farris Thompson suggests that Afro-Atlantic[4] altars are "inherently open and ecumenical . . . 'additive, eclectic, non-exclusive'" (Thompson 1993b, 20, quoting Richard Price in *Alabi's World*). In the languages of the Yoruba and related groups traditional altars are the "face," "countenance," or "forehead" of the gods, "the threshold for communication with the other world." However, this "face" was often hidden deep within the compounds of the devotees. The Yoruba people encoded the rank and secrecy of the gods by the way they organized their sacred space. In Yorubaland such spaces included a public outer courtyard, an inner court for initiates where, with music and dance, "persons turned into gods," and an innermost chamber where the "essential stones and other emblems rest upon an elevated dais" (Thompson 1993b, 146). Different people had different levels of access to these spaces. While the public outer courtyard was completely open to public view, access to the inner courtyard was restricted to the initiated worshippers of the particular Orisha. It was only in the innermost chamber that the actual presence of the Orisha was embedded in stones and other objects, "fetishes" as they became known to European travelers. Only priests had daily access to this inner sanctum. Others were only allowed into this area by invitation. As Drewal says, "Concealment constituted heightened spirituality. It is a way of conveying the ineffable qualities and boundless powers" of sacred beings (Drewal et al., 39).

In the innermost of these sacred rooms, the consecrated materials may sit directly on the ground or on a platform made of smoothed and shaped clay rising from twelve to eighteen inches high. Often, the most important objects on the altar are elevated further by being placed on cylindrical stands or other objects (for example, mortars, piles of calabashes, or calabashes on top of pottery) (Thompson 1993b, 146). Calabashes and pots held the essential objects associated with the deities so enthroned. Along with these sacred calabashes and pots, African altars contained other objects emblematic of the *ashé* or special power of the deities. These objects included "pots, cowry shells, pieces of iron, gourd bowls, stones, tree limbs, and branches. These things would be selected because of their symbolic association with the deity or function they were to serve" (Brandon, 12). However, when observing these sacred spaces one might notice that unlike the altars of Christian churches or Hindu temples, there are few human or humanlike figures, and those figures that can be observed are generally said to represent not the Orisha but their devotees. These images generally exhibit the appropriate acts and gestures one should assume in the proximity of the divine. They present a "school of being," spatial and iconic instructions on the "proper way to stand and kneel before the gods" (Drewal et al., 26; Thompson 1993a, 17; Thompson 1993b, 147).

Often these images are women in various postures. In Yoruba culture the female was seen as soft, cool, and tranquil, and images of women were believed to have a pacifying and assuasive influence on the deities. Women kneeling, offering their breasts, and feeding their children not only represented those qualities but also indicated the "love, tenderness, generosity, nurture, and protection" one hoped to obtain from the Orisha (Lawal, 25–26). Rosalind Hackett, a longtime scholar of Yoruba religious art, also suggests that the preponderance of female imagery signifies the role that women have as the nurturers of the gods. Within this tradition, and those that sprang from it, all priests, including men who are dedicated to the Orisha, are called *iyawo orisha*, that is, "wife of the Orisha," because of that special relationship they have with the Orisha (Lawal, 25). Thus we see that the Yoruba and other West Africans brought a new language of the sacred with them to the Americas. In the Yoruba worldview, what is most sacred is what is most hidden, the female or someone with female qualities is the most appropriate official of the sacred beings, and in the right circumstances human beings can turn into gods.

POSSESSION TRANCE

An important part of the religious and cultural life of the Yoruba people was the phenomenon scholars call possession trance. As described in the anthropological literature, possession is any altered or unusual state of consciousness indigenously understood in terms of the influence of an alien spirit, demon, or deity (Crapanzano, 7). People under such influence often exhibit dramatic changes in body language, speech patterns, and general behavior.

These changes might be perceived as grotesque or even blasphemous, especially by outsiders who don't know the characteristics of the possessing spirit. The legitimacy of any particular possession event, however, should be judged according to local standards that distinguish between this type of behavior and similar behavior that is the hallmark of mental illness. Although possession can be found around the world,[5] how the local culture understands the phenomenon determines its response to these behaviors. Most commonly possessing spirits are seen as spirits of deities or other holy beings, as unclean or demonic spirits, or as spirits of the dead. If the culture usually views possessing spirits as unclean or demonic, efforts are made to banish or exorcise them, ridding the individual of their influences and sometimes punishing the medium. However, if the spirit is seen as benevolent, for example, one's ancestor, a deity, or other holy being, the culture generally welcomes it, listens to any exhortation or demand it makes, and generally deals kindly with the possessed person. Indeed, in those societies where possession was positively valued, such a phenomenon was often intentionally induced so that the possessing spirits could communicate with members of the society.

Although many people are not as clear as they could be about the types of phenomena they are observing, scholars recognize three basic types of trance phenomena: conscious possession, trance possession, and shamanistic trance. In general, during trance events the consciousness of the individual is understood to be absent from the body, while during possession events, the individual's body is understood to have been overtaken by an outside consciousness. During conscious possession, the individual maintains some sort of consciousness during the possession event, although people often report that although they remain aware of their surroundings, they are in a meditative or dreamlike state. We're not sure what Dona Beatriz Kimpa Vita's experience was of her ongoing possession by Saint Anthony, but it would certainly fall under this classification.

In other types of trance, however, the individual loses consciousness during the duration of the trance event. During possession trance the individual's body is believed to be inhabited by the alien consciousness. Because his or her own consciousness is absent, the medium has no memory of what transpired while his or her body is possessed. Such an individual may or may not have some internal or mystical experience during the time his or her body is under the influence of the alien entity. During a shamanistic trance, on the other hand, the shaman's consciousness leaves the body and "travels" to other worlds or other planes. Although the shaman has no memory of what transpires to his or her body or physical environment during the trance event, he or she has vivid memories of traveling to that other place, meeting spirits or animal guides, and in general returns with new knowledge or awareness that can be used by him or her subsequent to the event. Swedenborg's mystical experiences talking to God and angels would be considered examples of shamanistic trances.

Among the Yoruba the most common type of these events falls in the realm of possession trance, during which the individual's consciousness is taken over by an ancestor or deity who uses the medium's body to interact with the observing community. The participants see this sort of possession as an affirmation of the divine presence and an opportunity to receive divine help and relief from individual or community struggles. These possession events usually take place in conjunction with religious rituals specifically or partially designed to induce them. Generally specific people who have been initiated into possession priesthoods or other secret societies become possessed so that they can serve as mediums for specific entities. There are different techniques for inducing possession among those so initiated, but the most common among the Yoruba was a combination of drumming and a form of call-and-response singing. Among the Yoruba people specifically and West African people in general drugs and intoxicants were not used to induce possession; rather the ritual environment itself was the trigger that induced these phenomena in susceptible individuals.

People from West and West Central Africa who were brought to the Americas maintained their ability to engage in possession activities. Even though the earliest American colonists did not recognize any religious activity among their bondspeople, they often reported the drumming and dancing Africans engaged in during their personal time. Some even tried to suppress such activities as "sinful" and recognized that such events could serve as the incubators of resistance and rebellion (Stuckey 1987, 25; Butler 2008, 101). For Africans dance (and the possession trance that often followed) was a means of establishing contact with the ancestors and the gods. Consequently, dancing was a common part of black funeral rituals (Stuckey 1987, 25; Frey and Wood, 25; Egerton, 157). As George Brandon says in reference to Cuba, "It would be surprising, indeed, given the intimate relationship which exists between music, dance and religion in African cultures, if these dances did not turn into religious ceremonies at times, complete with spirit possession" (Brandon, 71–72). It is unlikely that the European master class would have recognized these events as religious rituals, although in some sources they are described as "devil dances." It should not be surprising, then, to find that dance, in the form of the ring shout, call-and-response singing, and a type of trance, formed an integral part of the Christianized religiosity of African Americans in the nineteenth century (Frey and Wood, 145). As will be discussed more thoroughly in chapter 9, it was also this African style of worship that blacks taught their white counterparts during the revivals and in their mixed-race churches (Taves, 99). By the late nineteenth century, attempts to rid African American churches of the shout and its associated spirituals were impossible—their essential features were present in one form or another throughout the black cultures of the United States and within a portion of white American culture as well (Stuckey 1987, 95).

GENDER IN YORUBA SOCIETY

Gender designations among the Yoruba peoples appears to be much more fluid than Westerners are generally used to. Deities have both male and female aspects and human beings exhibit a form of gender mixing. Of course the term *gender* itself is somewhat slippery and problematic. However, Americans have what Harold Garfinkel calls the "natural attitude" toward gender, including the idea there are only two genders, that gender identity doesn't change, that genitals are the essential sign of gender, that a male/female gender dichotomy is natural, and that any deviation from these ideas is either a joke or a pathology (Garfinkel, 122–28). One of the ways the idea of gender is used among scholars is as an analytic tool for exploring cultural concepts. One such concept is that of prestige structures, that is, ideas about power relationships. Gender is often used to signify a set of binary opposites, such that man is to woman as culture is to nature, social good is to self-interest, and public is to domestic. According to these concepts, men are more aligned with culture while women are more aligned with the natural world; men have a more universalist orientation while women's interests are more private and particular; men care about the welfare of the whole society while women are more concerned about the well-being of themselves and their children. All of this leads to the stereotype that men should control the "social domain" while women should control the domestic sphere. In addition, those social activities associated with men tend to be more highly valued than those associated with women. Consequently, societies formulate prestige structures and power relationships that can be used to evaluate individuals and social organizations based on the gender associated with them (Clark, 30–31).

In her 1997 book *Invention of Women*, Oyèrónké Oyěwùmí, herself a Yoruba woman, has argued that "there were no *women*—defined in strictly gendered terms—in [traditional Yoruba society]," and that "the concept of 'woman' as it is used and as it is invoked in the scholarship is derived from Western experience and history" (Oyĕwùmí, xiii). She argues that relative age rather than body type (that is, one's genitals) was the basis for hierarchical organization in Yoruba society. Although, as I argue elsewhere (Clark, 35–44), I think Oyĕwùmí overstates her case; there are instances where gender is used, especially in a religious context, as a metaphor for other types of relationships.

Among the Yoruba, most relationships are described in terms of age relationships. Thus there is a single word for child, *omo*, which needs a modifier if one wants to designate the child's gender. Among adults one's place within any relationship or social gathering is dependent upon relative ages, who is older than whom. In social gatherings these relationships may change as individuals join or leave the group. When women marry they generally join the household of their husband's family. As a new bride the woman is addressed as *iyawo*, which means "wife, younger than the speaker," since as the most recent addition to the extended family she is considered younger than all the other members of the family, even children who may be physically younger. A new bride refers to all of the members of her husband's family as *oko*, "husband," regardless of their body type. Although we translate these terms, *iyawo* and *oko*, with gendered English words (wife and husband), among the Yoruba they indicate prestige relationships rather than strictly gender, that is, the new bride is "wife" to everyone in her husband's family and they are all "husband" to her. As new wives join the family and as she contributes her children to it, she gains in power and prestige so that over her lifetime she may move from being the least powerful to one of the most powerful members of the family (Bascom, 51; Clark 41–43). Within her birth family, the new bride maintains her prenuptial relationships. This means that while she is "wife" to everyone in her husband's family, she is "husband" to the spouses of her brothers and other male relatives. So her "gender" isn't fixed based on her genitals but varies according to the people with whom she is interacting.

In the religious realm these same terms are used to describe the relationships between the Orisha and their priests. Although there are some religious roles that are limited to either males or females, in general within Yoruba culture both men and women can take on most religious roles, including the priesthood of the various Orisha. In spite of the gender associated with them, all of the Orisha, whether considered male or female, as the more powerful being in the relationship, are considered to be the "husbands" of their priests. All newly initiated priests, regardless of their own body type, are given the title "iyawo" during their novitiate year as an indicator of this relationship. This means a man with several wives and children of his own would be called "iyawo Orisha," wife of the Orisha, when he is first initiated. He is "iyawo" relative to both his Orisha "husband" and all the other priests of that Orisha who are older than him in its service. Both male and female priests may also experience gender switching during possession events. Just as the young woman Kimpa Vita became Saint Anthony, a male being by Western criteria, so too the priests of the Orisha may become temporarily male or female when they are possessed by an Orisha. Thus a female priest possessed by Shango, the young virile king, takes on his male gender for the duration of the possession event. Similarly, a male priest possessed by the epitome of female sexuality, Oshun, takes on her gender.

Yoruba women not only have power within their own and their husband's families, they also have independent power as farmers and petty traders. Men and women work together on the family farms to grow food for themselves and their children, but in addition women often grow crops with the intent to sell either the raw produce or foodstuffs produced from them. Although men are usually responsible for long-distance trading, it is the women of the town who control the local marketplace and all the buying and selling that take place. As a businesswoman a woman is entitled to control her own money, and if she is successful it is possible for her to become richer than her husband.

CONCLUSION

Like the Kongolese who were brought from West Central Africa, very many of the Yoruba people who were brought here were young men caught up in the ongoing wars among the city-states of Yorubaland and between them and their neighbors, especially the Fon people, with whom they traded and fought for generations. Along with the young soldiers were others caught up in these wars, along with troublemakers who had been banished from their home areas and others unlucky enough to be in the wrong place at the wrong time. All of these people brought their own ideas about how societies should work, the nature of the cosmos with its different visible and invisible beings, how men and women should relate, and an instrumental view of the relationships between human beings, the deities, and the ancestors. This instrumental worldview reflects what Horton places on the more manipulative end of his continuum, situations in which individuals form connections with the deities and the ancestors with the goal of providing for the worldly needs of themselves, their families, and the larger society, that is, gaining the benefits of health, wealth, and increase (Horton, 33). Such a religious orientation was not completely absent from the European American mindset, but European Christianity of the time tended to be more on the communion side of Horton's continuum. Before the Great Awakening, the God of Anglican and other Protestant forms of Christianity was seen as absolutely transcendent, too far away and too different from humanity to be concerned about individual people's needs and concerns. As we have seen, this orientation changed and evolved toward a more manipulative, more immanent, more African approach toward God, especially the person of Jesus.

But the slaves from the Yoruba-speaking areas and their neighbors brought other ideas with them as well, including ideas about the differences between belief and knowledge, ideas about the place of women in society, and new ideas about witchcraft, its practitioners, and its uses.

6

THEN WHY NOT EVERY MAN?

> Didn't my Lord deliver Daniel, deliver Daniel, deliver Daniel.
> Didn't my Lord deliver Daniel, then why not every man?
> Didn't my Lord deliver Daniel, deliver Daniel, deliver Daniel.
> Didn't my Lord deliver Daniel, then why not every man?
> He delivered Daniel from the lion's den,
> Jonah from the belly of the whale,
> and the Hebrew children from the fiery furnace
> then why not every man?
>
> —Traditional Spiritual

Many of the earliest accounts of African American religiosity begin during the period of the Second Great Awakening, assuming that Africans lost all of their own religious ideas and traditions during the Middle Passage from Africa and the horrors of American slavery. However, from the earliest colonial period Africans were able to both pass on many of their religious sensibilities to their children and incorporate the sensibilities of those who continued to arrive from the West and West Central African coasts. It appears that Americans came out of the revival period not only with a more firmly held religiosity but also with a very different view of God, one more closely aligned with African than European ideas. As Karen Armstrong says, by the nineteenth century European biblical literalism had framed God both as the First Cause who created the cosmos according to the biblical account and as a vengeful tyrant that terrorized all of humanity with threats of eternal damnation either arbitrarily or because they refused or were unable to abide by his onerous rules (Armstrong, 380, 378). Europeans and many Euro-Americans found that science offered more satisfying answers to the questions about the creation of the cosmos, and many began to reject the tyrannical God of their past. Although Armstrong suggests that Jews, Muslims, and Eastern Orthodox Christians might have offered other views of God that could have replaced this one, Europeans instead rejected God completely. Americans on the whole, however, have not rejected God. In fact, in a 2006 Pew Research poll 95 percent of the respondents expressed a belief in God, a universal spirit, or a higher power; 92 percent believed that God was responsible for the creation of life on earth; and 84 percent said that religion was either very important or fairly important in their lives (Pew Research Center for People and the Press, questions 61, 62, and 71).

Instead of turning away from God and religion, Americans developed a different image of God and a different form of religiosity than their European cousins—one that was more similar to that of the enslaved Africans and African Americans among them. The Kongolese religious cosmos, like that of pre-Reformation European Christians, had a single deity, the great God Nzambi, and ancestral spirits who mediated as family agents. It was these spirits who were responsible both for rewarding or punishing the ethical conduct of their descendants and for protecting them from illness, bad luck, and other forms of *ndoki* (witchcraft). Although West African cosmologies included both a great God (Olodumare among the Yoruba and Mawi/Lisa among the Fon) and a pantheon of lesser deities, West African religiosity was characterized by concerns about achieving a good life and avoiding the wrath of unhappy deities, ancestors, and evildoers or witches. Both the ancestors and the lesser deities were powerful spiritual beings but both could be approached and placated with the appropriate offering and ritual attitudes. We find similar religious ideas in medieval (Catholic) Christianity, which saw certain holy people, such as the saints and especially Mary the mother of Jesus and Jesus himself, as intermediaries between individuals and almighty God, ruler and judge of the cosmos. But Protestant theology turned against the saints as intermediaries, leaving a deep gulf between the people and their God.

Christian-style ideas about sin and salvation were generally absent from West African religiosity, and even West Central Africans who had been Christians for generations focused their religious attention elsewhere. African religious rituals tended to center on maintaining a relationship with important otherworldly beings and working with those beings to make life in this world better by avoiding disease, bad luck, and the malevolence of others. Since the great God was too distant and powerful, it was the ancestors and the lesser deities to whom the people turned for help with the problems of their lives. West and West Central African cultures also had a different view of evil. While these cosmologies recognized evildoers and malicious beings in both the visible and invisible worlds, they didn't have any beings, such as the Christian devil, that embodied absolute evil. When applied to Christian theology, this way of thinking led to reducing the devil to a "busy old man" and placing Jesus in the role of personal mediator and "my bosom friend." One's personal hardships could be compared to those of Jesus's passion and death, and such comparisons could lead one to a personal resurrection or rebirth. Eventually this new way of looking at salvation led away from Calvinism toward a more universalist theology in which Christ died to save all peoples, who only needed to reject their sinful ways and turn toward him to be saved. Salvation was a gift one need only accept, once and forever.

These African religious ideas continue to permeate our culture, where according to many religious traditions salvation is open to all those who "accept Jesus as their personal savior" through an act of their own religious will. In many ways the work of the social gospel movement, and the so-called prosperity gospel, has continued the this-worldly orientation of West and West Central African religious traditions. Both of these movements endeavor to improve people's lives in this world. The social gospel is primarily a liberal religious movement that applies Christian ethics to social problems such as inequality, liquor, crime, racial tensions, bad hygiene, child labor, weak labor unions, poor schools, and the dangers of war in order to improve society in general and especially to improve the lives of its poorest citizens. The prosperity gospel, on the other hand, is a self-help movement suggesting that God provides not only salvation in the next life but the blessings of health and wealth in this one. Like African rituals where devotees make offerings to the ancestors or the deities in hopes of maintaining or improving their lives, proponents of prosperity theology believe that by positive confessions of faith and "sowing the seeds" through the payments of tithes and other offerings they can reap the blessings of the good life in the here and now. All of these ideas closely mirror the West African cosmological view that life in this world is meant to be good and that through their own efforts as well as by working with God, people can bring the blessings of the good life to themselves and others.

KNOWLEDGE AND BELIEF

In his 1992 book *The American Religion: The Emergence of the Post-Christian Nation* the literary critic Harold Bloom suggested that American religion is "irretrievably Gnostic," that is, based on one's personal experience of Christ rather than a set of theological beliefs or set rituals (Bloom, 49, 54). Christianity was not always Gnostic in its approach. During its long growth period on the European continent, from Roman times until the Protestant Reformation, Christianity was a way of life for the people. One was born, baptized, and indoctrinated into Christian rituals and traditions as part of one's daily life. Theology and theological disputes were the provenance of specialists but of little concern to the common people. With the birth of the Protestant Reformation in 1517, doctrine and beliefs became more important as different Protestant groups took issue with different points of Catholic doctrine and the Catholic hierarchy attempted to maintain doctrinal purity. During this period, people from all walks of life were willing to die, and did die, in support of what we today might consider minor theological points. During the British colonization of the Eastern Seaboard many of the earliest American colonists risked the hazards of the Atlantic passage and the rigors of colonial life in order to pursue their vision of a purified Christianity. Many of the Protestant denominations found throughout the United States today had their beginnings because of some doctrinal disagreement with others from their European homeland.

However, today few Americans outside of seminaries or schools of theology can articulate the differences between one denomination and another, as religiosity has moved from a focus on beliefs to a focus on a type of gnosis or religious knowledge—not theological knowledge but a personal intimate knowledge of God, usually in the form of Jesus Christ. This was a radical change in Christian religiosity. We can trace this change back to the religious revivals of the early nineteenth century, that period when African Americans had an important influence on the developing American religious sensibility. What ideas about knowledge in general and religious knowledge in particular did Africans bring with them to the Americas?

Few scholars have attempted any analysis of African philosophical ideas, including ideas about the differences between knowledge and belief, the difference between what one "knows" and what one "believes." The one exception can be found in the work of Barry Hallen and J. Olubi Sodipo, whose *Knowledge, Belief, and Witchcraft* (Hallen and Sodipo) lays out the ways in which Yoruba speakers express their ideas about knowledge and belief and how these ideas are different from those expressed by speakers of English. What they discovered is that the meaning of the Yoruba words generally translated as "to know" and "to believe" differs significantly from their English counterparts.

As it is used in everyday conversation, English recognizes three types of knowledge: firsthand information (knowing that), personal competence

(knowing how), and knowledge gained from others, what Hallen and Sodipo call knowledge by acquaintance (45–47). Such knowledge, gained from
secondhand sources such as books, media, the testimony of others (such as
preachers and teachers), and the Internet, is an important type of knowledge
in our modern, fast-paced society where we are unable to verify all that we
are told and must depend on the reliability of others for accurate information. Only a small percentage of our knowledge is based on direct, firsthand
experience, while much of what we know comes to us from others. In fact,
if we insisted upon verifying every piece of information for ourselves our
society would come to a dead stop. Instead we apply what Hallen and Sodipo call the principle of charity, which allows us to accept what we are told
unless we have a specific reason for doubting it (52–53). Accepting what
others tell us, whether in direct conversation or through our many information sources, allows us to expand our knowledge base significantly beyond
that provided by our own individual experiences.

Among English speakers "belief" is a slippery word whose many
meanings make it difficult to pin down and define accurately—even for
those of us who are native speakers and use it every day. According to Hallen and Sodipo, English recognizes three types of beliefs: firsthand belief, or
believing that (propositional belief, as in "I believe that it will rain tomor-
row"); testimony, or believing a person ("She told me it was raining and I
believed her"); and believing in. Since few of our beliefs are based on firsthand experience, belief based on testimony is extremely important. Like
knowledge based on secondhand sources, beliefs based on the testimony of
others can sometimes be verified and thus moved to a stronger sort of belief
or even knowledge, but generally these beliefs depend on the goodwill of
the source to not mislead us (50–53). While believing that and believing a
person may entail varying degrees of belief (I may be 75 percent sure of my
belief that it will rain or have a high level of confidence in what an individual has told me), believing in is absolute and often is used to refer to
religious and philosophical ideas. In those circumstances where belief in
prevails, anything less than 100 percent certainty moves the idea from a
belief to an opinion (53–55). Hallen and Sodipo rank the quality of our
knowledge and beliefs. Often the best kind of knowledge is firsthand information (knowing that). If a person says he or she knows that something is
true, then it must be true. This is different from a belief that may be false.
The second-best type of knowledge is knowledge gained from trusted others (knowledge by acquaintance), and the third best is propositional belief
(believing that). However, English speakers often trust third-party sources
over an individual's personal knowledge. If my friend tells me it rained yes-

terday but the TV weatherperson says it was sunny, I might choose to believe the weatherperson over my friend or use the Internet (another type of third-party source) to adjudicate between the two.

In general, beliefs, especially belief in, are not verifiable. However, among English speakers beliefs are often validated by presenting evidence that what is believed is reasonable or accepted by a large number of other people. Such beliefs are considered stronger than beliefs that can't be confirmed with such evidence. For example, if all my friends believe in UFO abductions, then my own belief will be stronger (56–58). English speakers do not generally describe their personal experience as "true," instead reserving the term for descriptions of propositions (76). Among English speakers, proof of the truthfulness of knowledge or reasonableness of beliefs tends to depend on second-order sources. That is, an individual may turn to a book, the Internet, or other authoritative sources rather than his or her personal experiences to satisfy a challenger and, in fact, we generally find such sources more authoritative than accounts of an individual's experience (57–60). When challenged about their beliefs, English speakers tend to appeal to other beliefs or to evidence derived from perception, memory, and the like (80).

Our tendency is to assume that all cultures have the same categories of knowledge and belief as we do, so that translation between one language and another is fairly straightforward. However, Hallen and Sodipo suggest that Yoruba-language speakers use the terms commonly translated as "knowledge" and "belief" differently. According to Hallen and Sodipo, *mọ̀,* the Yoruba word generally translated as "to know," requires that one have a firsthand experience, that is, I must see and comprehend something in order to be able to say I mọ̀ (know) it. Anything that meets these criteria, what I mọ̀ because I have seen and comprehended, becomes for me *òótọ́,* truth (60–62). I know it is raining because I have looked outside and seen the rain falling. If my knowledge is challenged, it can be tested by giving the challenger his or her own firsthand experience so that he or she can comprehend it and thus also mọ̀, know, it is raining by looking outside. If, however, the challenger cannot verify my knowledge for himself, there are ways that he might become convinced, but my *imọ̀* (noun form of mọ̀, that is, knowledge) cannot become his imọ̀ (knowledge); rather, the challenger can only *gbà,* agree to my assertion—that is, believe me. If I say it rained in Houston yesterday while I was there and you were not, you cannot verify this knowledge for yourself. You can only trust what I say and agree with my assertion. For a Yoruba speaker, looking up the weather report in the newspaper or on the Internet is not sufficient for you to gain this knowledge for yourself.

You can only agree with my assertion and the testimony of the other sources. This agreement is usually framed as *gbàgbó*, agreeing to accept what one hears from someone, and translated as "to believe" (63–64). Information that is the object of gbàgbó includes not only what another individual has shared but what we call traditional knowledge, as well as what one has learned in school, read in books, heard on TV or the radio, or seen on the Internet (65). When *igbàgbọ́* (belief) is challenged, the challengers may be able to witness the thing for themselves, thus claiming to mọ̀, or may regard the speaker as trustworthy and accept his or her word, or the speaker may be able to convince the challengers to accept his statement. However, only in the case where one can verify the statement "with his own eyes" can a challenger claim the statement as òótọ̀ (truth); if he or she accepts the statement without such verification, it remains igbàgbọ̀ (belief) (69–72).

English and Yoruba are similar in that there is an element of firsthand experience about knowledge and mọ̀ and something secondhand about belief and gbàgbó. That is, we attach greater certainty to knowledge and mọ̀ than to belief and gbàgbó, and it is possible for information to move from belief and gbàgbó to knowledge and mọ̀ (80). However, Yoruba speakers are much more stringent about what information is accepted as òótọ́, that is, true, reserving this designation for only information gleaned through personal experience. The Yoruba will claim mọ̀, to know, only what has been seen for oneself, while all other information remains in the realm of gbàgbó, belief. Hence, contrary to the common understanding of those of us who are members of Western culture, the Yoruba people are much less credulous than we are, accepting as truth a much smaller group of phenomena. Whereas we accept as truth information gleaned from third-party sources, especially such authoritative sources as books, including religious books, media, and the Internet, the Yoruba only accept personal experience as òótọ́, truth, while regarding all other information as igbàgbọ́, beliefs, making them, as Hallen and Sodipo argue, "more reflective, more theoretically attuned, more skeptical, and more empirical" than generally acknowledged (73).

How might these language differences affect religious belief and practice? Religious ideas sit squarely between our ideas of what is "known" and what is "believed." Many Christians use the terminology of knowledge to talk about their religious beliefs while using the testimony of scripture and religious authorities (priests, preachers, and ministers) to validate their beliefs. The precolonial experiences of Yoruba people (and perhaps other African peoples) didn't depend on such testimony but rather on their personal experiences. The Yoruba, for example, were regularly directly confronted by the Orisha and their ancestors, who spoke through personal dreams, possession trance, and divination. The proclamations received in these ways were tested against one's own experience. If one was told to perform a particular ritual or refrain from a certain behavior in order to manifest a better or less harsh destiny, one could choose to follow or ignore the advice received, thus testing it. When confronted by Christian missionaries, both Yoruba and Kongolese people judged the accuracy of their "prophecies" according to their own criteria. Biblical sources were less important to these African peoples than to their European counterparts, as African peoples saw them as information that was given to people who lived a long time ago, very far away. Instead these African peoples used their own contemporary experiences to validate the words of missionaries. Did the proclamations of missionaries lead to a better life in the here and now? Were their words confirmed by one's own dreams and visions? Were their lives examples of the "truth" they were preaching? The king of Kongo, for example, didn't convert to Christianity because of some belief in the words of the missionaries but because he had a vision that led to success against his enemies—his experience validated the message of the vision. Similarly, as we shall see, among African Americans conversions came when personal religious experience became important to missionaries and when the people began to have conversion experiences.

As the great awakenings, especially the second, moved forward, Americans of all colors and social classes began to base their religiosity not on doctrines but on practices, not on beliefs but on experiences. Thus like Bloom we can proclaim that American religiosity is a form of gnosis, a form of knowledge gained not through reading and study but through one's personal encounter with some form of Ultimate Reality. And if what one encountered doesn't correspond to the reality preached in church, Americans, then as now, either looked for a different church or tried to convince the preacher to change. These changes in American religiosity began in small backwoods churches but have spread throughout the country so that the religiosity of the American founders, both Congregationalists in the north and Anglicans in the south, seems strange to many of us, while that of the earliest American Baptists and Methodists resonates with contemporary Americans of all religious persuasions.

In many ways Americans are more similar to Africans in terms of their religiosity. Many chose to trust their own religious or spiritual experiences over the doctrines of any religious community. Unlike the Puritans, who even after their conversion experiences had been validated by the community of "saints" were never really sure they were saved, those converted during the Great Awakening revivals were sure not only of their experiences but also about their place within the company of the saved. As we shall see when we discuss the Pentecostal movement at the turn of the twentieth century, this form of religious experience and the knowledge it provokes continue.

WOMEN AND RELIGION

Particularly striking in an analysis of West and Central African religious traditions and, as we shall see, the African-based traditions that grew out of them, including the different varieties of Vodou, is the strong place of women in these traditions. Throughout the history of Western Christianity women have been among the most active participants in religion but excluded from the higher levels of leadership. During the medieval period two roles were generally open to religious women, that of wife and mother and that of a nun, cloistered in a convent. Strong women in both roles have managed to leave their mark on Christian religion, but in general men held the most important roles in medieval and early modern Christianity and are accorded the most recognition within the tradition. This gendered dichotomy was continued and even strengthened with the rise of Protestantism, which saw the overthrow and abandonment of monasteries and convents throughout Europe. When the leaders of this movement abolished clerical celibacy and the Christian monastic tradition, they simultaneously eliminated one of the mainstays of independent women's roles within society. In addition, when Protestant leaders banned the representation and veneration of saints within their congregations, women were left with few models of female religiosity to balance the male trinity of Father, Son, and the somewhat genderless Holy Spirit (Peach, 203). Rather than including strong religious-minded women within the institution of the Protestant clergy, leaders, invoking the Pauline tradition of female silence and submission, relegated all good Christian women to the role of wife, mother, and helpmate (Ruether, 221). On the one hand, Protestant theologians proclaimed the "priesthood of all believers" as foundational to their vision of Christianity. However, the most radical version of this vision of equality, based on the Pauline formula that there is neither "Jew nor Gentile, neither slave nor free, nor is there male and female, for you are all one in Christ Jesus" (Galatians 3:28), was not promoted as the ideal of the new Protestant social order. Instead Protestant leaders preferred to promote a hierarchy that placed men over women, parents over children, and masters over servants. Men were upheld as the heads of their households who could expect deference from their wives, children, and servants. As the model of the benevolent God within their families, men were encouraged to act in a kindly manner to their subordinates, but there was no recourse if they acted in a harsh or arbitrary manner (Ruether, 222). Within the family women were expected to acquiesce to their husbands' demands while encouraging them discreetly in piety and submission to the higher authority of God and his earthly representatives in the persons of the minister and the civil authorities. Women were also seen as the first teachers of the household, mediating between the husband-master and his children and servants.

Thus there were two conflicting drives within the Protestant tradition: on the one hand championing of the individual conscience for every believer; on the other, setting up an absolutist hierarchy that kept everyone within his or her designated social position. At different times during the earliest years of the Reformation, women were encouraged to emphasize one or the other of these drives. For example, women within dissenting congregations in England and the British Isles were often encouraged to take the lead in organizing congregations and providing the means to call and support the preachers, who were not supported by the official Anglican stipendiary system. During these early years gifts of prophecy and preaching were accepted as appropriate for both men and women. Quaker women were especially important preachers and often served as missionaries to the American colonies, the Caribbean, and the Middle East (Ruether). However, as dissenting congregations grew and became more established, especially when they established colonies in America, women were pushed away from leadership positions and expected to return to their "natural" positions in the home and to defer to the leadership of men. It wasn't until the nineteenth century, when women took their role as the moral and religious teachers in the home out into the wider world, that American women would again gain leadership roles within the Christian denominations, and even today the ordination of women as ministers and higher-level religious functionaries is considered unorthodox within the many conservative denominations.

We also find two other conflicting views of women during the colonial and Revolutionary periods. On the one hand, women were often considered to be more pious than men, exemplifying the Christian virtues of compliance and submission to higher authorities. On the other hand, there was always the suspicion that the most compliant of women (and, by extension, servants) were harboring secret rebellions against that authority. Women, like Anne Hutchinson and others who stepped out of their "place" within the hierarchy, were often accused not only of insubordination to their husbands or civil authorities but also of witchcraft. Such women could be disciplined even to the point of death on either account. Women and others who wanted to follow their own consciences, especially when those consciences ran in a path different from those expressed by their husbands, fathers, ministers, and the civil authorities, had to tread very carefully. True religious piety was considered the best means of ensuring women's good behavior, and many women embraced their role as the spiritual center of the home. They would eventually expand their definition of "home" to include the wider community in order to provide themselves an outlet beyond the domestic sphere.

Anne Hutchinson (1591–1643) is one of the best-known leaders of the antinomian movements within early Puritan society. She believed that one's spiritual life not only was not dependent upon ordained ministers but could be dispensed by any spiritually minded Christians, male or female. In 1635 she began by gathering a small group of women into her Boston home for prayer and spiritual guidance and soon was leading a group of both men and women who felt free to discuss and critique the opinions offered by their minister based upon their own reading of the Bible (Ruether, 225). These discussions, along with her general antinomian attitude, put Anne in conflict not only with the local clergy but also with the secular authorities. Women were expected to accept the leadership positions not only of their husbands and fathers but also of those other leaders of the community. It was bad enough when only women attended her weekly discussion group, but when men joined and put themselves under her leadership, John Winthrop, the governor and her neighbor, viewed her as causing conflict within the colony. She was eventually brought before both civil and religious courts, and in 1637 she was both banished from the Massachusetts colony by civil authorities and excommunicated from her congregation (LaPlante).

West and West African cultures, like that of the Yoruba-speaking peoples we just considered and others throughout the areas contributing to the slave trade, provided many more roles for women in their societies. Although in many ways traditional Yoruba society, for example, was as chauvinistic as European and Euro-American culture of the same time, Yoruba culture provided many more outlets for women's leadership than did these European-based societies. In the religious arena, not only were there strong female deities women could look to as role models in their own lives, there were many religious roles for women within the different worship communities. Within these communities leadership was not as gender identified, so both men and women could achieve many of the highest priestly roles.

In addition, the role of possession medium was often considered so identified with womanliness that men taking on that role were gendered female in respect to their deities and called "wife" of the Orisha (in spite of having wives and children of their own). Yoruba women, like Kimpa Vita in Kongo, also joined other types of secret societies whose main purpose was the welfare of the community. All of these religious roles gave women status power both within their worship communities and in the larger society.

African women from these cultures would have brought their understanding that appropriate religious behavior for women included direct leadership roles. Because our understanding of the religious roles among the enslaved before their conversion to Christianity is so vague, it is unclear how enslaved women might have actualized this understanding in their new environment, although there are records of both male and female conjurers, fortune-tellers, and mediums sprinkled throughout the records we do have. However, it is during the time of the Second Great Awakening that we can see African-heritage women both enslaved and free taking on strong leadership positions. Some women became exhorters and led services while others served as mentors and "godmothers" to those on the cusp of conversion, helping them through the conversion experience and supporting them in their new religious lives.

The nineteenth century saw an explosion of women's involvement, especially in the new Baptist and Methodist religious traditions that were most influential in the revivals that swept the country. By this time the colonial views that women were more pious than men had expanded so that religiosity became synonymous with femininity (Peach, 1). This viewpoint led to an increase in women's religious participation. As Martha Tomhave Blauvelt says, "An ideology which insisted that religion was natural to women implied that it was somehow unnatural to men. It subtly encourages men to relegate religion to their mothers, wives, and sisters; at the same time, it counseled women to regard religion as their duty. As a result, women participated in nineteenth century revivals in even greater proportions than they had during the colonial period" (Blauvelt, 3).

The ways in which northern and southern women participated in the religion of the nineteenth century differ significantly. For northern women, their conversion experiences were primarily internal and recorded in diaries and conversion accounts. However, we have few of these kinds of documents for southern women. The fact that revivals formed the core of southern religiosity in the nineteenth century suggests that southern women (and men) had more spontaneous, emotional, and public conversion experiences. Based on generalized accounts of revival conversions, southern women and men were more likely to express their conversion by shouting "Hallelujah!" and rolling on the floor during a tent revival (Blauvelt, 4).

In general, however, until the nineteenth century southerners were less religious than their northern brethren. Southern colonies were established for commercial rather than religious reasons and although the laws in both areas required regular attendance at religious services, southerners were less likely to attend church or participate in the religious life of the community. However, southerners seemed to have found the revivals of the Second Great Awakening particularly appealing. Whole families, including the enslaved, traveled to revival sites and spent the week worshipping together. Revival ministers preached a type of personalized evil embodied in the devil and exorcised during the conversion experience (Blauvelt, 5). This evil and its release were experienced in concrete terms during the revival meetings. Although black and white participants were often separated at these events, the proximity of the locations introduced white revivalists to the most exuberant and emotional form of black conversions. And sometimes the two groups did worship together, so that blacks and whites influenced each other's experiences and responses to ministerial exhortations. Revivals also provided participants the field in which to exercise their talents. Evangelical theology suggested that once an individual was converted, his or her everyday life should attest to the reality of that conversion. Thus individuals were encouraged not only to live good lives but also to evangelize to those around them, hold prayer meetings in their homes, and work at revivals (Blauvelt, 5). Some women and blacks became exhorters and traveling evangelists. Others worked within their own communities to prepare their friends and family members for conversion and to strengthen the newly converted as they made the transition from sinner to "saint."

Women, both black and white, often held prayer meetings in their homes, where they counseled the newly repentant, explained the steps toward salvation, helped overcome religious doubts, and provided support in times of doubt and despair. These meetings met nightly during revivals but often continued beyond the time of the revival so that individuals could support each other in their conversions (Blauvelt, 7). In some of the earliest Baptist and Methodist congregations, black and white women were allowed to hold such offices as deaconess and elderess in their congregations, and some women even became exhorters and preachers (Frey and Wood, 101, 114, 126–27). Black women also served as "missionaries" to their enslaved brethren, often assuming moral and religious leadership in the absence of male leaders (Frey and Wood, 104–5). The "emotional" style of revival worship favored the presence of women not only as members of the congregations but also as leaders. When religiosity became associated with religious enthusiasm, with all its trappings of mysticism and possession, women were able to carve out a place for themselves as specialists of this style of worship (Frey and Wood, 101, 122). According to Sylvia Frey and Betty Wood, not only did enslaved women establish a cultural presence at revival meetings, they were also credited with leading scores of men and women to the same type of "deeply personal, highly emotional affirmation of faith" they exhibited (Frey and Wood, 121). Using the revival theology of equality before God to their advantage, black women consistently fought for leadership roles in their religious communities. As churches were increasingly brought under the authority of regional and national organizations, women were often moved to second- and third-level roles but continued to maintain a strong presence (Frey and Wood, 169–71).

WITCHCRAFT: THE EUROPEAN VIEW

Anne Hutchinson was not the only colonial woman to challenge the social and religious restrictions of early American society, but her story shows how the drive for independent religious thought came in conflict with the desire on the part of colonial authorities for social conformity. The push for conformity, especially among women (and others on the lower rungs of the social hierarchy), overcame principles of independent thought and action that were so important to the earliest colonists. Although Hutchinson was not formally accused of witchcraft, many other insubordinate women were. As Rosemary Ruether says, "In the official Puritan mind, a woman who dissented from male church authority was not only a heretic, but very likely a witch as well, for only the promptings of the devil could strengthen the frail female that she would content against male authority in this way" (Ruether, 226). On the one hand, early colonists saw their new world as a blank slate, an Eden untouched by the religious perversions and controversies that had developed in Europe. On the other hand, when they arrived on these shores they found impenetrable forests, peopled by "savages" ignorant of religion and civilization, as they understood it. In this view, America was the home of Satan and his demons, which were waiting to snatch the heedless to their eternal damnation. Witchcraft could be seen everywhere. It explained the inexplicable, including droughts, epidemics, and deadly storms, even earthquakes. Witches threatened not only individuals but also the structure of the new communities themselves. Each of the communities in the Americas had its own view of what activities were encompassed within the term "witchcraft" and who within its community might be the perpetrator of those activities.

Colonial European ideas of witchcraft developed during the century-long period of search for witches and heretics that became known as the Inquisition. Although witchcraft was known during the pre-Christian era, its place in society was ambiguous. Everywhere there were certain "cunning folk" who had knowledge of local herbs and worked as healers and midwives. Often these same people, or others, also engaged in divination and fortune-telling that enabled them and their clients to see beyond their physical senses. From the fall of the Roman Empire until the post-Reformation period there was no history of religious tolerance in Europe. The early Christian church declared that belief in witches as people who were able to act against the will of God to affect the weather or change their shape was unchristian. To hold such beliefs suggested that some people (or their demonic masters) were more powerful than God. However, early in the second century, this view changed, and by the mid-second century witches were included among the heretics that were the focus of the inquisitors trying to solidify the authority of the Catholic church throughout Europe. Practices that were outside the norm for a community were often branded as "witchcraft" in an effort to eliminate them. As Christianity in the form of the Catholic church gained prominence throughout the continent during the late Roman and early medieval periods, it began persecuting those whose beliefs or rituals didn't fall within the limits set by the clergy. As early as the 1100s the church was issuing proclamations against individuals who seemed to cling to the old "pagan" ways, seemed to have special skills, especially in the healing arts; or put forward ideas deemed heretical. One of the first ecclesiastical inquisitions was established in 1184, and by the thirteenth century Pope Gregory IX had officially tasked members of the Dominican order to carry out inquisitions throughout Christendom (Europe) in order to root out and prosecute heretics and witches. The papal bull of Innocent VIII of 1484 suggested that

> many persons of both sexes, unmindful of their own salvation and straying
> from the Catholic Faith, have abandoned themselves to devils, incubi and
> succubi, and by their incantations, spells, conjurations, and other accursed
> charms and crafts, enormities and horrid offences, have slain infants yet in
> their mother's womb, as also the offspring of cattle, have blasted the pro-
> duce of the earth, the grapes of the vine, the fruit trees . . . blasphemously
> renounce that Faith which is theirs by the Sacrament of Baptism, and at
> the instigation of the Enemy of Mankind they do not shrink from com-
> mitting and perpetrating the foulest abominations and filthiest excesses to
> the peril of their own soul (Kramer and Sprenger, xliii).

The witch-hunter's manual, *Malleus Maleficarum* or *The Hammer of the Witches*, was written by a pair of Dominican priests and published in 1486 to aid German witch-hunters. It detailed procedures for identifying and convicting witches. Throughout most, but not all, of Europe, the witch-hunters were more likely to target women, especially women who were outside the protective custody of male family members, such as childless widows or unmarried women without a male protector. But women in general were considered to be more susceptible to the enticements offered by Satan in his recruitment of people to become his human agents, and over time the word "witch" has come to be a female-identified word that points to the quintessentially evil, antisocial, and deliberately hostile person. Eventually even persons with extraordinary skills who helped rather than harmed their neighbors were branded as witches, as they were believed to gain their power not from God but from his archenemy, the devil. Reviewing the records of the witchcraft trials throughout the continent we find that in general those accused of witchcraft tended to be from the lower classes, were more often women than men, were said to have a disagreeable and evil personality, and were believed to use witchcraft to gain advantage or persecute their neighbors by extraordinary means. Witches were evil persons who chose to repudiate their Christianity in order to associate with the devil, becoming his minions in the world. Interestingly, many of the activities we might today associate with witchcraft, such as astrology, alchemy, or augury, were the province of learned men and not generally considered witchcraft.

By the beginning of the sixteenth century the church's religious control was absolute, although minority traditions such as Judaism, Lollardy, and Islam continued in small, scattered pockets. However, that changed when Martin Luther nailed his ninety-five theses on the church door in Wittenberg, beginning a movement known today as the Protestant Reformation. Now doctrine and ritual became the concern not only of the educated clergy but also of the common person in the pews. The reformers disagreed not only with the leaders of the Roman church but among themselves, and persecutions of individuals and groups for "wrong" theology or practice were common. The blood of those martyred for their beliefs is sprinkled throughout Europe.

WITCHCRAFT: THE AFRICAN VIEW

West and West Central African societies also had ideas about persons who cause individual and communal disasters. E. E. Evans-Pritchard, who wrote one of the definitive anthropological texts about African witchcraft (Evans-Pritchard), describes witches as people who can injure others by virtue of an inherent quality, an inherited trait one carries as "witchcraft substance" within one's body (1). According to this viewpoint one does not choose to be a witch but instead is born with a physical substance that gives one access to extraordinary powers one can use for good or ill. This substance grows as the body grows so that as one grows older one's powers increase. One need not fear a child, whose witchcraft substance is small and weak, but there can be much to fear from an older person, who has stronger witchcraft substance as well as a more developed ability to use it (7–8). The antisocial person is not the only person in a community with this substance, but many powerful and successful people are assumed to have used their witchcraft power to become successful. Since those with witchcraft power are not necessarily evil, good people with this power can use it to achieve good ends. Witchcraft in these communities is not extraordinary but rather an everyday part of the world. Witches are not remarkable, since anyone might be a witch—in fact you may be one yourself, and certainly there are witches among your closest neighbors (19). As Evans-Pritchard says, in these societies "witchcraft is . . . a normal, and not an abnormal happening" (30). Although inexplicable events such as why a tree fell on one man and not another or why one farmer has a successful harvest while his neighbor's crops wither and die may be explained by witchcraft, as long as a witch's witchcraft does not kill another, the witch is permitted to live his or her life unmolested. If one has been discovered to have bewitched another, generally one is politely asked to withdraw one's witchcraft and cool one's witchcraft substance.[1] Often such a person is unaware that he has witchcraft substance. In fact, one can be born with witchcraft substance and be a good person and productive member of society (49–50). However, once one is made aware of one's witchcraft power, one may choose to use it benevolently or malevolently. The benevolent witch will learn to use his or her power for the good of the community, often learning to see and deflect the witchcraft of others and helping to heal the victims of deliberate or accidental witchcraft. Such a person may also gain a reputation within the community, so that those who feel that they have been bewitched can appeal to him or her for relief. In the African context, witchcraft was always seen within a context of the community. Each individual was caught in a web of interpersonal relationships that included not only the living but also those yet to be born and those ancestors who had died. Achieving at the expense of these others was always considered the mark of an inappropriate use of one's power. Thus among the Kongolese of the early 1700s the prophetess

Apolonia Mafuta could denounce the rich and powerful, including members of the nobility and the European priests, as witches for their participation in the ongoing civil war and the expanding slave trade.

Witchcraft and cannibalism were widely associated in West Africa. Witches were believed to visit individuals in the night to suck out their vital energy, leaving them progressively weaker and weaker. Many Africans believed that the European slave traders were also cannibals who used the bodies of the enslaved to produce their own goods: the red wine that the Portuguese and Spanish sailors favored was believed to be made from the blood of the enslaved, olive oil extracted from their bodies, cheese from their brains, and bullets from their bones (Young, 156). Some believed that the cowries that were used to buy the enslaved were grown on the bodies of those thrown into the waters in an early form of fish farming. Although we might smile at the naiveté of these descriptions, in actuality it wasn't far from the truth. Europeans did exploit the bodies of the enslaved to produce their rich material culture. It was the gold, sugar, tobacco, and other products of slave labor that enriched European individuals and made countries like Spain and Belgium and England world powers. As the slave trade progressed, those Africans who grew rich and powerful as a result were also often accused of inappropriate witchcraft. All of the rich and powerful were assumed to have what the Kongolese called ndoki, witchcraft power, but greed and selfishness were always the markers of using that power against the best interests of the community (Young, 157).

WITCHCRAFT: THE AMERICAN VIEW

Many of the early colonists in what was to become the United States made the dangerous journey to the New World in order to escape religious persecution. Each group hoped to establish in their own area a homeland free from the religious impurities of the old country. However, the colonists also brought their religious intolerance with them. Colonial churches were closely tied to the local secular authorities, which had the right and responsibility to maintain local religious purity. Those who wouldn't or couldn't adhere to the local religious standards were silenced, punished, banished, and sometimes killed. Even in the southern and middle colonies, not known for their religiosity, officials attempted to maintain the power of the church by harassing northern missionaries who dared to darken their shores. There are records of tenacious missionaries being repeatedly beaten, banished, and sometimes killed for proclaiming their religious ideas.

The most famous outbreak of "witchcraft" in the early colonies occurred in Salem, Massachusetts, in 1692. Much of the literature about this
outbreak and the trials and executions it engendered focuses on the testimony of an enslaved woman name Tituba. She was one of the first three
women accused in what became an orgy of witchcraft prosecutions that
eventuated in the arrests of over 150 men, women, and children, the deaths
of twenty-four, and the disruption of hundreds of lives not only in Salem
but in neighboring towns and villages as far away as Boston (Breslaw, 171).
Although Tituba is generally described as an African-heritage woman, it is
clearly evident according to the detailed research done by Elaine Breslaw
that Tituba was actually an Amerindian captured from the eastern coast of
South America. She was eventually sold to Samuel Parris in Barbados. Breslaw suggests that Tituba was captured as a child between nine and fourteen
years old (Breslaw, 30), so she would have been between thirteen and eighteen when Parris took her as part of his family to Boston four years later in
1680. When he accepted a ministerial post in Salem in 1689, she, together
with her Indian husband John, again traveled with the family to their new
home in Salem.

In spite of the accepted wisdom that suggests Tituba was a voodoo
priestess who indoctrinated a group of Salem girls into African folklore,
leading them in occult rituals, including naked dancing in the local woods,
the drinking of blood, and the sticking of pins into "voodoo" dolls, there is
no evidence in the seventeenth-century records that she ever took part in
any occult activities (Breslaw, xx–xxi). In fact, Tituba would have had little
knowledge of African-inspired rituals. During her earliest enslavement she
probably lived in a mixed African/Indian community and might have been
taken under the wing of one or more older African or Indian women. However, as she generally worked as a domestic, she would have spent the majority of her time in her master's home and not the slave quarters. By the time
of the witch trials, she appeared to have been fully acculturated into the
white Puritan world surrounding her, even speaking standard English rather
than a pidgin or creolized dialect (Breslaw, 161–65).

In contemporary America, African and European ideas of witchcraft
have become so intertwined that "voodoo" has become closely tied to our
ideas of "witchcraft"; often the two terms are used interchangeably. Prophecy, divination, and fortune-telling were deeply embedded in the English
cultural heritage colonists brought with them, although severely condemned by the Puritan and Anglican clergy. However, for both the common
people and the clergy, beliefs regarding the spiritual world permeated society and, as Breslaw says, the visible world was believed to be "as densely

populated with spiritual beings as any African or Amerindian village" (100). In all of these cultural areas, not only was the invisible world of spirits real, there was the understanding that it could be manipulated through magical practices for either good or ill. This commonality meant that African-heritage individuals could integrate European ideas and techniques without violating any of their essential features of their worldview, while Europeans could incorporate African magical techniques and practices without affecting their religious viewpoints (Breslaw, 101). Such magical techniques represented an instrumental approach that didn't depend on any religious or theological understanding but appealed to pragmatic desires to make one's own life better or to affect the lives of one's enemies.

However, among the educated, particularly the clergy, such manipulation of magical forces was beyond the abilities of ordinary people and required the assistance of an external diabolic force, the devil. Thus the same witchcraft activities that were morally neutral in Africa and among African-heritage peoples were considered evil and demonic, a crime against God, from a European, Christian point of view (Breslaw, 115). Breslaw suggests that Tituba's testimony instigated a subtle change in the witchcraft beliefs of all inhabitants of Salem and the surrounding society (122–32). Similarly, African witchcraft ideas and techniques have crept into the wider American society as practitioners and clients cross social boundaries.

Throughout the American south, for example, African-heritage people and others within the surrounding communities looked to individuals who seemed to have especially strong witchcraft substance to not only protect them from the vagaries of life but also heal physical, mental, and emotional dis-ease. African ideas of witchcraft are most apparent in descriptions of southern hoodoo. Hoodoo men and women were believed to have the power to both help and hurt their neighbors through the use of a variety of charms, tobies, and mojo bags. Some conjurers were believed to have an inherent power while others acquired their power from some other entity, often a dark man they met at the crossroads, in the forest, or in some other spiritually powerful location. We can often see in these descriptions traces of African deities, Orisha, Lwa, or nkisi spirits. (The little man one meets at the crossroads is surely a sort of Papa Legba figure.) As southern blacks moved away from their ancestral homes and into the urban north, a new market for hoodoo ingredients developed. No longer able to go into the woods to find essential ingredients, hoodoo practitioners and common people who wanted some extra help to make their lives better turned to "drugstores" and mail order companies to provide both the ingredients for their own "works" and ready-made items they could use. (See Carolyn Long's *Spiritual Merchants* for an in-depth description of the development of this marketplace.)

CONCLUSION

Immediately before and after the American Civil War, the Second Great Awakening saw important changes in American religious sensibilities. Fideism, belief in God, increased as the image of God softened and moved closer to human life at the same time that the purported power of the devil was diminished. The whole of the invisible world, including not only God but other spiritual beings, the ancestors, and beloved dead, became more accessible not only to religious specialists but also to the common people, whose conversion experience depended on having an intense personal encounter with God or his son Jesus. Important to this change was a new understanding of salvation. Instead of the very limited view of the northern Calvinists and southern Anglicans, these later Christians approached salvation from the point of view found in the spiritual that heads this chapter. It exemplifies a universalist view that suggests that every person could be included among the saved, the "saints" of the church. No longer would salvation be only for the selected few, the elite of the congregation, but for everyone who could find their way to Jesus, their bosom friend. Jesus himself was often imagined as a fellow traveler through life's vale of tears whose own suffering was mirrored in the day-to-day suffering of the members of the congregation. Such a view appealed to both the lower classes among the free white and black population and the enslaved. If the Lord could deliver Daniel from the lion's den, Jonah from the belly of the whale, and the Hebrew children from the fiery furnace, then why indeed wouldn't he deliver his American children from eternal damnation? As theology continued to develop through the nineteenth and twentieth centuries, damnation and eternal punishment became more and more downplayed. Instead the more African idea that all but the very worst of people would be welcomed into the heavenly abode became the popular theological position.

This period also saw an increase in religious tolerance. As personal experience rather than theological correctness determined one's place among the community of the saved, individuals moved freely between denominations, attracted more by the charisma of the preachers and exhorters than their denominational affiliations. It was during this period that Methodism and the Baptist traditions became major American denominations, leaving behind the more staid Anglican/Episcopalian traditions. There also appeared a certain level of polymorphism as individuals, families, and communities engaged in a variety of religiously identified experiences. Not only did people attend church more regularly, many were associated either simultaneously or serially with the many new religious movements that developed during this period, including the Spiritualist movement. This willingness to try different religious forms, often without completely separating from existing forms, exemplifies Americans' tendency to experiment with new beliefs and practices that promise not only spiritual salvation but also some succor in their day-to-day lives. This doesn't mean that new religious forms were universally welcomed or appreciated; they weren't. In fact, many of the new religious traditions experienced virulent persecution. However, many of those groups persisted in the face of persecution, and even those that didn't survive into the new century left their mark on American Christianity.

Women's place in society also began to change during this period. At least partially led by participation in these new religious movements, as well as their participation in both the abolitionist and suffragist movements, women from all walks of life began to campaign for a wider role within their societies and churches. African American women were often on the forefront of all these movements. Sojourner Truth's famous speech at the 1851 Women's Convention in Akron, Ohio, entitled "Ain't I a Woman?," epitomizes the African and African American woman's view of her place in society, not as a shrinking violet that needed to be "helped in to carriages, and lifted over ditches," but as a fully functioning member of society who could "work as much and eat as much as a man" (Halsall). Although Truth's speech is probably based principally on her own experience in slavery, it exemplifies the African view of womanhood. In many ways West and West Central African women were subordinated to their male relatives; however, in general they had much more of the freedom the suffragists were campaigning for in terms of personal autonomy and personal power and authority. African women were not shrinking violets on either continent. We can see that in the lives of Kimpa Vita and Apolonia Mafuta in Kongo, in the places women found for themselves in Yoruba, and in the lives of both elite and ordinary Fon women, who not only ran the palaces of their kingly husbands but also fought in elite military regiments.

7

CHILDREN OF THE LEOPARD

Kingdom of Dahomey

"Dahomey epitomized everything negative that the Euro-American imagination of the nineteenth and twentieth centuries wanted to believe about Africa. Dahomey was said to be a state grown rich through the slave trade . . . But slavery in the Western Hemisphere was a blessing compared with life in the kingdom, at least as Euro-American observers described it" (Edna Bay).[1]

The Kingdom of Dahomey has given us one of the most well-known images of black religion—voodoo. The term "voodoo" is multifaceted. In the popular imagination "voodoo" refers to a strange Caribbean cult replete with magical charms, midnight rituals, pins sticking out of dolls, and zombies. It has been the fodder for bad television shows and movies. The term is often used to denigrate ideas outside the religious realm, as when George H. W. Bush referred to Ronald Reagan's economic policies as "voodoo economics." Within the religious realm, voodoo, more properly spelled *Vodou* or *Vodun*, refers to a religious tradition centered on the island of Haiti, its African predecessor, and the spirits of that tradition. Although many threads came together to form the religious tradition known today as Haitian Vodou, including both Kongolese and Yoruba religious concepts, one of the most important of these strands was that provided by the enslaved peoples brought from the Kingdom of Dahomey.

During the nineteenth and twentieth centuries, the Kingdom of Dahomey served as the embodiment of the negative stereotypes Europeans and Americans had of Africa. In Dahomey, it was said, slaves were captured by an army of amazons (women warriors) who served as the frontline soldiers in the service of a bloodthirsty king. Captives not sold into slavery were butchered as human sacrifices on voodoo altars to snakes and trees. Those who escaped into the slave trade were the lucky ones, for among the Dahomeans were slaves of the absolute monarch who presided over all this brutality (Bay 1998, 1–2). Although exaggerated, much of this account has some basis in fact, while some is a gross misrepresentation of the real life in the Kingdom of Dahomey. According to the standards of the time in both Europe and the Americas, the Kingdom of Dahomey was a well-functioning state. It guaranteed its citizens certain basic rights, including a means of livelihood and surpluses of both food and other goods, while meeting their fundamental material and spiritual needs. Although militaristic, like many nations of that time (and of ours), Dahomey was neither an oppressive state that terrorized its citizens nor a perfectly idyllic country (Bay 1998, 3).

As in the case of Kongo, the bulk of what we know of Dahomey is based on the reports of European explorers and traders who visited in the sixteen and seventeen hundreds. Many of the elites of the area that would become Dahomey could speak European languages, usually Portuguese, and some were educated by European missionaries. (In fact, the catechism prepared by Spanish missionaries in 1658 for their mission in Allada is the earliest text in any West African language [Law, 11]). As with the Kongolese, ambassadors from this area were sent to Europe to represent the interests of their monarchy abroad. However, there does not remain any written material from the point of view of the king of Dahomey or his people (Law, 3) so the account of the earliest history of the area depends on the work of foreigners and local mythology.

We do know that the Kingdom of Dahomey was established along the West African coast sometime before 1600, purportedly by the descendants of a son of a princess of the royal family of Tado who mated with a leopard, but probably by migrants, perhaps from the southern state of Allada. According to the founding myth of Dahomey, three sons of this original dynasty argued and separated to found the kingdoms of Allada, Porto Novo, and Dahomey (although historically Allada probably was older). Scholars question this mythical account and suggest that the outlaw band of strangers who settled in Wawa formed alliances among themselves and with the indigenous people to establish the nucleus of what would become the Kingdom of Dahomey. Under these circumstances it was important for the interlopers, who became known as the Fon people, to establish themselves as quickly as possible. They did this through several institutions that had important ramifications for the development of their kingdom.

Although we don't generally think of it in those terms, the continent of Europe is a relatively small landmass with a large population. As a consequence, throughout its history, European prestige and wealth were determined by the amount of land one owned. Kings, lesser nobles, and those

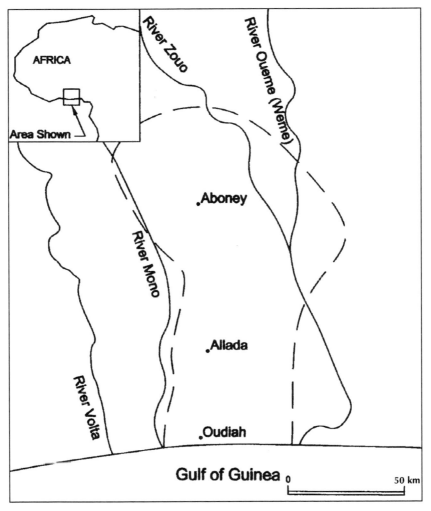

West African Kingdom of Dahomey

ambitious to advance in the social hierarchy fought to bring adjacent lands under their control and thus increase their standing among the elites of the continent. Africa, however, is a huge continent where land was easy to acquire but the labor to make it productive was not. Thus, throughout West Africa, prestige—and the wealth that followed—was established not by the control of land but by the control of people. In such a world, where wealth and prestige were linked to the number of individuals under a person's control, the royal clan that would eventually control Dahomey, the "children of the leopard," tried to increase its size as quickly as possible. It did this by acquiring both slaves and wives from the surrounding peoples. By 1724, for example, it was estimated that the palace women known as the "king's wives" numbered more than two thousand.

From its humble beginnings, what became the Kingdom of Dahomey was expansionist and brought new lands and their peoples under its control through warfare and raiding. Throughout its history, these wars were financed by selling a portion of the conquered peoples south to Allada and into the Atlantic slave trade. By 1727 the Kingdom of Dahomey had expanded from the center of a plateau about sixty miles from the West African coast, conquered neighboring Allada, and taken control of the coastal city of Whydah, which would become the center for its Atlantic trading activities. By absorbing Allada and Whydah, Dahomey was able to cut out the middlemen of its slave trading and begin to deal directly with the European merchants. Before the rise of the Kingdom of Dahomey, Allada, which was situated along what was then called the Slave Coast, was the largest and most powerful of the kingdoms along this portion of the West African coast. Both Allada and Whydah were important trading centers from the mid-1600s. At least one early king of Allada understood Portuguese, having been educated at a monastery on the island of São Tomé (Law, 3). Although slaves from this area were considered inferior to those from the West Central states of Kongo and Angola, Allada was one of the largest and most important of the states along the west coast of Africa and probably the principal supplier of enslaved peoples from within West Africa (Law, 11, 87–88). A large percentage of the enslaved sold out of Allada were purchased or captured farther inland and many were documented as coming from the lands of the Yoruba (principally from the city of Oyo) or the Fon, from Dahomey (Law, 101). Although many sorts of people got caught up in the slave trade, including foreigners and those condemned to slavery for failing to repay their debts, the majority of those exported out of these areas were prisoners of war, sold by the victors as booty (Law, 104).

The main function of the Kingdom of Dahomey was the conduct of war for the purpose of bringing more people under the authority of the king and providing more individuals to the domestic and external slave trade. The militaristic Dahomeans continued to raid surrounding areas, bringing back numerous prisoners as well as the heads of their defeated enemies. While some of the prisoners might be sacrificed, the bulk of them were given as slaves to courtiers and officers or sold into the overseas trade (Bay 1998, 63–67). Such captives formed the economic foundation for the kingdom. However, the internal slave regimes were also important in that they supplied the basic workforce in Dahomey. Often, captives from a single area were resettled into new villages within Dahomey to work as farmers on the king's land (Herskovits 1967, 99). In 1724, the kingdom, which had been becoming increasingly militarized both to expand its reach and to supply people to the slave markets in Allada, was able to conquer its southern neighbor and appropriate the trading port for itself (Law, 116). The bulk of the foreigners brought into the Dahomean orbit were sold overseas. However, those who remained became essential to the developing Dahomean culture. Ethnically the people of Dahomey, who became known as Fon, were a mix of peoples from the surrounding areas. Most spoke a variant of the Gbe language (and later Yoruba) and shared cultural similarities so that it was relatively easy to integrate the newcomers into the developing Fon culture. In fact, Edna Bay suggests that Fon culture provided many opportunities for newcomers with talent and ambition to amass great wealth and power (Bay 2008, 3). The ability of these peoples to create a society that incorporated an ethnically diverse population points to the eclectic nature of Fon culture and one of its primary strengths. The Fon delighted in change and innovation. Not only did they incorporate neighboring peoples, including those from the Yoruba-speaking lands to the north and east and the Akan peoples to the west, they also welcomed European influences brought to them by way of the Atlantic coast to the south, and in the nineteenth century they welcomed back the *Aguda* or Afro-Brazilians who returned from slavery in South America (Bay 2008, 79). The Fon people were always ready to learn to use new materials, ideas, and techniques and to modify them to suit their own tastes (Bay 2008, 64). Fon eclecticism, including their material culture, technologies, deities, and principles of state organization, was grafted onto an existing worldview associated with the Vodun. We should not think of Fon religiosity as fixed or static. Instead, ritual practices and the principal deities changed and evolved during both precolonial and colonial periods as the monarchy creatively invented new rituals and chose which deities to honor in order to strengthen its own power as the political situation changed. Since no commoner ceremonies could be performed until the annual "Customs" (religious rituals) of the monarchy were complete, changes among the most elite probably also affected the rituals and beliefs of the more common people as they decided which Vodun and ancestors were worthy of continued service (Bay 2008, 4–5, 24–25, 56).

Although the many wars fought by the Fon were not religious in nature, they had a religious component. The Dahomeans both depended on their own Vodun (gods) and ancestors to aid in their war efforts and attempted to neutralize the Vodun and ancestors of their opponents. Elaborate ritual preparations were required before a campaign could begin, oracles were consulted, and certain ceremonies were performed. In the meantime, men were sent to the enemy's country both to spy on their power and preparations and to attempt to destroy the power of the enemy's protective Vodun by making poisoned offerings and by burying "medicine," mystical packets designed to sow discord among the people, in strategic areas. When the Dahomeans returned victorious from such wars, they brought with them the leaders of the defeated towns, who were then slain as offerings to the Vodun and ancestors who helped ensure victory. Those not offered as sacrifices were sold into slavery. It was assumed that the losers in such battles were not only weaker militarily but also had not sufficiently propitiated their supernatural guardians (Argyle, 83–86).

It is estimated that the Kingdom of Dahomey contributed as many as fifteen thousand persons to the slave trade annually. Many of these were enslaved as a result of wars and raids into neighboring territories. Some of the enslaved were condemned criminals and some were politically trouble-some persons sold into exile. Although it was illegal to sell honorable citizens into slavery, rumors continued to persist that both the king and merchants filled out slave cargos with such people (Bay 1998, 48). Scholars agree that the slave trade was a central source of state revenue for at least half of the life of the kingdom. Brazil and Saint-Domingue/Haiti were the most common debarkation sites for the people sold away from Dahomey. As we have seen in Kongo, trade between Dahomey and their European partners was not a one-sided affair. The king of Dahomey and his ministers had considerable power in deciding when and with whom they would trade, in setting the prices for trade goods, including the human beings that formed the bulk of their trade, and in controlling the quality of the goods they received in return. If the king was dissatisfied with what a ship's captain offered in trade, the king would either refuse to deal with him at all or require that he sweeten his offer with more or higher-quality goods.

WOMEN IN DAHOMEAN SOCIETY

Two institutions within Dahomean society were startling to their European partners. The first was the place of women, both within the household of the king and in the army. The second was the tradition of sacrifice made to the deities, the Vodun. Many of the most important people within the monarchy, the group headed by the king that ruled Dahomey, were women, the wives and daughters of the reigning king and his predecessors and the so-called queen mother (who was neither the wife nor the mother of the king) who reigned alongside the king as a royal partner.

Within the Kingdom of Dahomey, women had important political and social power. Edna Bay argues that during the period of the slave trade Dahomey was ruled by a coalition of forces collectively known as the "monarchy" and represented by the king in whose name the country was governed. Rather than being a single individual with absolute power, the Dahomean monarchy was a small and fluid group of the political elite consisting of both men and women from various family lineages and social strata who wielded various powers in the governance of the kingdom. The king himself was neither a puppet nor a prisoner of this group but its head. One did not become the king of Dahomey merely by an accident of birth, as in Europe, where the oldest son generally succeeded his father. Nor was leadership passed from brother to brother until all of the men of one generation died out, as was the normal practice in the rest of Dahomey. Instead a small group of the reigning king's sons were eligible to succeed him. In order to become king a son had to form alliances with his siblings, important commoners, and the powerful women of the palace, the princesses and wives of his father, the former king.

We often think of the wives in polygamous households as pampered women, sequestered away from public view in the depths of the residence, as women whose only function was to satisfy the sexual pleasure of their husband. But the wives of the King of Dahomey were not a harem in that classical sense. Instead, they were fully active members of the Dahomean society. They cultivated fields, made and sold goods in their own names, and were involved in the administration of the kingdom (Bay 1998, 48–51). It has been estimated that by the late nineteenth century eight thousand people lived in the royal residences scattered across the kingdom, the majority of whom were women (Bay 1998, 8).

The children of the palace, including the daughters, were socially male in what was a patrilineal society. Generally in such a society, and as we saw among the Yoruba, men were heads of households and the most powerful members of their families. Any children born into a patrilineal household "belonged" to the family of the father. In such a society, when women married they often moved into the household of their husband's family but had little status, since they remained outsiders to the family and were always under the social and political control of their husband or his relatives. Women might, however, retain political control within the households of their birth families, from which they were never totally separated. This was generally the social organization throughout the Kingdom of Dahomey.

However, in the Dahomean royal household (and certain other privileged lineages [Bay 2008, 61]) both the male and female children, the princes and princesses, were politically autonomous, could be the heads of their own households with their own entourages, and were in control of their own sexuality, retaining their children in their own lineage. This means that regardless of whom their mothers married when they married (or if they married at all) any children born to these princesses belonged to the royal lineage rather than that of their husbands or consorts (Bay 1998, 52). As adults, these princesses often served as wife-ambassadors to neighboring states, and during the time between the death of one king and the promotion of the new king from among his children, it was the princesses who were the mediators among the eligible sons vying to be named the next king (Bay 1998, 53). The most senior of the daughters of each king, known as the *na daho* (great princess), was a central player in palace politics. She had authority over all of the sisters and daughters of the reigning king, supervising their marriages and mediating their disputes. Although ineligible to become the king herself, she could use her power and authority to mediate between rival princes and promote the claims of her favorite (Bay 1998, 53).

There were two types of women in the palace. The so-called wives of the king (literally, the term *ahosi* meant dependent, follower, or subordinate of the king) were drawn from all levels of Dahomean society, including slaves and war captives, freeborn women, and women from elite households.[2] Women who became members of the royal household in this manner entered the hierarchy based on their social status of origin. However, once within the monarchy, they could advance in power based on their own ambition and merit. As it turned out, it was often commoner women who had the greatest potential for gaining and exercising power and authority within the monarchy. The other powerful group within the palace was the children born there (known as *ahovi* or children of the king). The ahovi included all those who were born to the king or one of his royal sons. While only royal sons could aspire to kingship, the eldest daughters or senior sisters of the reigning king were especially important in the selection of future kings and their installation into that office. No man could aspire to kingship without the political support of his sisters and aunts (Bay 1998, 8–9).

Many of these royal institutions were also found to a lesser degree throughout Dahomean society. For example, the oldest woman in a lineage was enstooled along with the lineage head and served, as did the queen mother, as his partner and advisor. The queen mother of a lineage, along with several other men and women, formed a council of elders who assisted and advised the lineage head (Argyle, 130). In some instances, too, elite but nonroyal women participated in a form of marriage similar to that of the princesses. In such a case the woman and her lineage, rather than the lineage of her husband, retained the right to any children born to her. Such women could form their own household and pass control of it to one of their daughters (Argyle, 149–50).

Also well documented in the literature were the regiments of female soldiers often called "amazons" that fought in the many Dahomean wars. These women were an elite and effective fighting force who considered themselves superior to their male counterparts. Like the women of the palace, they were called wives of the king and served in the palace between wars. Although these women were expected to remain celibate during their time of service, like the princesses they maintained possession of any children they bore.

TRADITIONAL FON RELIGION

If European visitors were surprised by the power wielded by the "amazons" and women of the palace, they were scandalized by the sacrifices, both human and animal, offered to the gods of Dahomey. This is surprising in retrospect, since at this same time Europeans were engaging in their own bloody wars and the tribunals known generally as the Inquisition were responsible for thousands, some say millions, of people being tortured, burned at the stake, or killed in other horrible ways because of their actual or purported religious beliefs. In North America, too, people were ostracized, beaten, and even killed for espousing the "wrong religion" or wrong version of Christianity. Edna Bay suggests that in a world like the Kingdom of Dahomey where wealth was measured in terms of the number of persons under one's control, human beings were the most precious of the gifts one could give to propitiate the divine powers and encourage them to act favorably toward the society. Rather than being a sign that life was cheap, as was suggested by some sources, these sacrifices showed the willingness of the king to give of his wealth for the good of the people (Bay 1998, 66).

In precolonial times (and after) the religion of the people of Dahomey was focused on the thousands of spiritual beings known as Vodun, who gave their name to the most widely recognized African-based religion in the Americas—Vodou. The Vodun were the link between the visible world of humanity and the invisible world of the spirits. People could communicate with the denizens of that invisible world through sacrifice, prayer, possession, and divination (Bay 2008, 5). The Vodun included the so-called

Great Gods, who were formed into pantheons with specialized functions, as well as deified ancestors and the lesser gods who had been sent to live among the worshippers and in some cases mate with them (Herskovits and Herskovits, 10–11). Some scholars divide the Vodun into two general categories: popular and royal. The royal Vodun, which were called the *Nesuhwe*, included the deified members of the royal family, family members of their ministers and high-ranking officials, and the spirits of magical monsters known as *Tohosu* (Bay 2008, 21). Among the popular Vodun known as the Great Gods, Melville and Frances Herskovits identified three major pantheons: a sky pantheon, an earth pantheon, and a thunder pantheon. Heading the sky pantheon was Mawu-Lisa, the female/male creator pair that commands the night and the day and that gave birth to many of the other deities. Also included in this group are Legba, the trickster deity who is the "personal spirit of man and gods"; Ga, the god of metal and war; Age, the god of the bush who commands the birds and animals; Aido-Hwedo, the rainbow serpent also known as Dambala that works with the thunder god; and several others (Herskovits and Herskovits, 14–16). The earth pantheon is headed by Sagbata, the first-born son of Mawu-Lisa and the elder brother of Xevioso, the thunder god. Sagbata is said to own smallpox and other skin diseases. He is considered to be a great king who rewards followers with the fruits of the earth, especially grains such as maize and millet, and punishes through diseases, such as smallpox, that cause rashes and granular eruptions of the skin (Herskovits and Herskovits, 16–19). Xevioso, the head of the thunder pantheon, is also the ruler of the seas (Herskovits and Herskovits, 19–22). Several of these deities have direct cognates with Yoruba deities, including Legba (Eleggba), Ga (Ogun), Sagbata (Shopona/ Babaluaiye), and Xevioso (Shango).

While these deities drew worshippers from all sectors of society, no single person worshipped all of them. Rather worship was organized into groups that the Herskovitses characterize as "churches," modern anthropologists often call "cults," and we'll characterize as congregations of those who served the Vodun. Each such congregation had its own shrine, priests, rituals, and ceremonies (Herskovits and Herskovits, 35). Even the smallest village had modest shrines to the earth and sky deities, especially Legba, and each family compound had a shrine to its more important ancestors, the spirit of twins, and the spirits of any abnormally born children of the lineage (Herskovits 1967, 4–5). The village chief was the head of the principal family of the village as well as the political and often spiritual leader of the village as a whole. While he would have considerable power within his own village, he was also obliged to respect the will of both the king from whom he derived his power and the elders of the community, who served as his advisory council and represented their own lineages and the village as a whole (Herskovits 1967, 9). A congregation might include only the descendants of a deified ancestor or a large number of worshippers drawn from across families. For each congregation the deity or deities that they worshipped were considered to be the most important members of the pantheon. We call this form of religion, in which individuals worship a subset of a larger pantheon, henotheism. In a henotheistic culture individuals focus their religious attention on some small number of deities, perhaps only one, while acknowledging the deities worshipped by others. At the same time, an individual might be a member of several congregations, worshipping several different sets of deities in turn. As Nobel Prize–winning author Wole Soyinka suggests in a conversation with Ulli Beier concerning the Yoruba people published in 1997, such a religious culture fosters a tolerance for multiplicity and an acceptance of each individual's search for religious truth and meaning in his or her life (Soyinka 1997).

The Vodun were literally innumerable, both present in natural objects and installed in shrines by their devotees. They were not however locked into these locations and could move about at will. The Vodun could reveal themselves in dreams, through possession, and in other ways. They could be found not only in natural objects but also in manufactured items, both those from Dahomey and other parts of West Africa and those brought to the area by outsiders. Consequently the Vodun could conceivably be installed or discovered in Christian, Islamic, and even Hindu religious objects. Because the Vodun themselves could travel as well as exist in the sacred vessels in which they were placed, their worship could easily move from one region to another as their devotees traveled or were carried away to new areas. This made the religious system based on the worship of the Vodun eclectic and flexible enough to continually adapt, adjust, invent, and modify itself to new locales and environments (Bay 2008, 5–6). Like their cousins, the Orisha of the Yoruba people, the Vodun are seen as a bundle of characteristics, some admirable or even heroic and others petty and disreputable. They serve as moral exemplars in spite of their all-too-human weaknesses and failings. They are capable of both rewarding and punishing those who serve them, but their most important function is to provide protection from the dangers of life (Bay 2008, 16).

Religious practice among the people in the Kingdom of Dahomey, known as the Fon, was pragmatic and eclectic, and the Vodun were linked to humanity through complex relationships of mutual dependence. Sacrifices made to the Vodun nourished them so that they could continue to aid their devotees in the future. Contemporary worshippers of the Vodun describe their offerings using a metaphor of feeding, and most offerings could be classified as food and drink, including water, the essential initial offering; alcohol; sacrificial blood; and a wide range of solid foods. Each Vodun has both favorite foods and foods that are forbidden or considered poisonous (Bay 2008, 171n13). Both the Vodun and the honored dead were seen as having access to *ashé* or power, a power that could be used for good or ill, to reward or punish those in the visible world. Through their acts of service to both the Vodun and the ancestral dead, individuals and families could harness that power for themselves and their families. The Vodun and the dead were not all-powerful; they depended on the offerings of their devotees and descendants to provide the strength they needed to protect those who served them. Vodun without devotees and the dead without worshipful descendants weakened and eventually withered and died (Bay 2008, 5). Each of the Vodun had gifts that could make the lives of his or her worshippers more pleasant and punishments that could be used when he or she was displeased. In the eyes of the Fon, the gods were like human beings, perhaps like their own rulers, who could be willful and impetuous but who could also be won over by patience so as to show favoritism toward loyal worshippers. The ultimate test of a Vodun was whether it worked well to make the lives of devotees better. A Vodun that produced good results for its followers was given continued worship and sacrifice, while one who failed to provide for its followers would find its worship decreased or abandoned. Spirits from other areas who were shown to work well were welcomed into the community and incorporated into the cosmology of the Vodun. War captives and brides often brought their deities to a new community, while people might be sent to neighboring areas to be trained in the worship of new deities (Bay 1998, 22). Deities and rituals from Yorubaland were introduced among the Fon, principally through women who were absorbed into Fon families and artisans who migrated to Dahomey (Bay 1998, 190). So many deities and rituals were borrowed from the neighboring Yoruba-speaking peoples that Edna Bay suggests that the Fon and Yoruba religious systems could be considered to be a single religious universe (Bay 2008, 170n3).

In addition to the Vodun, the spirit world also included ancestors, who, if appropriately placated, could work for the good of their descendants. Among many West African societies, the elderly were accorded special privileges due to the great knowledge and power they had accumulated over a lifetime. When they died they became even more powerful ancestors, who continued to be interested in the well-being of their families. Many of the same types of rituals and offerings that could placate and satisfy the

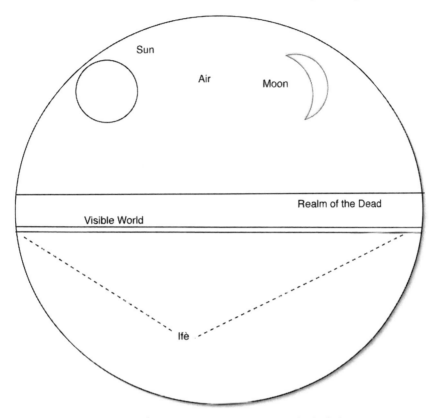

Calabash of the cosmos, Dahomey cosmological view

deities could also be used to appease and appeal to the ancestors. Ancestors entered the afterlife with the same status level they had in life. However, ancestors with powerful descendants themselves became more powerful, while those whose worship was neglected or those with no living descendants ceased to exist (Bay 1998, 23). Each family compound had a *deho* or family shrine where the entire lineage gathered from time to time to honor its ancestors with many different types of food and drink, including water, alcoholic and other beverages, fresh blood and cooked meat from sacrificed animals, grains, vegetables, and prepared dishes. After the completion of the rituals, during which the ancestors "ate" these offerings, the family members shared the leftovers, performing a type of communion ceremony (Bay 2008, 6–7). Individuals could also visit the *deho* at other times in order to present the ancestors with questions of importance to the family, get their approval for marriages, discover who had been reincarnated into a new child, and obtain their blessings for other changes within the lineage. Divination provided a method for ongoing communication between the living and their ancestors (Bay 2008, 7).

Edna Bay reports that one of her informants, who had been an advisor to two kings in the late nineteenth century, described the cosmos as being like a closed gourd, which contained earth, sky, water, and the realms not only of the living but also of the dead and the Vodun. As he described it,

> Earth is a flat surface that floats on waters at the point where the calabash top meets the bottom. The sky and heavenly bodies are on the inner surface of the calabash lid, and most of the dead live in an indeterminate space somewhere above the surface of the earth. The Vodun, along with "the best" of the dead, occupy a world called Ifè, which is located underneath the earth's surface. The sinuka as the vessel of offering and sacrifice symbolizes the point of communication between the visible and invisible worlds, the sacred interaction between the living and the dead, the Vodun and those who serve them (Bay 2008, 40).

Both the ancestors and the Vodun lived in a kingdom of shadows known as *kutome*, literally the land of the dead. Life in Kutome was similar to life in the world of the living, *gbetome*. The ancestors of the monarchy ruled in Kutome as their descendants ruled in the visible world. Everyone in Kutome maintained the same relative social status as his or her living descendants, and each world could affect those living in the other. Thus angered ancestors could wreak havoc in a family, while those who were happy and appropriately placated could bless their descendants, giving them successful harvests and many children.

While theoretically anyone might be called to the worship of any of these Vodun, the responsibilities for the organization and maintenance of the individual congregations were often tied to families. Each congregation was controlled by the *hungan* (the chief for a Vodun), one or more priests, who could be either male or female or a male-female pair. Another type of priest was known as *vodunon*, meaning mother or person responsible for the Vodun. Others were identified as *vodunsi*, that is, a wife of one of the deities. It was the Vodunsi who spoke for the Vodun through the mechanism of trance possession. Often the Vodunsi were descendants of earlier Vodunsi, the title and responsibility passing down through a family. As with the Yoruba, both male and female priests carried these female-identified titles of "mother" or "wife." While a single lineage might control the worship of a Vodun, anyone called by the Vodun could become a member of the congregation and participate in its rituals. Thus these worship communities were organizations that crossed family and possibly class lines. As with the Yoruba, individuals might be called to the worship of a Vodun for any number of reasons, not only because the Vodun belonged to their lineage but also because of their own individual life circumstances. For example, mothers of twins, and later the twins themselves, often became involved in the worship of the *hoho*, the protector of twins (Bay 2008, 21).

PROPHECY, DIVINATION, AND RELIGIOUS PRAGMATISM

An understanding of personal destiny that came to Dahomey from Yoruba-land was also an important element of Fon religion. The cult of Fa (known as Ifa among the Yoruba) used a system for discovering one's destiny and its best manifestation through a divination system based on sixteen palm nuts or kernels (Herskovits 1937, 30). The Fa priest, called a *bokonon*, used palm nuts in a set of sixteen or linked together on a chain of eight to tie the client's questions about his or her life to one of a series of stories associated with the 256 possible combinations of numbers embedded in narrative verse. A competent priest had memorized at least one story for each number combination, and master priests knew significantly more. The stories tell of an individual, deity, or anthropomorphized plant or animal that approached a Fa priest with a difficulty and describe how the difficulty was resolved. Included in each story are the offerings or other actions that helped the protagonist solve his problem. Using the story as a model, the priest and the client developed a plan to answer the client's question and move him along the path of his best destiny. In addition to approaching the Fa priest during times of personal crisis such as illnesses or bad luck, individuals and families also consulted Fa at milestone occasions like births and marriages to learn the first outlines of the child's destiny or to determine whether a proposed marriage fit within the partners' destinies.

By the nineteenth century the cult of Fa flourished in Dahomey and became one of the most important cult groups among the Fon. It was strengthened by the migration of diviners who were escaping the disintegration of the Oyo Empire. In addition, many Fon children were sent to study Ifa among the families of their Yoruba-speaking mothers (Bay 1998, 255). The Fa cult was unique among Fon cults in that its priesthood was exclusively male and its divination focused on the individual rather than a larger social unit such as the family, lineage, town, or kingdom. Fa diviners encouraged men to learn their personal destinies in order to promote their own advantage and that of their lineage. Women's destinies were seen as tied to those of the men in their lives, their husbands and fathers, and Fa encouraged male control of woman, especially their sexuality (Bay 1998, 256, 257).

In contrast, women were the principal followers of the other Vodun and their primary priests. Women were more likely to be the Vodunsi, the possession priests who spoke for the Vodun, and even men who occupied these priestly positions were given womanly titles. Whereas Fa divination tended to be secretive and private, possession utterances were public and communal, spoken in open spaces in the town and forest, and accompanied by musicians and dancers as well as the community at large. Fa diviners also distanced the devotee from the Vodun, since they stood as mediators between the human and the divine. Whereas devotees of the other Vodun might have shrines in their own homes or could visit public shrines on their own, Fa always required the services of a diviner to contact the invisible world (Bay 1998, 256).

Both divination and possession trance served the function of prophecy within West and West Central African societies. Americans' acceptance of closed revelation has waxed and waned over time. As a group Americans tend to be open to new religious revelations, as can be seen by the many new religious traditions that have developed here, particularly after the Second Great Awakening, a time when African ideas of religiosity were incorporated into the developing American religious sensibilities. Pragmatism, the tendency to judge new ideas by the results they produce, serves as an emblematic method of thinking and acting in American culture. In the religious sphere, a pragmatic mindset leads one to judge religious traditions not according to the "truth" of their dogmas and creeds, not according to the splendor or evocativeness of their rituals and practices, but by whether the tradition works to provide spiritual fulfillment to the individual. Throughout most of their history, Americans have been religious pragmatists who have been quick to experiment with new traditions when they have felt that their old religious traditions no longer served their spiritual needs.

How much did Fon (and other African) religious ideas about continuous revelation affect this American propensity to judge new religious ideas against a pragmatic standard? In comparing the relative positions of European and African clergy, John Thornton suggests that European clergy were able to control revelatory pronouncements because of their strong political base and ties to secular authority. Throughout West and West Central Africa, traditional priests lacked such authority, and even in Kongo, where the Catholic clergy had strong ties to the secular elite, ongoing revelation was an accepted element of religious life (Thornton 1992, chapter 9). Among British colonists in North America circumstances prevented the development of a strong, independent clergy. Ministers were often subject to the economic control of their vestry or other lay leaders of the congregation and thus lacked the ability to strictly control revelation among their congregations. In fact the established clergy were unable to stop the waves of new revelations coming out of the First and Second Great Awakenings (1730s and 1740s and then between 1790 and 1840) and the many new American religions that were spawned during this period. General American religiosity was greatly changed during this time, and African religious cultures seemed to have been very influential in this regard.

Although both Methodist and Baptists were instrumental in the antebellum revival movement known as the Great Awakening, by the dawn of the Civil War the majority of the enslaved were converted to the Baptist faith (Young, 77–78). Baptism became an especially important Christian ritual during this period. Among the Kongolese, salt rather than water formed the essential element of Catholic baptism; however water and water spirits were also important in the cosmological systems of both the Kongolese and Fon. In both Africa and the Americas water served as the boundary between this world and the world of spirits. The horizontal line of the Kongolese cross and the watery realm at the boundary between the two halves of the Fon cosmological diagram represented the water out of which humans were born and over which they must pass on their way to the land of the dead. Many believed that one could see God or meet other spirits in or near water. In the American environment, such visions were an important part of the conversion experience. Conversion for the enslaved was often preceded by great distress, an illness or weakness followed by a vision or dream where one was shown both the fires of hell and the beauties of heaven. Sin was a sickness, the cure for which was baptism. For many, such visions were a prerequisite for conversion—until one had such a vision, one was not considered ready for baptism.

Throughout West and West Central Africa, secret societies served important social, political, and religious functions. Initiation into these societies often required a death-and-rebirth experience that left one with new otherworldly powers. River baptism followed a similar death-and-rebirth form of initiation into Christianity. During this ritual one was pushed underwater, symbolically drowned, and then pulled back to life by the initiating minister and his assistants, who subsequently integrated the reborn into the community of believers. Many saw God or had other ecstatic experiences while underwater. Maintaining that relationship between spiritual and physical death and rebirth, some people even kept their white baptismal robes to use as their burial shrouds sometime in the future. During the visionary experiences leading up to their baptisms, the enslaved often saw themselves, heaven, Jesus, the angels, and God as symbolically white. Like much of the religious symbolism of African American experience, this whiteness is double-coded. On the one hand, in Kongo and throughout much of West Africa, white is the color of the dead, the other world, and the spiritual. For example, as a child the prophet Kimpa Vita had a vision in which she played with two "white" children. Their color was interpreted as a spiritual, rather than racial, marker, and her childhood vision identified her as a future spiritual leader. In the Americas, African-heritage people continued this notion of whiteness and spirituality. Among West and West Central African societies, blackness was not, however, associated with evil. Instead it often represented the material, as opposed to the spiritual, realm or was used to mark something as mysterious or enigmatic. White also represents spirituality among Europeans, but also what is good and pure, while black is often used to represent evil. During the earliest colonial period indenture and slavery were not completely racial, as bondspeople were often indentured Europeans rather than enslaved Africans. However, as America became more racially conscious, these color connotations began to be applied to racial groups so that people judged "white" by the culture were assumed to be part of the master class and by extension more intelligent, ethical, and so on, while darker skin became associated with the lower, enslaved classes, who were perceived as less intelligent and less ethical. Thus, living in a racially segregated world in which white skin color was associated with the master class, visualizing the spiritual world as white greatly disadvantaged black converts and led to a form of self-loathing that for some people has continued to the present time.

CONCLUSION

Fon religious ideas have permeated American culture in both positive and negative ways. Fon culture was an important part of the traditions that became known as Vodou, Voudou, and hoodoo in Haiti, in New Orleans, and throughout the American south. In addition, "voodoo," the American stereotype of these traditions, continues to play an important part of what Richard Dawkins calls an American cultural "meme," a concept that carries cultural ideas, symbols, and practices. As we shall see, even in the twenty-first century, Americans can use the term "voodoo" to characterize ideas they wish to demonize and denigrate. In the twenty-first century, the concept of the zombie, another idea from the Fon and Kongolese by way of Haiti, has gained new life as a literary and film genre. Although the meme of the zombie has evolved from its nineteenth-century precedents, the fear of being turned into a primitive, mindless being continues, as we shall discuss, to carry great weight in American society.

But ideas from the Fon and other West and West Central African cultures about divination and prophecy have also been influential on the development of a distinctive American religious worldview. We will look at both of these influences in the next chapter and consider how they have been instrumental in the development of American religious sensibilities.

8

THAT VOODOO THAT YOU DO

Nothing sparks the American imagination like the term "voodoo." Not only does voodoo have religious connotations, it has been used to describe everything from music and musical traditions to conspiracy theories and economic and fiscal policies. Americans who know nothing else about Haiti or New Orleans recognized voodoo dolls, zombies, and the name of Marie Laveau, the Voodou Queen. To call something a form of voodoo, as George H. W. Bush did in disparaging Ronald Reagan's economic theories in 1980, is to classify it as superstitious nonsense without applying any other critical analysis. But the term "voodoo" and the religious complex behind it have an important history both in the development of Haiti and New Orleans and in the wider American context.

The word "voodoo" comes from the Fon term to describe Fon deities. The name of these deities has variously been spelled "voodoo," "vodou," "voudou," and "vodoun," among others. Twenty-first-century scholars have settled on the spelling "vodou" to describe both the deities and the religious traditions they have spawned in Haiti and "voudou" for the sister tradition in New Orleans. The vodou and their worshippers made their biggest impact in the Americas on the religious development of Haiti, the first independent black nation in the Americas, and in New Orleans, the destination of many slaveholders and their chattel after the Haitian Revolution. Used as a pejorative for centuries, "voodoo" has entered common American culture, albeit with distorted and inaccurate connotations. This chapter will review the development of Vodou in Haiti as well as its manifestation in New Orleans and Louisiana and the place of the southern African American tradition known as hoodoo in this story. We will also explore the impact "voodoo" has had as the ultimate demonic category in American culture in general and Vodou's place in the contemporary American religious landscape.

No African religious tradition survived fully in North America; however, the set of "superstitions" known as Haitian Vodou, its Louisiana counterpart New Orleans Voudou, and the rural African American cultural elements known as "hoodoo" continue to influence American culture. A superstition is usually described as belief in some sort of activity not supported by reason or knowledge. Superstitious actions often develop when individuals or communities attempt to affect some aspect of their lives that appears to be outside rational control. People like athletes, soldiers, and salespeople whose lives or livelihoods seem to be controlled by luck or irrational forces may turn to activities described as superstitious. For example, athletes may refuse to wash their clothes or themselves after a win in order to prolong their good luck, or they may engage in elaborate rituals prior to pitching or hitting in baseball, throwing free throws in basketball, or kicking field goals in football. Soldiers and salespeople may carry good luck charms, dress in a certain order, eat or not eat certain foods, step out of the house or onto the field of action in a certain way, or perform other ritualistic activities in preparation for engaging their opponent or approaching a prospect. All of these activities lend the feeling of having some control in situations where skill and expertise are not enough. Definitions of superstitious activities are always difficult. What is irrational to one is completely rational to another. Some people think all religious activity should be classified as superstition, while for others only those activities outside their own religious tradition are superstitious. Hence, for some people praying for rain in the local church may be considered a completely rational activity, while doing a rain dance out in the fields may be called superstitious. Christian missionaries have been notorious for decrying the religious activities of the people they encounter as superstitious while promoting their own religious beliefs and practices.

During the earliest years of the colonization of what was to become the United States, life was extremely uncertain: disease swept through settlements, killing whole families or taking some and not others, crops succeeded or failed, the natives were friendly or attacked seemingly without provocation. Although historians can often look back and see the logical flow of events leading to prosperity or disaster, for the colonists cause and effect were much less visible. We tend to think of the European colonists as part of the rational elite of the eighteenth-century Enlightenment, but many of the earliest settlers came from the pre-Enlightenment eras of the sixteenth and seventeenth centuries. They brought their own superstitions, spells, and the like with them. These were joined, especially in the south, with those of the natives as well as those brought from Africa by the enslaved.

Slavery was an especially perilous existence. Not only were the enslaved subjected to the uncertainties that beset all the colonists, they were also dependent on the whims of often distant and alien masters or overseers whose actions and reactions may have been unfathomable. For example, masters or overseers often used whipping and threats of whippings to control and motivate the enslaved, but in many cases the number of threats greatly exceeded the actual whippings. Slaves who often ran afoul of their masters or overseers would use fellow slaves, often known as conjurers and hoodoo masters, to predict and attempt to prevent threatened whippings. When these actions appeared to deflect punishments, they were more likely to be repeated and passed around within and among slave communities. Although we tend to think of these types of activities as irrational, such activities were constantly being tested. Those that appeared to succeed were repeated while those that did not were not. However, the literature of superstitions (as well as that of prayer and similar activities) is rife with justification of why an activity appeared to succeed in one instance but failed in another. Often when such an activity fails the individual is accused of not performing it correctly or failure is blamed on the interference of another physical or spiritual being, or it might be suggested that the being invoked chose not to comply—"God has other plans."

HAITIAN VODOU

The island of Saint-Domingue (now know as Hispaniola), and particularly the country of Haiti, which occupies its western portion, is generally recognized as the home of Vodou in the Americas. During its earliest history the island was one of the largest sugar producers in the world and consequently the destination not only of European planters but also of enslaved Africans destined to work their many plantations. Africans from all three of our areas of interest were shipped in large numbers to the island. Between 1725 and 1755 almost 40 percent of the slave ships landing on Saint-Domingue were from the Bay of Benin, bringing Fon, Yoruba, and other peoples from Allada and other West African ports, while massive numbers of West Central Africans began arriving in the last half of the eighteenth century (Hall, 169–70). By 1790 the western, French-controlled portion of the island was the richest French colony in the New World, gaining its great wealth from sugar, coffee, and indigo. On the eve of what would eventually be called the Haitian Revolution, there were more than a half million enslaved Africans in Saint-Domingue, between half and two-thirds of whom were African-born and African-socialized. Of these more than half were from the Central African kingdoms of Kongo and Angola (Rey 2004, 10; Vanhee, 246). However, it appears that in spite of the encouragement from both the Vatican and the Spanish and later French crowns there was little inclination on the part of the planters and businesspeople of the island to provide religious instruction to the enslaved or build on their existing religious backgrounds. Here as in North America, religious instruction and practice took away valuable time from the productive labor of the enslaved and so was often neglected.

In 1791, after a midnight ceremony during which a black pig was offered to the Fon spirit of Ezili Dantò and all those present pledged themselves to the fight for freedom, the black majority revolted and was able to establish the first independent black nation in the Americas. On January 1, 1804, final independence was declared for the new nation. They named their new country Ayiti, based on an Arawak name which meant "land of mountains." This revolution triggered a massive exodus from the island by the French, their slaves, and other free people of color. Many settled in New Orleans, doubling its population and forever influencing the cultural development of that city, the future state of Louisiana, and the United States as a whole. From the earliest days of the nation of Haiti, the ruling elite have had an ambivalent relationship with Vodou and its practitioners, sometimes embracing portions of the tradition, sometimes ignoring it, and sometimes attempting to repress it.

The religion we know today as Vodou was born out of the beliefs and practices of enslaved Africans brought to the island, principally from the kingdoms of Dahomey and Kongo and the empire of the Yoruba. The religion takes its name from the Fon word for Fon deities, the Vodou, although in Haiti the deities are generally known as *Lwa* (or *Loa*). The English corruption of the word, voodoo, has entered American culture as a way to derogate an activity as some form of black magic, sorcery, or witchcraft, or as associated with inappropriately ecstatic religious or superstitious activity. What might be called Hollywood voodoo, because of the plethora of movies using the concept, is often typified by generally black bodies dancing around a bonfire in an effort to control such supernatural forces as zombies and other evil spirits and using the power of these spirits to harass and murder whites who happen to stumble upon their secrets.

Vodou and its sister religion of Santería, which we will discuss in chapter 9, are often used to exemplify the idea of religious syncretism, that is, the inappropriate mixing of incompatible symbols, such as mythology, ritual, and deities. Vodou appears to combine French Catholicism with primarily

Fon "paganism" to produce a new tradition that is not faithful to either of its parent traditions. Scholars point to the preponderance of West African language and cosmology and the association of Vodou deities with Catholic saints and their iconography as well as the incorporation of Catholic prayers into Vodou rituals as easily understood examples of such syncretism. Generally this syncretism is explained as the way oppressed West Africans were able to hide their own religious sensibilities from the view of the dominant and oppressive European religious culture.

However, research by Terry Rey of Temple University, Hein Vanhee of the Royal Museum for Central Africa in Belgium, and others suggests Vodou is the result of a unique collaboration among the African peoples who found themselves enslaved on the island and that European religiosity had little influence on its development. Instead, according to Rey, the several-generations-old embrace of Catholicism by the Kongolese people and the syncretism between age-old Kongolese religious ideas and those introduced by Catholic missionaries in Africa served as "a prototype and a taproot of New World Afro-Catholic religious syncretism." He suggests that "enslaved Africans were very much capable of synthetic theological reflection, which enabled them to carve new religions out of the old ones of two worlds, that of Africa and that of Europe" (Rey 2004, 9–10).

Scholars generally agree that Vodou as we know it today developed between 1760 and 1860. During approximately half of this period the people of what would become the nation of Haiti were denied any access to official Catholicism or Catholic religious instruction. After the Haitian Revolution in 1791, the Vatican refused to recognize Haiti as an independent nation, withdrew most of the priests from the island, and declined to send new priests to minister to the Haitian people until the concordat of 1860. This left Haiti with a strongly Kongolese society (by some estimates over a quarter of the people were born and raised in Catholic Kongo) but few Catholic priests to administrator the sacraments or spread and maintain Catholic beliefs and practices. As we discussed in chapter 3, the Kongolese people have from the beginning of their existence as a Catholic kingdom been merging Catholicism with their traditional religious beliefs and practices and have provided spiritual leadership for themselves by way of the laity in the absence of sufficient priests to administer the sacraments and provide spiritual guidance. As in Kongo itself, it fell to catechists and other African religious specialists to minister to the mass of African Christians in Haiti (Rey 2004, 13, citing Vanhee and Laguerre).

The earliest mention of "Vaudoux" can be found in a work by the Creole lawyer Moreau de Saint-Méry. He discusses the slave dances, including what appears to already be a longtime favorite called Vaudoux. However, as he describes it, this was more than simply a dance tradition but instead was "one of those institutions largely consisting of 'superstitions and bizarre practices'" on the part of the enslaved. He says that the word refers to "an almighty and supernatural being" represented by a snake kept in a box and petitioned for control of the enslaveds' masters as well as for money, the recovery of a sick relative, or the love of another. He describes a Vaudoux ceremony led by a king and a queen who used possession trance to transmit the words of the spirit to its devotees (Vanhee, 246–47, quoting from Saint-Méry, 63–68). It appears that at this time the religious practices of the enslaved were a largely heterogeneous mix that was just at the beginning of the process of merging or creolizing the traditions of the various African cultures found on the island. Some of these new or existing practices were used by the rebel leaders to bring together the disparate groups of fighters. It was these fighters who were able not only to throw off the yoke of slavery and colonialism but also to defeat the great Napoleon Bonaparte when he attempted to regain the island for France in 1803.

After independence, there was a long period of isolation as many of the elite whites and free blacks fled the island, the Catholic church withdrew all but a few of its clergy, and the European powers refused to trade with the new nation. Freed from colonial repression, Haitians were able to construct their own culture. It was during this period, Rey and Vanhee suggest, that the religious tradition known today as Vodou developed. Citing Alfred Métraux's 1959 classic *Voodoo in Haiti,* Rey notes the "veritable seizure of Catholicism" by Haitian Vodou between 1804 and 1860, that period when official Catholicism was absent from Haiti and there were few Vatican-sanctioned priests in the new country (Rey 2002, 265, citing Métraux, 331). Why Catholicism made such inroads into Vodou practice during the time when European dominance and Catholic influence were at their lowest point has never been adequately explained. Scholars have generally preferred to attribute the appropriation of European culture by Africans throughout the Americas to the result of European dominance and oppression than to the purposeful actions of African-heritage peoples. However, in this case it appears that the majority-Kongolese Haitians were able to apply their own ways of integrating Catholic religious sensibilities with those from other African cultures to influence the development of Haitian Vodou.

Contemporary Vodou consists of three disparate cosmologies that are combined but not mixed together. These can be identified as two different series of deities, the Rada spirits and the Petwo spirits, under almighty God. In Yoruba, Dahomey, and Kongo cosmologies the deities or spirits are generally divided into two categories. Among the Yoruba, deities such as Ogun and Shango are described as "hot," "red," and male while others, such as Obatala, Yemaya, and Oshun, are considered "cool," "white," and generally female (although some Orisha, such as Obatala, have both male and female manifestations). Similarly, among the Kongolese some minkisi are said to be "those of the above" while others are "those of the below." Those of the above are associated with fire, thunderstorms, and birds of prey and are generally considered retributive and masculine, while those of the below are associated with feminine concerns, fertility, and terrestrial waters. Vodou uses similar categories. The Rada spirits, whose name comes from the town of Allada, are predominately associated with the traditions of Dahomey and the Yoruba-speaking people that were their neighbors. They are "cool" deities marked by feminine concerns and are related to the right hand, the downward direction, water, and healing (MacGaffey, 225). Petwo spirits, who are more likely to have Kongo associations, are "hot," related to the left hand, the upward direction, fire, and violence. Somewhat disconcerting, at least to scholars of Kongolese cultures, is the placement of the *simbi*, who are "cool" water spirits, in the "hot" Petwo family, but their Kongo heritage seems to take precedence over their other associations (MacGaffey, 225). Similarly, several Yoruba/Fon deities who are considered "hot" in their homeland were included in the "cool" Rada family. These two families of spirits are headed by the monotheistic God of Christianity, who is honored by Catholic prayers, rituals, images, and iconography. The pantheons of Rada and Petwo spirits are not intertwined; rather, the two groups of spirits are defined in opposition to each other, and while the Rada and Petwo spirits are the concern of the *oungan* or *manbo* (male and female Vodou priest respectively), Catholicism is represented by the work of the *prêtsavann* (bush priest), who serves many of the functions performed by the nonclerical leaders in precolonial Kongo. He seeks the blessing of God, called *Bondye* (Good God), at the beginning of Vodou ceremonies, recites Catholic prayers and chants during initiation events, and accompanies the funeral procession from the home to the church and later to the cemetery, where again he leads the congregation in the Catholic prayers. The prêtsavann also officiates at the subsequent novenas for the deceased. While earlier scholars of Vodou considered the role of the prêtsavann a sort of compromise between Vodou devotees and the Catholicism of the surrounding colonial culture, Vanhee says instead that it represents the incorporation of similar religious roles from precolonial Kongo (Vanhee, 262).

At the top of the Vodou cosmos is Bondye, who is responsible for creating and maintaining the universe. However, like the Fon and Yoruba high gods Mawu-Lisa and Olodumare, Bondye is not actively involved in human affairs and little ritual attention is paid to him. Instead Vodou rituals are focused on the Lwa, also known as *les Mystere*, and/or the ancestors, *les Morts*. There are hundreds of Lwa, many associated with elements of the natural environment, for example, the ocean, rivers, and the rainbow, and others associated with human archetypes such as the trickster, the farmer, or the soldier. Often the Lwa are also associated with particular Catholic saints, although the associations are somewhat idiosyncratic, varying from place to place. As he is in Yoruba and Fon mythology, Legba (Eshu/Elegba among the Yoruba) or Papa Legba is a pivotal figure. Often associated with Christ or Saint Peter, Papa Legba is the trickster and intermediary figure that is the keeper of the gate and the crossroads. Like Peter, who carries the keys to heaven, Legba opens or closes the lines of communication between the Lwa and their devotees and carries messages between the visible and invisible realms. Papa Legba's *veve* or sacred drawing includes a cross, reminiscent of the Kongolese Four Moments of the Sun.

The earliest record of Vodou in Haiti speaks of "an almighty and supernatural being" represented by a snake. Danbala, Damballah Hwedo, Danbala Wèdo, or simply Da, who is associated with the rainbow and often manifests as a snake, is considered the father or head of the Lwa. His Christian association is God the Father, as well as Saint Patrick, whose iconography shows him preaching to the tangle of snakes at the water's edge (not banishing them, which is the more common Christian interpretation of Patrick's iconography). Danbala represents the life force, as Karen Brown says, "the coiling, sinuous movement that is life's movement" (Brown, 273). Like the rainbow, Danbala unites the land above and the water, the home of the ancestors, below, as well as the ocean and the mountains. Similar to the Yoruba Orisha Obatala, Danbala is seen as an old man whose food is natural, raw, and white, typically *òjat*, a thick almond and sugar syrup, or an unblemished egg balanced on bleached flour (Brown, 274).

Other Vodou spirits include Agwe, the Lwa of the ocean; Cousin Zaka or Azaka, the Lwa of agriculture; Papa Loko, the guardian of the fields and vegetation; Erzili or Mistress Erzili, the Lwa of love, beauty, and sexuality; Ogou, the Lwa of iron; and Gede, the Lwa who is lord of the cemetery and is also associated with sexual prowess and fertility. Gede is actually the head of his own small pantheon, the Guedes or Guede spirits. Among the Guedes are Baron Samdi and his wife Gran Brigit. Baron Samdi is perhaps the most commonly portrayed Lwa, easily identifiable in his black clothing, black top hat, and sunglasses, often with one lens missing.[1] The rituals for the Guedes serve as the bridge between the Rada Lwa and those of the Petwo pantheon.

Associated with the Lwa but somewhat separated are the Marasa or divine twins. The Yoruba people are reputed to have the highest rate of twinning in the world, and throughout West Africa twins are afforded special status. In some cultures, twin births are considered unnatural and the babies are rejected by the society. In other cultures, like the Yoruba and Fon, twins are considered semidivine. According to Karen Brown, "twins symbolize human nature: half matter and half soul," and they are often related to the Christ figure, who is half God and half man. Many of the Dahomean deities, especially those associated with the formation of the world, are twin figures, and among contemporary Vodou devotees, the Marasa are considered to be both the first of God's children and the first to die (Brown, 23–24).

Whereas the Rada deities are considered "cool" and gentle, the Petwo Lwa are "hot" and violent. Scholars have long debated the source of the Petwo Lwa. Maya Deren, who did research on the island in the late 1940s under a Guggenheim Fellowship, suggested that they come from the Native Americans who still lived on the island when the first Europeans and Africans arrived (Deren, 67). Karen Brown says that since the Dahomean Lwa were too benevolent, the Petwo rites were developed in the New World when aggressive, exacting Lwa capable of violent activities were needed to protect devotees from a society bent on their destruction (Brown, 24). However, Vanhee and MacGaffey both suggest that the Petwo cult was Kongolese in origin (Vanhee, 261; MacGaffey, 223) based on the similarity between the names of many Petwo Lwa and those of similar beings among the Kongolese.

Similarly, the origin of the name Petwo, Petro, or Don Petro has been subject to scholarly dispute. However, Pedro was a common Kongolese name during this period and Don a common honorific. In fact, the king that condemned Dona Beatriz Kimpa Vita was named Pedro I. Like their Kongolese ancestors, the Petwo spirits are not as distinctive and separate as those of the Rada pantheon, although there are several Petwo spirits who have direct relationships with their Rada counterparts, including Kafou Legba, Ezili Je-Rouge and Ezili Dantò, Ogou Ferary, and over thirty manifestations of Gede energy (Pinn, 24–25). Also included among the Petwo spirits is Simbi, who is the keeper of springs and ponds and facilitates communication between the living and the dead. The Rada and Petwo deities and their rituals are generally kept separate from each other. Even though Vodou uses the African hot/cool categories of deities, most of the Yoruba/ Dahomey deities, regardless of their original classification, are included among the cool Rada deities, while most of the Kongolese spirits are included among the hot Petwo deities. Importantly, these two sets of spiritual beings are not classified as "good" and "bad." They are ambiguous—members of both groups can impose and remove afflictions; both can heal and harm (MacGaffey, 225).

Just as the contemporary Vodou pantheon is divided into these three types of spirits (Bondye, Rada, and Petwo spirits), so too are contemporary Vodou rituals typically divided into three movements. Rituals start first with Catholic prayers led by the prêtsavann. These are followed by the invocation of the cooler Rada spirits and finally the invocation of the harsher Petwo spirits. Opening prayers typically include the Our Father, Hail Mary, and Apostle's Creed in French followed by Christian hymns. As the energy of the ritual picks up, the language moves from French to Creole intermixed with Fon and Yoruba words, the language of the Lwa. First to be invoked during this transition from Catholicism is Saint Peter (Legba), who opens the doors and removes the barriers between the visible and invisible worlds. The oungan or manbo continues the transition by picking up the *ason*, the sacred rattle, and invoking a litany of important saints, first male, then female. When these final Christian prayers conclude, the drumming and the invocation of the Lwa begin, first for the Rada spirits and then later for the Petwo spirits (Brown, 275–80).

NEW ORLEANS VOUDOU

Folk tradition suggests that it was a Petwo-style ritual that inaugurated the Haitian Revolution in 1791. Fear for their lives and the loss of their property prompted a vast migration of French colonists and their enslaved chattel as well as some of the more elite free people of color from the island. Many of these settled in the nearby French colony of New Orleans, where they reestablished their lives and made their fortunes. Vodou, too, migrated from its island home to the mouth of the Mississippi. Here, in the style of early Haitian Vodou rituals, New Orleans Voudou developed independent of the systemization that occurred on the island after the revolution.

Although Voudou-type activities are recorded in New Orleans as early as 1743 (Ward, 32), the history of New Orleans Voudou is the history of its Voudou Queens, especially the two Marie Laveaus, mother and daughter.[2] The first Marie Laveau was born in 1801 to Marguerite Darcantel. Both her mother and grandmother were free women of color, both having been freed in the late 1700s. Like her city, Marie was possibly "a mixture of race and colors—white, black, red, French, Spanish, West African, Central African and Native American" (Ward, 10). Carolyn Long suggests that Marie's grandmother may have been a member of the Wolof African group brought to Louisiana in 1743 as a child (Long 2006, 9, 17, 19). Contrary to popular belief, most of the Africans brought to the Louisiana colony in the 1700s came directly from West Africa rather than through the Caribbean. Between 1719 and 1743 more than 29 percent of the slaves imported into the New Orleans area were from the Dahomey port of Ouidah (also known as Whydah) on the Bight of Benin and approximately 66 percent were from Senegambia. These people brought extensive knowledge of tropical agriculture, irrigation, metallurgy, marketing, and medical care geared for the semitropical climate they found at the mouth of the Mississippi River. The second-largest group of Africans came from the Kingdom of Kongo. The Kongolese people added their unique form of Catholicism to the religious mix already present in New Orleans. After the Haitian Revolution (1791–1804) many French planters immigrated to the area along with their black slaves. The Yoruba and Igbo people also contributed to the development of New Orleans Voudou.

As free women of color, Marie's mother and grandmother joined a growing "colored" middle class in New Orleans. Unlike English colonies of the same time period, New Orleans, by this time under the control of Spain, provided several ways in which the enslaved could be emancipated. Once freed, former slaves could work for wages, buy and sell property, and pass that property on to their children. Many free women of color entered into marriage-like arrangements known as *plaçage* with elite white men. Such relationships were instrumental in the formation of a tripartite racial society in New Orleans in which not all whites were elites, and many members of the so-called "colored" class of mixed-race persons became quite prosperous. Marie's mother entered into such a relationship with Henri D'Arcantel but later formed a relationship with Charles Laveau, a free man of color, who became Marie's father (Long 2006, 22–23).

By the time Marie was born, approximately 20 percent of the eight thousand citizens of New Orleans were free people of color like Marie herself (Ward, 12). Although the two Marie Laveaus (mother and daughter) were important to the development of Voudou in New Orleans, they didn't invent it. Voudou was already alive and vigorous long before the first Marie's birth in 1801. The first Marie was, however, instrumental in the development of Voudou at a critical point in the history of New Orleans, as she lived during the period when the city was moving from being a French colony where a free black middle class held influential positions in the social life of the city to being part of the Jim Crow era after the American Civil War, when black peoples and their cultures were severely repressed. By 1817 the New Orleans City Council had set aside an area across from Rampart Street known as Congo Square as a place where both free and enslaved black residents could gather, trade, and entertain themselves. A common form of this "entertainment" included the tribal songs and dances that disguised the religious celebrations of local Voudou practitioners, including the Laveaus. Eyewitness accounts tell of the first Marie dancing with a snake during these weekly celebrations. Later these ceremonies were moved away from the urban area and onto the shores of nearby Lake Pontchartrain.

Most of what we know about Voudou in New Orleans comes from newspaper coverage of arrests, reports of ceremonies, and the eyewitness accounts provided to the Louisiana Writers' Project. The Louisiana Writers' Project was the local branch of the Federal Writers' Project created as part of the Works Progress Administration during the Great Depression of the 1930s to provide employment for journalists, creative writers, and other white-collar workers. The Federal Writers' Project was tasked with compiling local histories, oral histories, ethnographies, children's books, and other works. In New Orleans field workers attempted to unearth the true story of Marie Laveau by locating and transcribing civil and ecclesiastical records related to her, her family, and her associates as well as newspaper articles related to Voudou. Field workers also interviewed New Orleanians who remembered Marie or her successor, commonly referred to as Marie II. This documentation provides a very uneven account of New Orleans Voudou. Although we can agree with Carolyn Long that Voudou must have had a complex theology, a pantheon of deities and spirits, a priesthood, and a congregation of believers, we know little of these religious aspects (Ward, xvii, 93).

We do know that by her late twenties the first Marie Laveau was beginning to be referred to as the "head of the Voudou sisterhoods" or the "mother of the Voudou orders" (Ward, 61). It appears that New Orleans Voudou was primarily a women-led religious tradition. Women were important leaders in most West and West Central African religious traditions. Both men and women led religious communities in Haiti. It is possible that Marie Laveau the elder learned much from her own mother, who may have been recognized as a conjure woman, a healer, and a nurse. Marie herself exhibited strong charismatic characteristics that drew people to both her public rituals and her private healing practice. As a Voudou leader she invited the spirits into her own body and was said to have spoken with the voice of La Grand Zombi, embodied in her snake companion. She also was herself "a root doctor and healer with knowledge of both medicinal and the magical qualities of numerous herbs" as well as "a spiritual guide and teacher" who attracted followers from across New Orleans society, both black and white (Ward, 61, quoting Glassman, 21).

Voudou in New Orleans does not appear to have been a unified set of beliefs and practices. Instead it appears to have been an eclectic combination of African-inspired rituals, elements of Haitian Vodou, European Catholic rituals, European popular folk practices, and Native American beliefs and practices. Like other African-based traditions, New Orleans Voudou focused on improving the lives of those who used the services of practitioners. People from all walks of life went to the Laveaus and other Voudou leaders to improve their health or job prospects; to find or keep a lover, wife, or husband; or generally to improve their lot in life. Voudou rituals were concerned with serving the deities and the ancestors; however, many individuals also engaged in activities meant to enhance their personal well-being, influence the actions of others, and control the forces of luck. Using the principles of imitative and contagious magic, Voudou charms contained ingredients chosen for the way their physical appearance, their names, or their everyday functions mirrored the desired attribute or action.

In addition to the large public rituals performed on Kongo Square and the shores of Lake Pontchartrain, it appears that Voudou leaders like Marie held rituals in their own homes. An article in the *Louisiana Gazette* from August 1820 talks about a home in the Faubourg Tremé that was "used as a temple for certain occult practices and the idolatrous worship of an African deity called Vaudoo. It is said that many slaves and some free people repaired there of nights to practice superstitious, idolatrous rites, to dance, carouse, &c." (Ward, 102). Louisiana Writers' Project informants talk of an altar in the front room of the Laveau home with many candles, saints' pictures, and a large statue of Saint Anthony as well as statues of Saint Peter and Saint Marron. In both Haitian Vodou and New Orleans Voudou there are Catholic saints associated with the most important spirits and deities. Although we don't know what association Saint Anthony may have had for Madame Laveau, "Anthony" would have been an important saint among the many Africans of Kongolese descent that were sent to the Americas after the death of the Kongolese Saint Anthony, Dona Beatriz Kimpa Vita, and Anthony continues to be an important folk saint among the people of New Orleans (Ward, 51). Saint Peter, who holds the keys to heaven in his common iconography, is associated in both Haiti and New Orleans with the guardian of the crossroads and the keeper of the gate to the spirit world and is known as Elegba among the Yoruba, Legba in Haiti, and Limba, La Bas, Liba, and Lébat in New Orleans. Some version of this deity is found in almost every African-based religion that developed in the Americas. Saint Marron is nei-

ther an African deity nor a saint of the Catholic church but rather a folk
saint unique to New Orleans. His name comes from the French word *marron*, which refers to a runaway slave. Marron's image is similar to that of Saint
Anthony. While Anthony is known for finding lost objects, Marron helps
those who "got lost" on purpose to avoid and evade capture and a return to
slavery (Ward, 109).

One of the most famous pilgrimage sites in New Orleans is the purported tomb of Marie Laveau in the Saint Louis Cemetery One on Basin
Street. To this day people leave gifts for the Voudou Queen, including flowers, wine, food, Mardi Gras beads, and other offerings. Many mark an *X* on
the front and side of the above-ground tomb. Ward suggests that these marks
invoke not only the Christian crucifix but also the Kongolese Four Moments of the Sun and perhaps other icons of the intersection between the
visible and invisible worlds (Ward, 13). The form of Voudou practiced by the
Marie Laveaus and their contemporaries vanished under the yoke of Jim
Crow in the early twentieth century, and Voudou as a religious tradition has
all but died out in New Orleans and Louisiana. What remains are the voodoo shops and museums throughout the French Quarter for the amusement
of tourists. Practitioners of African traditional religion in New Orleans today are more likely to be devotees of the Yoruba Orisha than La Grand
Zombi. In addition, the African healing arts, conjure, and spiritual counsel-
ing survive throughout the southern United States and in northern cities
with large black populations in the form of hoodoo, the rural Protestant
version of Voudou.

AMERICAN HOODOO

The West and West Central African cosmological systems associated with
Vodou and Voudou were not limited to Haiti and New Orleans but also
extended up the Mississippi Valley and through the rural southern portions
of the United States. Hoodoo, or as it is sometimes called, conjure, seems to
have lost the system of beliefs, gods, priests, and sacred ceremonies that were
maintained most obviously in Haiti and instead exists in creative tension with
the surrounding rural black Protestant culture. As Jeffrey Anderson, author of
Hoodoo, Voodoo, and Conjure, says, the term "hoodoo" refers to merely a set of
magical beliefs without the trappings of religiosity.[3] This attitude may also
look back to a Kongolese precedent where indigenous pre-Christian culture
successfully coexisted with a vibrant Catholicism. As discussed earlier, the
Kongolese religious cosmos was not focused on gods, priests, and rituals but

rather on the use of *minkisi* to provide spiritual and physical healing. Hoodoo adepts tend toward a strong Old Testament–based form of Christianity, and many see the Bible as a "conjure book" and repository of especially strong spells. Practitioners of hoodoo limit themselves to fortune-telling, spell-casting, and charm-making (Anderson, xi). Like its more systemized relatives, hoodoo is a system for producing good fortune, punishing enemies, and protecting oneself or one's clients from the evil machinations of others. Adepts are variously known as cunning doctors, trick doctors, high men and women, root workers, or conjure men or women. Most adepts have been African Americans; however, there have been some white, Latino, and Native American practitioners as well. Hoodoo has followed the migration of African Americans from the rural south to the urban north, so one can find shops catering to practitioners throughout the United States as well as on the World Wide Web (Long 2001). Some hoodoo spells are the special expertise of adepts, but many fall into the realm of folk remedies and thus are well known within African American and southern communities. As with most magical traditions, hoodoo draws freely on all of the cultures of the American melting pot, including European, African, and Native American ideas, spells, talismans, images, and symbols.

An important part of hoodoo practice is the construction of ritual objects, variously known as conjure bags, tricks, hands, charms, and tobies and often described in the literature as fetishes. Nkisi-like objects can be found throughout the Americas, highlighting the creative ways enslaved Kongolese and their compatriots used these ideas in their new American environments. In Cuba, they created a kettle or pot called a *prenda* filled with all types of objects empowered, like the nkisi, to work for them. The Cubans also created carved figurines that were used to magically attack slaveholders and other enemies. In Haiti medicines wrapped in silk, cotton, or raffia cloth and secured with pins and ribbons, called *wanga*, were invested with spirits who work for adepts. In Brazil, similar objects wrapped in cloth and tied tightly with cords, called *ponto de segurar* (securing points), were created. Among hoodoo adepts conjure bags, tricks, charms, and tobies were created to heal the sick, harm enemies, reveal the unknown, and protect their owners from the ravages of slavery. We can generically call these hoodoo objects "conjure bottles," since they are most often made out of discarded bottles of various types. Conjure bottles resemble the Kongolese minkisi in both their construction and use. The use of conjure bottles was decried as based on ignorance, irrational superstition, and a presupposed hazy set of ideas about the world and its workings. However, a less biased analysis shows that they correspond to a coherent set of ritual beliefs and practices brought by the enslaved from Kongo and other parts of West and West Central Africa.

Hoodoo men and women did not merely copy African minkisi; instead, they constructed their conjure bottles from locally available materials (African, European, and American) according to the needs of their clients based on a certain set of core principles. These principles point back to their African prototypes and include the ideas of containment, color symbolism, and other symbolism we discussed earlier in conjunction with Kongolese minkisi. However, it's also important to mention that conjure bottles were not merely minkisi revised but a constellation of West and West Central African beliefs and practices brought together in slave barracks throughout the United States. Conjure bags might contain pins, needles, and rusty nails along with hair and nail clippings. Crudely made human effigies reminiscent of the figurative minkisi were constructed to act as the images of conjure victims. These dolls, prototypes of the so-called "voodoo dolls," might have sharp objects sewn inside them or stuck in various parts of their anatomy. Another essential ingredient in southern conjure bottles was graveyard dirt (*goofer* dust), recalling the connection to and invocation of the spirits of the dead (Young, 163–64). In Kongolese society, earth from a grave has an especially strong connection to the interred person (Thompson 1984, 105), and goofer dust continues to invoke the power of the ancestors in the construction of conjure bags and bottles. The use of conjure bottles is still alive in the twenty-first century. Not only are books such as Anthony's readily available, a quick Internet search will provide hours of reading on the construction and use of all the various types of conjure bottles.

THINKING OF VOODOO

In his book *The Selfish Gene*, Richard Dawkins coined the term "meme" to represent a cultural concept, behavior, or style that is passed from person to person within a culture. Memes are analogous to genes in that they self-replicate, mutate, and respond to selective pressures as they move through a culture carrying ideas, symbols, and practices that are transmitted through writing, speech, gestures, rituals, or other types of phenomena. The meme of "voodoo" entered American culture as a way to denigrate an idea as, to use the definition from the online Merriam-Webster dictionary, "based on highly improbable suppositions" that are "extremely implausible or unrealistic" (Britannica). "Voodoo" carries other connotations as well. It is a form of "black" magic that is both evil and of Africa. Black magic as the use of unnatural means to gain unsavory ends may originate anywhere in the world. However, the African magic embedded within the idea of voodoo is often perceived as especially disgusting and mysterious, involving midnight rituals, death hexes, and zombification. These ideas are so entrenched within American culture that in a *New York Times* opinion page discussion on May 25, 2011, between David Brooks and Gail Collins, Brooks suggested that both the Democratic and Republican ideas were "truly voodoo fiscal policy." And Collins responded, "Ah, they do do that voodoo that they do so well" (Brooks and Collins). What exactly is "voodoo fiscal policy"? Brooks and Collins don't say, but apparently it's implausible or unrealistic. Their use of this meme also suggests elements of superstition and irrational savagery. Without further explaining the terms of the argument, columnists like Brooks and Collins can denigrate these policies, and readers feel as though they know what is being said (and implied).

When American troops occupied Haiti between 1915 and 1934 they dismantled the constitutional system and instituted a virtual return to slavery in order to rebuild the national infrastructure. Before that time the religious activities that had been brought under the umbrella of Vodou had been alternately valorized and demonized on the island. During the American occupation, there was an effort made both to wipe out this tradition and to institute a more rational Protestant Haitian culture. However, "voodoo" as a pejorative that represented black magic, ecstatic dancing around midnight bonfires, blood sacrifice, and zombies had already become an American meme. White observers in the seventeenth, eighteenth, and nineteenth centuries never fully understood this as a religious tradition; instead, they feared it as a particularly insidious type of magic that gave the powerless peoples of the island the ability to both kill their oppressors and turn them into zombies. A zombie is a uniquely Haitian construction. A zombie is a person who appears to have died but is revived after burial and compelled to do the bidding of the reviver, including criminal acts and heavy manual labor. Movies like *White Zombie* (1932), *Dead Men Walk* (1943), *King of the Zombies* (1941), *Night of the Living Dead* (1968), *Voodoo Dawn* (1990), and others have crystallized our ideas both of zombies and the culture of Haiti.

The word "zombie" may come from either *nzambi*, the Kongo word for spirit, or *zumbi*, the ghost (spirit) of one not appropriately buried (Frey and Wood). However, as popularly understood, zombies have no soul or spirit but instead are animated by a spell or the magical power of another, usually a voodoo priest or sorcerer. Alternatively, the sorcerer might capture the soul or mind of a living person and so be able to control his or her actions. To invoke our earlier discussion of possession trance, zombies are half possessed—their own spirits have vacated their bodies, but no new spirit has taken possession of them. Instead, they are controlled by an outside force. As mindless bodies, zombies are able to perform both arduous work without pause and evil actions without moral qualms. Not surprisingly, zombies are not too much different from one common perception of the enslaved as mindless bodies that require constant supervision in order to perform relatively simple but physically demanding tasks. Like zombies, the enslaved were seen as brutish with no independent will or consciousness. When members of the white elite are zombified by black sorcerers, the culture of slavery is inverted. Such inversion can only be resolved through the breaking of the spell and the restoration of the zombie to himself or the destruction of his physical body through decapitation or cremation.

The revival of zombification in the twenty-first century keeps many of the motifs of the early genre but substitutes virulent plagues and out-of-control scientific research instead of magic in producing zombies. Contemporary zombies typically are the result of a "zombie plague" that is self-replicating—human beings attacked by zombies become zombies themselves. In the contemporary zombie literature, such progressive zombification leads to the downfall of civilization and a return to a preindustrial society. Even when there are no racial undertones in the work, zombification always implies the destruction of Western (white) culture and the return to the brutality of barbarous (black) anarchy.

9

NEW AFRICAN BRANCHES

"Òrìṣà is the voice, the very embodiment of Tolerance," says Nobel Prize–winning author Wole Soyinka. "The accommodative spirit of the Yorùbá Gods remains the eternal bequest of a world riven by the spirit of intolerance, of xenophobia and suspicion."[1]

African religious thinking and the religions that developed in the Americas from the traditional religions of Africa continue to influence American religious and cultural sensibilities. Because of their late entrance onto the American religious stage, the Yoruba were very influential in the development of African-inspired traditions, especially in the Caribbean. There is the perception that because of their temporal closeness to Africa these traditions, especially the tradition known as Santería or Lukumí, along with Vodou and Voudou, are more pure (less diluted) than other traditions. However, the Yoruba arrived into what was already a great mixing pot of both African and European religious sensibilities. Thus these Yoruba-identified traditions are most often used as the most visible examples of religious syncretism. Although they developed outside our North American area of interest, several authors have suggested that these Yoruba-based traditions are poised to become one of the most important world religions of the twenty-first century. What influences might these traditions have on the ongoing development of American religious sensibilities?

African religious sensibilities have also continued to influence the American Protestant religious scene in the late nineteenth, twentieth, and twenty-first centuries. The most visible of these influences was the Pentecostal movement, centered on the Azusa Street Revival in Los Angeles. As in the earlier revivals of the Great Awakenings, blacks and whites worshipped and learned these new religious technologies together in mixed-race congregations, and Pentecostals of all races continue to engage in the experiential religious practices developed there. But let's look first at the African-identified religion of Santería.

SANTERÍA, A CONTEMPORARY
AFRICAN-BASED RELIGION

Most studies of black religion in America focus on the mainstream churches, notably the Baptist and Methodist traditions that claim the majority of churchgoing African Americans. However, religion within the black community is not uniform or monolithic. Instead, it is as variable as religion within the wider American culture. African Americans participate in a great many of the more religiously unconventional groups in America, often in black-identified subgroups. Many of these subgroups were developed in the early twentieth century, perhaps in response to the challenges of the Great Migration of blacks from the rural south to the urban north.

Hans Baer and Merrill Singer have developed a typology of black religious groups based on their strategies of social action and attitudinal orientation. They suggest that the content, structure, and variability of African American religious groups have three sources: the African cultures whose people were brought to the Americas, the Euro-American cultures that developed here, and the religious response of African Americans to their minority status in American culture. They delineated four types of black religious groups, including what they call Thaumaturgical/Manipulationist groups that attempt to achieve socially desired ends by engaging in various magico-religious rituals or by acquiring esoteric knowledge (Baer, 8–9, citing Baer and Singer). Although not identified by Baer and Singer, the African-inspired traditions, such as Vodou, Voudou, and Santería, should be included within this group. Of these three traditions Santería may be poised to have the most influence on contemporary American culture. Santería, developed on the island of Cuba between the late 1800s and the early 1900s, is one of the many religious traditions that arose in the Caribbean and South America based on the religious traditions of the African people, especially Yoruba speakers, who were brought there as slaves between the sixteenth and the late nineteenth centuries. Today there are followers of Santería and its sister Orisha-worshipping traditions throughout the world, including Europe, Asia, Africa, and North and South America. It is estimated that there are millions of practitioners of these traditions in the Americas alone. The worship of the Orisha has become so important that in their book *Orisa Devotion as World Religion* Jacob Olupona and Terry Rey argue that the Orisha-based traditions ought to unseat such demographically minor traditions as Jainism and Zoroastrianism in the catalog of so-called world religions (Olupona and Rey, 8). Although Santería in the United States started in the Cuban exile communities, it has spread to include members of all racial and economic groups throughout the country.

"Santería" is the most familiar name for these traditions; however, many practitioners find the term offensive and prefer other designations. Some of these include Regla de Ocha or simply Ocha; this is a mixture of Spanish and Yoruba terms that means the rule (*regla*) of the Orisha (*ocha* is a contraction of "Orisha"). Another is Lukumí (or Lucumi), based on the name given to the people from the city of Oyo, the center of the Oyo Empire at the time of the slave trade. In Cuba, all Yoruba-speaking people become Lukumí. In the late twentieth and early twenty-first centuries, Ifa, the name of the premier Yoruba divination system, is used by many as the name of the tradition. Finally, many prefer the designation "Orisha religion," which makes the deities the center of the religion. As this is the most general name, it is the one I will use here.

After the Haitian Revolution, the center of Caribbean sugar production moved from Haiti to Cuba, where increased production called for an increase in the number of laborers. The combination of many Yoruba-speaking captives available in the West African slave markets and the greater demand for labor in Cuba caused the greatest influx of Yoruba peoples to Cuba in its history. By 1886 (when slavery was officially abolished in Cuba) between five hundred thousand and seven hundred thousand Africans had been transported to the island. Between 1850 and 1870 over a third of these people were members of the Yoruba language group. From as early as 1573 free and enslaved Africans formed social clubs called *cabildos* in the cities of Cuba, especially Havana. By law these clubs were limited to members of a single culture group or "nation." As members of these clubs, people could socialize with others who spoke their language and shared their culture. These clubs were encouraged to maintain elements of their culture, including their drumming and dancing traditions, and members of one cabildo were not supposed to use the drum rhythms or dance steps of another cabildo. Thus the members of the cabildos were able to reestablish some of their cultural and the spiritual traditions, which depended on drumming and dancing to invoke the deities, in a relatively benign cultural context.

Things changed in the nineteenth century, however, as the authorities began to see the cabildos as breeding grounds for anticolonial and abolitionist activity. After slavery was finally abolished in 1886 and Cuba gained its independence from Spain in 1898, the new governmental authorities feared the power of the cabildos and began to persecute them more strongly. So in the late nineteenth and early twentieth centuries, cabildo members, including the Orisha devotees, moved their worship activities from the cabildo buildings to private homes to avoid government oversight and persecution. Throughout the nineteenth and twentieth centuries the religion experienced alternating periods of repression and tolerance. When Fidel Castro took control of the government after the Cuban Revolution in 1959, many Cubans left the island and settled throughout the Caribbean basin and in the United States, and when the Cuban government opened the port of Mariel to anyone who wanted to leave the island in the early 1980s another large group of Orisha worshippers from Cuba entered the United States. Originally both sets of these immigrants settled in south Florida and the New York City areas; however, over the ensuing years they spread throughout the United States so that by the end of the century, you could find Orisha-worshipping communities in many large and medium-sized cities throughout the country.

Orisha religion has many sources, but it is primarily based on the traditions of the Yoruba-speaking people from what is now southeastern Nigeria. The Yoruba people of the eighteenth and nineteenth centuries were not a single group but citizens of different city-states who spoke dialects of a common language and fought bloody wars against each other and their neighbors in the Kingdom of Dahomey. Because they looked to a similar set of sacred stories, and worshipped deities who belonged to a common pantheon, they were able to join together to preserve what they could of their cultures in Cuba. In addition to the traditions of the Yoruba-speaking peoples, early devotees of the Orisha in Cuba also embraced some aspects of the other cultures of the island, including the Kongo culture of the people who had been brought there since the sixteenth and seventeenth centuries, the Catholic Christianity practiced by the dominant European culture, and the native traditions of the Caribbean islands.

One of the most visible ways traditional Yoruba religious practice has incorporated European religious traditions has been the use of Catholic saints to represent the Orisha. Throughout Cuba (as well as Brazil and Haiti, other locations with significant Yoruba immigration), the African deities have been associated with the Catholic saints popular during the colonial period. These associations have long been used as one of the most obvious examples of religious syncretism. Syncretism is formally defined as the attempt to combine two or more different systems of belief and practices together into a single system. Often the two belief systems are logically incompatible, although individual devotees seldom question the internal inconsistencies. Sometimes such combinations are seen as transitions between the old and new ways of being religious, such as when missionaries allow converts to include elements of their old culture in their new religious practices. Examples of syncretism might include African drumming and dancing during Christian religious services or the use of Native American smudging rituals by non-Native peoples. Sometimes syncretic practices are considered a betrayal of the original purity of one or the other of the traditions, an example of ignorance, or an example of theological confusion. The Orisha traditions are often described as syncretistic religions that combine elements of West African Orisha cults and Spanish colonial Catholic practice. Practitioners are commonly accused of either corrupting Catholicism with their own cosmology, practices, and language or inappropriately assimilating Catholicism into their practice of Orisha worship.

Yoruba culture, like the other African cultures we have analyzed, is open, flexible, and incorporative rather than closed, rigid, and conservative. Thus it was common for Yoruba-speaking people to incorporate new ideas and practices into their own way of life. In Africa the stories and practices associated with many of the Orisha can be traced to neighboring African groups. In the Americas, too, the Yoruba-speaking people continued to incorporate elements from the surrounding community into their religious culture. Thus we find statues of Catholic saints on Orisha altars and the use of holy water as well as tobacco and rum (New World products) in religious ceremonies. However, these elements do not seem to have significantly changed either the cosmology binding together devotees' beliefs and practices or the essential forms of their rituals. The names and images of the Catholic saints, for example, have been used as a substitute for the names and images of the Orisha, especially in times of persecution. However, when it comes time to propitiate those objects that are believed to contain the presence of the Orisha, the statues are left outside the ritual space, as they are conceived of as merely decorative and not sacred objects. In the United States, some of these syncretic elements have been consciously discarded. For those coming to the religion from Protestant or secular environments, the Catholic icons are strange and meaningless. In addition, for many African Americans, these Cuban-Catholic objects are uncomfortable reminders of the colonial heritage of the tradition.

Accusations of syncretism usually center on ideas of purity within a tradition. Syncretism is often described as the attempt by practitioners of an incomplete or lesser tradition to assimilate the concepts of a more advanced or more highly developed tradition. Often, this assimilation is assumed to have taken place under duress. Thus it is common to read that the Orisha devotees in nineteenth-century Cuba who had been enslaved and forcibly taken to a foreign and repressive culture incorporated elements of that culture in order to survive. Early observers thought that this incorporation was due to an incomplete understanding of Cuban Christianity and that when these people, or their descendants, were more fully knowledgeable about the majority religion they would let go of their previously syncretic beliefs and practices.

Contemporary practitioners of the Orisha traditions frame this story differently. They suggest that sometime in the distant past in Africa or in the early years of the development of the religion in Cuba there was a pure version of the tradition that has been degraded and corrupted, either by the forcible removal of practitioners from Africa or the subsequent development of the religion in Cuba or the United States. Changes in the tradition are thought to be the result of either repression and persecution on the part of the Catholic Spanish culture of Cuba or the work of unscrupulous or ignorant practitioners in subsequent generations. However, Henry Drewal's research on the contemporary cultures of West Africa (Drewal) suggests a third, more deliberate story. The flexible, incorporative nature of Yoruba culture as well as the evidence from the Ifa divination texts suggests that the religious traditions the Yoruba-speaking people developed in Africa and brought with them to Cuba were already syncretic. According to the cosmology described in the divination verses, many of the Orisha and their rituals had their origins not in Yorubaland but in the surrounding territories. Many of the peoples of western Africa freely borrowed deities, rituals, and cosmological elements from each other, without any concern for religious purity or orthodoxy. In addition, there was no unified Yoruba traditional religious culture during the period of the slave trade. Rather "Yoruba culture" and its religious traditions only developed as a single entity in the Cuban cabildos of the late nineteenth and early twentieth centuries and other South and Central American locations. The incorporation of European Christian elements into Orisha religious practice, then, can be seen as a continuation of the tendency to incorporate new elements into Yoruba religious practice. Rather than being forced upon practitioners or the result of ignorance or corruption, this story suggests that the incorporation of Christian elements was the freely undertaken work of knowledgeable priests and practitioners. Whether or not an Orisha community accepts any particular innovation is always a point of contestation determined by the members of that community.

If this religious tradition had stayed in Cuba, it would be of little interest in our project of discovering African influences on the religious traditions of the United States. Relatively few of the enslaved who landed on American shores came from the Yoruba heartland, although as we discussed in chapter 7, shipments from the Kingdom of Dahomey often included people from Yoruba-speaking areas. However, there has always been movement between Cuba and the United States. The 1910 census shows that there were officially fifteen thousand Cubans living in the United States, although a report on immigration given to Congress at the same time estimated the total at forty-four thousand. Immigration increased dramatically after the revolution in 1959 and again in 1980. Today it is estimated that over a million Cubans or their descendants live in the United States (Cultural Orientation Resource Center). Along with their other cultural traditions, these immigrants have brought with them the religious beliefs and practices of this religious tradition—and have shared them with their neighbors not only in the Latino community but also beyond. In 1998 *Christianity Today* estimated that there were eight hundred thousand adherents of this tradition of different nationalities in the United States alone (*Christianity Today*).[2]

As in both Yorubaland and Cuba there is no centralized authority or single monolithic Orisha tradition in the United States. Rather the Orisha tradition is characterized by religious communities who share a common cosmology and similar religious practices. These communities continue to be members of one of the fastest-growing religious complexes in the United States today. Every week more and more people from all social, racial, and economic groups are discovering these traditions, seeking and receiving initiations. Where once these traditions were limited to the Cuban-exile communities, today there are communities in most major and many smaller communities from coast to coast. Many people's primary interaction with the Orisha traditions is through participation in rituals of blessing and healing. Healing rituals are commonly performed whenever someone feels that his or her life is out of balance spiritually, emotionally, mentally, or physically. Since devotees believe that much physical and emotional distress is the result of spiritual imbalance, they recommend baths, head blessings, or other sorts of spiritual cleansing to remove negative energies from an individual and bring him or her back into line with his or her highest and best destiny. One may be cleansed with almost any natural object and many manufactured objects, including the leaves of plants, fruit, flowers, candy, cooked and raw food, meat, cloth, and, of course, water. Bathing in water infused with some number of these materials may also be recommended.

Although the Orisha communities in Cuba and the United States tend to be private and relatively invisible to the larger culture, several communities have played an important part in the public history of the religion in late-twentieth-century America, especially Oyotunji Village in South Carolina and the Church of the Lukumi Babalu Aye (CLBA) in south Florida. These two communities represent the two major strands of Orisha religion: one centered in the Hispanic communities of our largest metropolitan areas (CLBA) and the other composed of African Americans trying to rediscover their African religious heritage (Oyotunji Village). In 1992 CLBA won the Supreme Court case challenging their sacrificial practices, including the right to sacrifice animals in the service of their religion. In the majority opinion written by Justice Kennedy, the Court said that "religious belief need not be acceptable, logical, consistent, or comprehensible to others in order to merit First Amendment protection" (Greenhouse). It remains to be seen how this ruling may affect how First Amendment protections are extended to other religious traditions. In addition, beginning in the 1980s scholars and artists began studying and teaching about this tradition in both academic and public venues. Many departments of religious studies, music, and dance have scholars who are studying the different versions of this tradition, and in areas with a strong presence of Orisha devotees it is easy to find classes on the Yoruba language, culture, music, dance, and religion, often with either an African or a Cuban orientation.

As with many other non-European groups in the United States, Orisha worship communities who want to be recognized as legitimate religious organizations have had to make themselves conform more closely to the organizational structure of American Protestant churches. In general this has meant identifying one or more religious leaders (similar to ministers, rabbis, imams, and the like), having regular religious services, providing pastoral care, and setting up a governing board responsible for the secular life of the church (finances, building maintenance, etc.). Orisha churches like the Church of the Lukumi Babalu Aye (CLBA) and the Lukumi Church of Orishas in New York City are examples of this movement of protestantization. By setting up visible physical locations and holding regular services, these groups are moving away from the secretive, home-based organizations that are more typical of Orisha communities.

Another movement in Orisha-worshipping communities is the desire to re-Africanize the tradition and remove those syncretic elements that some practitioners believe were added during its sojourn in Cuba. These efforts include the replacement of Catholic and Spanish trappings with those from Africa, including the use of Yoruba rather than Spanish vocabulary, the production of Africanized images to replace Catholic ones, the incorporation of African-style clothing, and the move to return to Nigeria, rather than staying in the United States or going to Cuba, for rituals and initiation. Although

West Africa has been subjected to its own colonial challenges, there is a feeling among some Orisha devotees that the Yoruba people there have retained a purer and more authentic version of worship than can be found in the Americas. Not everyone agrees. Some say that the Cuban and American traditions are actually closer to some mythical original because they were not influenced by the colonial missionary project of early-twentieth-century Africa.

One of the most important rituals in the Orisha traditions is the drumming party known by the Spanish term *tambor* or the Yoruba word *bembe*. The primary purpose of these rituals is, through drumming, singing, and dancing, to entice one or more of the Orisha to join their devotees through the process of possession trance. Possession trance not only allows devotees to talk to their deities but allows the Orisha to talk back, to respond in a clearly tangible way. Drumming and dancing are integral to Orisha religion. They also are one of the ways that this tradition is making inroads into mainstream American culture. Yoruba music has formed the basis for several Cuban musical traditions, and CDs of this work are easily available, especially in the world music genre. However, this music is also finding its way into other types of collections. I was surprised to hear the refrain "Asesu Yemaya" from a song for the Orisha Yemaya played as part of the background music during a recent yoga class at my local community college, for example.

Not only has Yoruba religious music infiltrated the American music scene, scholars of religion are also beginning to take to heart Olupona and Rey's suggestion that the Orisha traditions be included among the major world religions. In his recent book *God Is Not One: The Eight Rival Religions That Run the World*, Stephen Prothero, a religious studies professor at Boston University, included Yoruba religion, which he characterizes as "the way of connection," as one of those eight traditions. He says that according to Yoruba religious understanding the problem of human existence is "disconnection" and "the solution to this problem is to reconnect ourselves to our destinies, to one another and to sacred power." He specifically identifies the techniques of divination, sacrifice, and possession trance as the methods for achieving this reconnection (Prothero, 206). The popularity of this book will introduce even more people to the Orisha and their religious traditions.

AFRICAN INFLUENCES ON CONTEMPORARY RELIGIOUS EXPERIENCES

Santería and its sister tradition of Vodou may be making inroads into the American religious consciousness. However, the African religious techniques leading to the type of possession characterized as speaking in tongues that were first introduced during the Second Great Awakening continued to influence mainstream American religious sensibilities into the twentieth century. In his 1974 article in the *Concordia Theological Monthly*, David Beckmann argues that the Pentecostal movement that developed at the turn of the last century has important African American and African antecedents that are usually ignored in descriptions of this phenomenon. As he says, commonly this movement is understood as "a 20th century extension of white revivalist Protestantism: Wesleyanism in England, the Great Awakenings in this country, more revivalism in the 19th century and the Holiness movement" (Beckmann, 11). Pentecostalism is characterized by speaking in tongues, faith healing, spirited music, certain theologies, and a typical piety. Beckmann focuses particularly on the phenomenon of speaking in tongues as the movement's most distinctive feature. "Speaking in tongues" or glossolalia is the behavior where an individual speaks either in a language that is unknown to him or in a series of fluent speech-like syllables. Within the context of religious services such behavior is considered sacred and the speech holy language. Among twentieth-century Pentecostals speaking in tongues was considered evidence of the Holy Spirit's indwelling presence (Beckmann, 12).

Glossolalia can be viewed as a form of possession experience. As outlined in chapter 5, scholars describe such experiences as altered or unusual states of consciousness, indigenously understood in terms of the influence of some other being that causes dramatic behavior. Possession, when another being controls the actions of an individual, is similar to typical religious behavior among West and West Central African societies, including those societies that made major contributions of their populations to the Atlantic slave trade. These behaviors are a way that spiritual beings, such as gods and ancestors, can speak to their devotees or descendants and provide spiritual or material aid. During African possession events these spiritual beings speak through individuals. Sometimes this is in the local or a foreign language; sometimes it is in a "sacred" pseudolanguage that has to be interpreted by nonpossessed devotees (Beckmann et al.).

Although there are examples of possession behavior among Mediterranean societies, such behavior was rare among those groups who contributed most to the development of the Judeo-Christian tradition. There are few instances in either the Hebrew Bible (Old Testament) or the Christian Bible (New Testament), and within the Christian tradition there are few examples of positive possession behavior before the period of the Second Great Awakening. There were some examples of Christians speaking in tongues noted in the epistles of Paul and during the early Christian era;

however, by the end of the fourth century positive examples of possession had disappeared from Christian religious practice. Typically, later European Christian societies attributed any possession-like behavior to demons or, after the late nineteenth century, disease. There are almost no examples of positive possession behaviors recorded during the European medieval period; instead, Christian mystics engaged in meditative trance, while possession behavior was attributed to the influence of demons.

The eighteenth century saw the rise of two very different Christian movements that involved trance. One was a group of Huguenots (French Protestants) called the Camisards, and the other was another group of French Protestants known as the Jansenists. The Camisards were stirred to rebellion against the religious establishment by child preachers who spoke from an entranced state. After their movement was crushed in 1701, some Camisard exiles settled in England. The Jansenists were followers of a saint at whose tomb cures were accompanied by convulsions. According to Beckmann, before it was shut down, the saint's cemetery became "crowded with people rolling, leaping, shaking, and dancing" (Beckmann, 16). It may have been John Wesley, the founder of Methodism, who brought possession behavior closer to respectability in a Christian context. When he visited a Camisard prophet in January of 1739, Wesley questioned in his diary whether the behavior he witnessed was a real or artificial trance and whether it was of God or not. However, soon those listening to Wesley preach began to exhibit similar behaviors, and "shouting, falling, and even convulsions" began to punctuate his revivals (Beckmann, 16). Such occurrences were rare, however, and often interpreted by Wesley and his followers as the last violent struggles of the devil being driven from the individual as the sinner moved toward repentance and peace with God rather than as positive possession events. It was only when Wesley's Methodism was brought to the free and enslaved blacks of antebellum America that these phenomena became common and expected occurrences not only at revivals but also during regular church services. By the time of the Second Great Awakening around the turn of the nineteenth century, blacks were beginning to have a discernable effect on the American religious landscape. According to the first national census of 1790, a fifth of the country's population was black, with the majority of those enslaved, generally but not exclusively in the southern states. Although the revivals were widely documented, what happened after people returned to their homes was not. This was especially true for the enslaved, whose religiosity continued to be ignored by the planter class. However, it was during this period that the formal and informal gathering places for the enslaved known as praise houses were being built.

PRAISE HOUSES AND RING DANCES

Many scholars see the praise houses and hush arbors of this period as the beginnings of what would become, after emancipation, the black church. As missionaries made inroads in their Christian conversion attempts, the enslaved often built their own religious buildings, called praise houses.[3] Here, away from the oversight of the master class, the enslaved could worship in their own way. Owners of larger plantations sometimes built these structures so that the enslaved could worship on their own property and would not have the opportunity to gather together with slaves from other locations and perhaps foment rebellion. Generally the praise houses were built deep in the woods or in marshy areas, often in or near the slave cemetery, far enough from the Big House that members could worship in a style of their own and close to the world of the spirits, who were believed to reside in graves and waterways. Far from the scrutiny of the masters and missionaries, these structures may also have served to reenact something like the middle religious space we saw in the structure of Yoruba shrines. As described earlier, the Yoruba often had a three-level organization to their sacred spaces that included a public courtyard; an inner court for initiates where, with music and dance, "persons turned into gods"; and the innermost chamber where the "essential stones and other emblems rest upon an elevated dais" (Thompson 1993b, 146). Protestantism didn't include the embodiment of sacred beings in stones or other emblems. However, in many ways the praise houses served as that inner court where initiates could sing and dance in their own way, drawing the sacred into themselves and worshipping in what they saw as a more appropriate manner than what they found in white churches.

Michael Gomez is probably correct to suggest that although we have no direct account of ring ceremonies before this period, enslaved Africans and their descendants participated in similar ceremonies from their first arrival on these shores. Of course in the earlier periods the shout would have been focused not on the Christian God but on the different African deities, ancestors, and spirits (Gomez, 268; see also Sweet, 74–76). Although these structures were often built under the authority of masters and missionaries, those who worshipped in them controlled their design and use. Unlike the services in the local white-controlled church, which the enslaved were also often compelled to attend, services in the praise house were full of song, dance, ecstatic shouting, and trance. Backless, rough-hewn benches rather than pews or seats with back rails allowed members enough room to pray in their very physical manner. Here the enslaved could escape the pains of daily life and for a time be free. Because these structure were roughly constructed, like the huts of their members, they were often overlooked both by the master class and visiting missionaries. In addition, their partial invisibility may have served to preserve the relationship of concealment to spirituality found in West African religious sensibilities (Drewal et al., 39).

The enslaved clearly saw the difference between their own form of joyous worship and the staid preaching of the master's church. They also recognized the hypocrisy of the master class, whose Sunday morning preaching about the meek and lowly Jesus was at complete odds with their everyday brutality. Although a white minister or missionary might come to the praise house to preach, generally the services were led by members of the congregation. Often these local "preachers" or "deacons" were illiterate, so reading or recitation of scripture and preaching from a prepared text gave way to spontaneous testimony and a form of trancelike behavior that came to be known as the ring shout.

The ring shout was one of the most important rituals developed in the praise house. During the service the congregation pushed the benches aside and formed a circle in the middle of the room. Shuffling in a counterclockwise circle (the direction of the Four Moments of the Sun in the Southern Hemisphere of Kongo and Angola), they sang until overtaken by ecstasy. The form of the ring dance was very controlled. One must not raise the foot from the floor but shuffle along, maintaining contact with the earth, the realm of the ancestral dead, punctuating each step with a sharp slap of the heel, mimicking the drums that were so important in African religious celebrations but forbidden throughout the American south. This led to a jerking, hitching motion that agitated the shouters until streams of perspiration poured from their bodies and wild shouts of joy and praise emanated from their lips. In his book *Slave Culture*, Sterling Stuckey argues that the ring shout was based on types of religious circle dances found throughout West and West Central Africa. Those rituals were led by drummers and used a call-and-response song style. For example, in Kongolese society, circle rituals were commonly used to honor the ancestors and to invoke for participants the Four Moments of the Sun. It shouldn't be surprising, then, to find enslaved Africans using similar rituals in the Americas (Stuckey 1987, 11).

The spiritual ecstasy experienced in the praise house was a particular type of possession trance. To the observer it appeared that the individuals had lost complete control of themselves and were flailing and flinging themselves around in a random and dangerous manner. However, to the faithful, the trance was a controlled community event. Unlike certain mental states to which it has been compared (epilepsy, for example), the trance event was limited to times and places where the community had put into place the conditions that supported it. Only under the influence of a certain percussive rhythm, a certain hymn, or a special ritual practice (for example, baptism or the ring shout) did ecstasy occur. Such trance was not an individual experience but a communal one. God spoke *through* the entranced individual to the community as a whole. At the same time, the community was responsible not only to *hear* the word of God but also to *protect* the person of the entranced individual. For the individual, the moment of trance might have been a release from the regime of slavery; for a time his or her body was outside the control of the master or his agents. At the same time, it was not a moment of complete, unbridled freedom, for the entranced person was under the complete control of the possessing Spirit who spoke and acted through him or her.

The type of singing known as spirituals may also have been born in the praise houses. The rhythm of the song and hand clapping reinforced the foot stomping, replacing the drum ensembles of Africa. (Drums were generally forbidden in the United States, but the enslaved found many creative ways around such prohibitions.) Because the spirituals supported the ring dance and the movement of the Spirit among the people, the words were less important than the percussive rhythms that were designed to give way to shouting and finally possession. But certain theological ideas were encoded in the words as well. Stuckey describes one occasion observed by Lydia Parrish and documented in *Slave Songs of the Georgia Sea Islands* where "a black man got on his knees, his head against the floor, and pivoted as members of the group around him moved in a circle, holding his head 'down to the mire,' singing 'Jesus been down to de mire.' The arms of those circling reached out to give a push and from overhead looked somewhat like spokes in a wheel."

> You must bow low
> Jesus been down
> to de mire
> Jesus been down
> to de mire
> Jesus been down
> to de mire
> You must bow low
> to de mire
> Honor Jesus
> to de mire
> Lowrah lowrah

to de mire
Lowrah lowrah
to de mire
Lowrah lowrah
to de mire
Jesus been down
to de mire
You must bow low
to de mire
low
to de mire

Stuckey suggests that the song depicts an awareness that Jesus, like the singers and the man on the floor, knew despair, but we can also suggest a strong Kongolese element here (Stuckey 1987, 25–26, citing Parrish). As Robert Farris Thompson suggests, such a head-on-the-ground position connects the individual to the dead in their upside-down world. The song invokes the watery region characteristic of that realm, visited by Jesus the great nganga and potentially by the individual at the center of the circle (Thompson 1996).

As with other rituals among the enslaved, the ring shout may have been an attempt to use the protective covering of putative Christianity to camouflage other more complex religious ideas that drew on the African heritages of those participating. This is not to say that those worshipping in the praise houses didn't consider themselves to be faithful Christians, but rather that the form their Christianity took was unorthodox to the extent that it drew on African precedents. It may also be that those worshipping in this way were practicing a form of polymorphism, that is, they were combining Christianity, as they understood it, with the religious beliefs and practices of their (or their parents') homelands.

However, what happened within the praise houses was not entirely hidden from either the master class or traveling missionaries. Because the rituals performed in praise houses often happened away from pastoral oversight, they became the symbol of black heathenism for Christian missionaries both black and white. Dancing was not a religious activity in European society and neither was possession. While dance was considered secular and frivolous, possession could only be the activity of the devil according to European sensibilities. In Africa, however, dance was often religious and was the means by which individuals and groups opened the door to communication with spiritual beings, gods, ancestors, and the like. White reaction to the activities of the praise house was mixed. Missionaries, in general, were appalled at the activities of the praise house, seeing them as barbarous expressions of African religiosity, lascivious frolic, savagery, and idol worship (Young, 98). From the slaveholders' point of view the activities of the praise house were more ambiguous. From the masters' point of view the praise house may have been considered a positive addition to the plantation regime. Through these activities, it was believed, the enslaved were being kept under social control and were able to work out their frustrations in the ring dance and other rituals. However, any gathering of slaves had the potential of fomenting rebellion, particularly when emotions became inflamed, as they appeared to be during these services. After Nat Turner's rebellion in 1831, many plantation owners dismantled their praise houses and required their slaves to worship with them in their own churches, reserving the balconies and galleries for them. However, the forms of worship developed in the praise houses of the south were soon to infiltrate into the churches established as part of the revival movement. Regardless of the status of the local praise house, the form of worship developed there continued and continues to inform African American, and to a lesser extent non–African American, worship styles in the twentieth and twenty-first centuries.

It is important to realize that just as the African-heritage persons in Haiti and Cuba freely constructed their own religious praxis out of the ideas they brought from their various African societies as well as those of the surrounding culture, African-heritage peoples in North America constructed their own form of Christianity out of their preexisting religious ideas and those provided by the surrounding culture, particularly traveling missionaries, preachers, and exhorters. But African Americans didn't keep these ideas and practices to themselves. During the revivalist periods and that short time when many worshipped in biracial congregations, blacks taught their white counterparts a new, more universalist theology and new, more enthusiastic worship forms. And even when these congregations eventually dis-integrated, white congregations kept many of the ideas and practices they learned from their black coreligionists. David Beckmann argues that the Second Great Awakening "set the mold for American Protestantism." He mentions specifically the nineteenth-century revivals, including Charles Grandison Finney's in the first half of the century, Dwight L. Moody's at the end of the century, and the Holiness movement that developed a theology of "baptism in the Holy Spirit" (Beckmann, 21–22). These movements came together in the twentieth century at the influential Azusa Street Mission, the birthplace of the modern Pentecostal movement.

PENTECOSTALISM

The antebellum period of religious revivals seems to have opened the door to an explosion of religious diversity in United States. Even after the revival movement ended, its emotionalism and enthusiasm continued, as did its ideas about sanctification, justification, and salvation. Although the term "mainstream religions" has traditionally referred to European versions of Protestantism (and after the influx of Southern Europeans, Catholicism), America has also been the home to many innovative religious traditions. This became even more true after the Civil War, when the United States moved from an agrarian to an urban culture. Whereas rural areas may have many very small churches, in urban areas churches tend to be larger and more prosperous. In addition, the urban environment lends itself to the development and support of groups outside the cultural mainstream, including the religious cultural mainstream. In his analysis of black congregations around the turn of the twentieth century, W. E. B. Du Bois, himself raised in a staid Congregationalist church in New England, surveyed both rural and urban black congregations. In the rural south he was struck by the emotionalism of the black congregations he visited (Du Bois, 58). Services in these churches were characterized by shouting, dancing, crying, being slain by the spirit, rhythmic sermons, shrieks, and contortions—all of the marks of religious "enthusiasm" so commonly found in the revival tents of the antebellum south. When rural blacks moved north in what is often called the Great Migration (1910 to 1930), they brought these emotional forms of religiosity with them. It should not be surprising, then, that these manifestations of the Spirit erupted again in the early twentieth century in the Pentecostalism movement outside the southern rural environment.

Although not the first manifestation of this new form of religiosity, the California-based Azusa Street Revival was probably most important for its development and spread not only to black but also to white churches. William J. Seymour, founder of the Azusa Street congregation, was introduced to Pentecostal doctrine by the white preacher Charles Fox Parham. Coming out of a Holiness tradition, Fox developed the idea that "speaking in tongues" or glossolalia was the initial evidence of one's baptism in the Holy Spirit. In 1906, after a short period enrolled in Parham's seminary in Houston, Texas, Seymour was invited to preach Parham's form of Pentecostalism at an old AME church and livery stable on Azusa Street in Los Angeles. The church he ended up founding there, the Apostolic Faith Mission, is widely considered to be the birthplace of worldwide Pentecostalism. This form of religion attracted many members of Holiness, Baptist, and Methodist churches, whose own histories look back to those earlier revivals of the nineteenth century. Not only was glossolalia important to the Azusa experience, Seymour and his congregation also developed and refined other practices already familiar to us, including prophecy and divine healing. As an interracial congregation, Azusa served as the training ground for many black and white Pentecostal preachers, who learned its unique worship style and were instrumental in the spread of Pentecostalism worldwide.

In his analysis of the different theological visions of the early Pentecostal movement, Douglas Jacobsen lists several characteristics of Pentecostalism that he suggests are the reasons for its success not only in the American religious landscape but also around the world (Jacobsen). Importantly, early Pentecostalism had an open view of theology based on the perceived ongoing input from God (354) and the continuation of his miracle-working activities. This puts Pentecostals at odds with the fundamentalists, with whom they are often confused. Fundamentalists limit supernaturalism to the past and reject the possibility of new miracles or prophecy in the present times (356). This marks a very different view of God between the two traditions. For fundamentalists, God's relationship to the world is constant and unchanging, while for Pentecostals that relationship is dynamic, even though God's own being is not subject to change. Pentecostals have great respect for the Bible, but rather than seeing it as the literal and unalterable word of God they see it as the foundation for what might yet be revealed and the touchstone that can be used to evaluate new revelations (357). Jacobsen also argues that there was overlap between early Pentecostalism and the social gospel in that Pentecostals believe that sin and redemption have social as well as personal aspects and that working for social change can also lead to individual spiritual change (359). Finally, Jacobsen suggests that Pentecostalism is essentially empirical. Pentecostals are more interested in what God is doing in the world today than what any traditional formulation of theology says he was or should be doing. Among Pentecostals one's personal spiritual experience always takes precedent over rational definitions of faith or creedal statements. The best marker of one's spiritual rebirth, the baptism in the Spirit, is an "outward, visibly observable action such as speaking in tongues" (360). Each of these points has important African precedents, including the ideas about ongoing revelation; a manipulationist approach that values not only spiritual but also social change; a better life—health, wealth, and increase, as Horton said (Horton, 33); and the importance of personal spiritual experience.

In his book about Pentecostalism and religion in the twenty-first century, *Fire from Heaven*, Harvard theologian Harvey Cox suggests that there are two major responses to the challenge scientific modernity offers to traditional religion: fundamentalism and what he calls experimentalism (H. Cox, 300). While fundamentalists of every religious stripe tend to be zealous, unswerving, and impassioned proponents of their particular sect or creed, experimentalists make their own personal experience the cornerstone of their religiosity. People in this group are drawn to a "spiritual bricolage" of an "eclectic, pulled-together bundle of ideas and practices" that probe beneath rationality (H. Cox, 305; Jacobsen, 362). Experimentalists have little regard for religious functionaries who want to focus on elegant doctrinal systems instead of allowing each individual the opportunity to pursue his or her own spiritual quest. Experimentalists are also more interested in practical results, the ways their faith helps them find their way in the here and now (306). Cox suggests that this form of religious experimentalism has a substrata of "primal spirituality" that has allowed Pentecostalism to flourish, not only in America but also around the world. Key to this primal spirituality are primal speech (glossolalia); primal piety expressed through trance, vision, healing, dreams, dance, and similar religious practices; and primal hope, the insistence that a radical new, and better, world is coming into being (82–83). What is striking about this description of Pentecostalism and the comparisons to fundamentalism is its parallels to John Thornton's comparisons between the spiritual understandings of the fifteenth- and sixteenth-century Kongolese people and those of the European priests who served them. Although the Kongolese people saw themselves as a thoroughly Christian (Catholic) people, they approached the pronouncements of the priests that served them in a way that would have been comfortable for nineteenth- and early-twentieth-century Pentecostals. Like the Pentecostals, the Kongolese did not believe that revelation ended during biblical times but instead believed that both God and their beloved ancestors continued to speak to them through their dreams and visions as well as through the pronouncements of those identified as nganga, intermediaries to the Other World. To the discomfort of the Catholic clergy, the pronouncements of both Catholic and traditional priests were judged not against a strict biblical standard but against one of efficacy. If these messages led to the betterment of the individual or the community, they were accepted as true and legitimate. If they were self-serving or harmful to the community, they were rejected—regardless of the status or position of the messenger. Like their Kongolese predecessors, early Pentecostals exhibited an open, flexible, and incorporative religious sensibility that is similar to that found in the religious traditions of West and West Central Africa.

RELIGIOUS INTOLERANCE

As we discussed in chapter 5, religious tolerance is an important aspect of traditional Yoruba and other West and West Central African traditions. Although many of the earliest American colonists left England or the Netherlands for America in order to practice their religion in what they felt was the best way possible, the colonists themselves were generally less tolerant of religious diversity than some of the people they were leaving behind. The groups known today as the Pilgrims and the Puritans set up theocracies where church and state were tightly intertwined, and although the Virginia colony was more secular than religious, it too was extremely intolerant. Anyone who deviated from the local theological positions and was not willing to change was exiled or even killed for his or her beliefs. Because each group thought that it had the one true view of Christianity, they often sent missionaries to neighboring colonies to convert them to "true religion." These missionaries were generally badly treated. Some were even killed as heretics.

The story of Anne Hutchinson, who was born in England around 1591 and migrated to the Massachusetts colony in 1634, can be used to set the stage for the story of how ideas about religious tolerance changed in America. Anne Hutchinson did not considered herself a heretic, yet she alienated the local churchmen both by her views and by her willingness to teach them to others. To twenty-first-century ears, the theological position taken by Anne, her mentor the Reverend John Cotton, and her followers seems only trivially different from the orthodox view of the Massachusetts Bay Colony, yet the position was considered important enough to make her (and others) stand trial and endure censure or exile.

As the daughter of a dissenting minister who himself suffered censure and imprisonment for his unorthodox views in England, Anne was both educated and encouraged to express her own views and opinions, especially in matters of religion and culture. After she and her husband moved to the Massachusetts Bay Colony in 1634, she began to hold weekly sessions in her home for women to discuss the minister's sermons and other religious topics. Soon these sessions grew from once a week to two and three times a week and local men began to join their wives in attending. Anne was not only able to explicate biblical passages but often found her views at odds with the establishment ministers. As an antinomian thinker, Anne felt that she should be free to interpret the Bible according to her own divine inspiration, even if her interpretation was considered less than orthodox by the local clergy. In 1637 she was called before the General Court of Massachusetts presided over by the governor John Winthrop, who accused her of stepping out of her ascribed role within colonial society. Her challenge to the local clergy and increasing political influence were also perceived as a threat to the continued well-being of the entire society of Massachusetts Bay. Since the Bible served as the legal foundation for Puritan society, much of her trial consisted of dueling biblical quotations. For example, Winthrop accused Hutchinson of not following the injunction that women should remain silent in church (1 Cor. 14:34–35). She however, responded that the Bible authorized her teaching when it said "elder women should instruct the younger" (Titus 2:4). Throughout the several-day course of her trial she was able to aptly defend herself, although it soon became apparent that the judgment of the court had been determined before the beginning of testimony. She was banished from the colony by the court and excommunicated from the Puritan church at her subsequent religious trial. Along with her husband and a small band of followers, she moved to Rhode Island. After the death of her husband in 1642, she moved again to what is now the Bronx area of New York City, then New Netherland, where she was killed in an Indian attack in 1643.

Hutchinson was not the only colonial woman to challenge the social and religious constrictions of early American society, but her story shows how the drive for independent religious thought could come in conflict with the desire on the part of colonial authorities for social conformity. The push for conformity, especially for women (and others on the lower rungs of the social hierarchy), overcame principles of independent thought and action during early colonial times. Hutchinson's principal error was not her teaching about the place of "faith" versus "works" in Christian life or even her antinomian views, it was her willingness to step out of her place as a Christian woman to share these views with both the women and men of her community.

Even after the Revolution and the ratification of the Bill of Rights over a hundred years later, members of the different religious denominations tended to vilify and denigrate each other. It was only after the religious revival known as the Second Great Awakening, which swept the country in the first half of the nineteenth century, that Americans developed a more tolerant attitude toward each other's religious ideas. In the piece by Soyinka, the winner of the 1986 Nobel Prize in literature, cited at the beginning of this chapter, he suggests that Yoruba traditional religion can provide a model of religious tolerance in an increasingly divisive world. Within traditional Yoruba culture (and we can suggest, to a certain extent, Kongolese and Fon cultures as well) there was an openness to all types of spirituality. Even today, although the country of Nigeria is divided between Christian and Muslim communities, there continue to be shrines to a variety of Orisha scattered around the towns and even shrines to different Orisha within the same family compound.[4] That the devotees of these different Orisha are living and worshipping together peacefully would have been amazing to our America forefathers, who all worshipped the same one God but fought and died over minor theological points. We find a more African type of tolerance appearing on the American scene during the Second Great Awakening and again during the Pentecostal movements, when theology became less important than one's personal religious experience. Suddenly people were worshipping together regardless of their previous religious affiliation, station, or status in life. Although religious tolerance was written into the American constitution in the First Amendment, the actual practice of accepting and honoring the religious views and practices of those out of the religious mainstream continues to be a challenge in the larger American society. As Soyinka suggests, the traditional African societies that contributed so much to American culture can also provide a model for not only tolerating but welcoming newcomers and their ideas into society.

CONCLUSION

Traditionally, scholars looking at African-based traditions throughout the Americas have seen the European elements in such groups as an attempt on the part of early practitioners to hide their continued African religious forms behind a thin veneer of Christianity. Yet our view of Haitian Vodou, Cuban Santería, and even the American black church suggests that the devotees of these traditions actually took what they wanted from European traditions and integrated it into an existing African cosmology and praxis. This is maybe most obvious in the case of Vodou, where, as Rey and Vanhee have argued, the religion obtained its final form—including the use of Christian prayers, iconography, and religious forms—after the revolution and in the absence of a Catholic clergy. In an environment where devotees were free to accept or reject any religious element, early servitors of the Lwa chose to include the elements of Christianity that fit within their idea of appropriate religious beliefs and practices. Although it is harder to see, we can suggest that American Christianity and American culture in general have also been greatly influenced by African cosmology and practices.

In all of the cultural elements explored in this text, Americans have moved from a European to a more African way of thinking and acting in the world. Those six sensibilities we originally identified as forming a uniquely American religious sensibility—individualism, fideism, polymorphism, experientialism, tolerance, and pragmatism—were influenced by both African and European ideas of religious beliefs and practices. This is also true of burial practices and understanding of the relationship between the living and the dead. As we have seen, as American religious sensibilities developed, worship styles became more "enthusiastic" even in the most staid mainstream congregations. Not only have worship styles changed in the presence of the great numbers of African Americans who participated in the Great Awakenings, so did beliefs about this life and the next. Whereas the European American view of salvation tended to be Calvinistic, limiting the saved to some few predestined by God, African Americans agreed with the traditional spiritual "Didn't my Lord deliver Daniel, then why not every man?" and believed that they all were destined for salvation and eventual reunion with their families and friends after death. They also believed that the hardships of their lives weren't indicators that they were less likely to be among the saved, but rather that their rich and powerful but cruel masters would find themselves left out of God's saving mercy. Of these two competing viewpoints—salvation for the lucky few or salvation for the majority—it is the more African position that has gained ascendance in the American religious sensibility, regardless of denomination.

Haitian Vodou, New Orleans Voudou, hoodoo, and Santería have all made inroads into American religious culture, opening up new vistas in American religion and exposing more Americans to African ways of thinking. A practical, instrumental view of religion permeates the culture. When asked why they prefer one church or denomination or religious practice over another, many will simply say that it works for them, that it provides the personal spiritual experience that they find comforting in their lives. A religion that "works" and the willingness to change religious communities when one way of being religious no longer works for the individual is an innovation within the history of Western Christianity. Few in the contemporary world join or change religious communities because of minor theological differences; instead they look for which congregation "feels right" and provides the religious experience they are looking for. Such pragmatism is both a philosophical and a theological position that has deep roots within American culture. Although it isn't a purely African idea, pragmatism as a philosophical concept developed alongside change in burial practices, the movement from doctrinal to experiential religion, ideas about women in religion, the place of prophecy, and religious tolerance—all the American religious sensibilities that have important African precedents. Like roots hidden deep within the earth, these African ideas have nourished American religious sensibilities that diverged widely from their European antecedents.

NOTES

CHAPTER ONE: A MOST RELIGIOUS NATION

1. Alexis de Tocqueville, *Democracy in America*, trans. Henry Reeve (New York: D. Appleton and Company, 1904), 331.

2. "World Values Survey." http://www.worldvaluessurvey.org/.

3. At a speech at Western Michigan University of Kalamazoo, the Reverend Dr. Martin Luther King observed that 11:00 a.m. Sunday was "the most segregated hour in this nation." (See the Western Michigan University archives at http://www.wmich.edu/library/archives/mlk/q-a.html for a copy of the question-and-answer session following Dr. King's speech where he made this observation.)

4. The catechism produced in Spain in the language of Allada, the kingdom that served as the port for the bulk of the slaves captured by the Fon of Dahomey, was published in Madrid in 1658 and is the earliest text published in a West African language. Robin Law, *The Kingdom of Allada* (Leiden, The Netherlands: CNWS Publications, 1997), 10.

5. For those who are interested in exploring the nuances of this debate more fully, Joseph E. Holloway does an excellent job of summarizing it in the introduction to *Africanisms in American Culture* (Holloway, ix–xxi) as does Jason Young with an updated bibliography of the major works (Young, Introduction).

6. In addition to Herskovits's own work, I have found Holloway's *Africanisms in American Culture*, Eugene Genovese's *Roll, Jordan Roll*, and Mechal Sobal's *The World They Made Together* good introductions into the study of African contributions to American culture.

7. To his credit, Raboteau describes African religious retentions in the Catholic countries of South America and the Caribbean (11–14).

8. Europeans with the latest armaments but without African allies were routinely massacred in Kongo and Angola. John Thornton, *Africa and Africans in the Making of the Atlantic World, 1400–1680* (Cambridge: Cambridge University Press, 1992), 112–16.

9. We'll discuss *nkisi* in more detail in chapter 3.

10 The term "Voodoo/Vodou/Voudou" has many different spellings and connotations, as we'll discuss more fully in chapter 8. "Voodoo," although the most commonly used variant in the United States, is considered derogatory by many scholars and most practitioners of these religious traditions.

CHAPTER TWO: JESUS IS MY BOSOM FRIEND

1. Albert J. Raboteau, *Slave Religion: The "Invisible Institution" in the Antebellum South* (New York: Oxford University Press, 1978), 257–58, quoted from *Slave Songs of the United States*, 216–17.

2. Today the thousands of Muslim immigrants who bring not only their own ideas about God and appropriate relationships between God and humanity but also strongly held religious sensibilities are challenging contemporary European secularism. These Muslim religious sensibilities are often at odds with those of their European hosts, who are attempting to use governmental action to bring these religious immigrants into line with existing European secular sensibilities. How this conflict in religious values will be resolved is still an open question, but one beyond where we are going in this text.

3. Both audio and written versions of this sermon are also readily available on the Internet, including SermonAudio.com (www.sermonaudio.com/sermoninfo. asp?SID=770213541) and ReligionFacts (religionfacts.com).

CHAPTER THREE: AFRICAN CHRISTIANITY

1. John K. Thornton, *The Kongolese Saint Anthony: Dona Beatriz Kimpa Vita and the Antonian Movement, 1684–1706* (Cambridge: Cambridge University Press, 1998), 2.

2. As an aside, it is interesting to note that while the Europeans couldn't conceive of an object elevated to a semihuman state, they could and did regularly demote human beings to the level of semiobjects in the course of their slave-trading and slaveholding activities.

3. Interestingly, among the Kongolese the fact that she was a woman possessed by a masculine saint was not an issue or area for concern, even though the local priest questioned how this gender switching could be possible. This same question is used by the contemporary Catholic church as one of its arguments against women in the priesthood. In one's role as priest, one is believed to take on the persona of Jesus, impossible for a woman according to European understanding.

CHAPTER FOUR: THE DEAD ARE NOT DEAD

1. Birago Diop, quoted in Albert J. Raboteau, *Slave Religion: The "Invisible Institution" in the Antebellum South* (New York: Oxford University Press, 1978), 2.

2. For more information about the New York City African Burial Ground, one of the best-known such sites, see www.africanburialground.gov/ABG_Main.htm.

3. David Roediger's "And Die in Dixie: Funerals, Death, and Heaven in the Slave Community 1700–1865" provides the most concise description of the funeral customs of the enslaved, although I disagree with his emphasis on West African customs as precedent. David R. Roediger, "And Die in Dixie: Funerals, Death, and Heaven in the Slave Community 1700–1865," *Massachusetts Review* 22 (1981).

4. Skeptics continue to question whether this was an elaborate April Fool's joke on the part of the young Fox sisters, but the ensuing Spiritualist tradition was no joke for the thousands drawn into its orbit.

CHAPTER FIVE: CHILDREN OF ODUDUWA

1. Wande Abimbola, *Ifá: An Exposition of Ifá Literary Corpus* (New York: Athelia Henrietta Press, 1997), 141.

2. A similar process of unification happened on the peninsula we know today as Italy. During the medieval and early modern periods, there was no "Italy," simply a group of independent city-states—Rome, Venice, Milan, etc.—who were only unified into a single entity in 1861.

3. Although there are many variant spellings of these Yoruba words, in general I will use the common American variants with no accents or tonal markers and use *sh* to represent the sound indicated by *s* with a dot below it.

4. This is the terminology he uses to incorporate West African, Caribbean, and Brazilian culture into a single inclusive term.

5. In her 1973 study of possession phenomena, Erika Bourguignon found various types of possession phenomena in 75 percent of the 488 societies she studied. The highest incidents of possession phenomena of all types were in the Pacific culture; the lowest were in North and South American indigenous cultures. This phenomenon was especially common among societies in Eurasia, sub-Saharan Africa, and circum-Mediterranean regions and descendents of Africa in the Americas (Bourguignon, 31).

CHAPTER SIX: THEN WHY NOT EVERY MAN?

1. It is interesting that witchcraft in contemporary Africa seems to follow a more European model, as those accused are often publicly attacked and burned by mobs of their angry neighbors.

CHAPTER SEVEN: CHILDREN OF THE LEOPARD

1. Edna G. Bay, *Wives of the Leopard: Gender, Politics, and Culture in the Kingdom of Dahomey* (Charlottesville: University of Virginia Press, 1998), 1.

2. Ministers of the king, those who represented him outside the palace, were also called *ahosi*, so we should probably use the more general translation, "one who is absolutely dependent on the king," rather than "wife."

CHAPTER EIGHT: THAT VOODOO THAT YOU DO

1. This image is so well known that the New Orleans Arena Football team, named the VooDoo, has as its mascot a human skull wearing a black top hat and sunglasses.

2. There is some question among scholars about who the younger Marie Laveau was. Carolyn Morrow Long suggests that rather than being the elder Marie's daughter, the second Marie might actually have been a half sister, a different daughter, a niece, a granddaughter, or another unrelated woman. Martha Ward, *Voodoo Queen: The Spirited Lives of Marie Laveau* (Jackson: University Press of Mississippi, 2004), 200–5.

3. Anderson distinguishes between hoodoo, which he locates primarily in the Mississippi Valley, and conjure, which is found elsewhere in the United States. However, he conflates the two terms, and I will as well.

CHAPTER NINE: NEW AFRICAN BRANCHES

1. Wole Soyinka, "The Tolerant Gods," in *Orisa Devotion as World Religion: The Globalization of Yoruba Religious Culture*, ed. Jacob K. Olupona and Terry Rey (Madison: University of Wisconsin Press, 2007), 40, 41.

2. Other sources provide different estimates. Nigerian babalawo Wande Abimbola suggested at the World Yoruba Congress in 1981 that there were one hundred million devotees worldwide (Boadle, Anthony, "Yoruba Deity Worshipers Open Congress in Havana," http://nigeriavillagesquare.com/forum/main-square/926-yoruba-deity-worshipers-open-congress-havana.html), while Mary Pat Fisher in her best-selling textbook *Living Religions* estimates one hundred million in North and South America alone (Fisher, Mary Pat, *Living Religions* [Upper Saddle River, NJ: Prentice-Hall, 1999], 425). Part of the problem in determining the number of practitioners is deciding what level of participation is required in order to include an individual in these statistics.

3. Although generally known as "praise houses," Margaret Washington Creel argues that these were originally known as "pray" or "prays" houses. In actuality, both names accurately reflect their functions (Creel, *A Peculiar People*, 391n44).

4. As Soyinka is painfully aware, today's Nigeria, home to the Yoruba people, is not a model of religious tolerance, as Christians in the south regularly battle with Muslims in the north for political and social control. Part of his work has been to try to bring the people back to their traditional, more tolerant culture.

GLOSSARY

Cr. = Haitian Creole
En. = English
Fn. = Fon
Fr. = French
Kg. = Kongolese
Lk. = Lukumi
Pt. = Portuguese
Sp. = Spanish
Vd. = Vodou
Yr. = Yoruba

Aguda	Fn.	People of African descent who returned to Dahomey from Brazil.
Agwe	Vd.	Deity of the ocean.
ahosi	Fn.	"Dependent or subordinate of the king." Wife or minister of the king of Dahomey.
ahovi	Fn.	Child of the Fon king or his sons.
Aido-Hwedo	Fn.	Rainbow serpent deity. See also *Damballah*.
aiye	Yr.	Visible world, this world, the earth. Opposite of orun, the invisible world (also *aye*).
aje	Yr.	Witch, witches; more correctly, those who possess witchcraft substance.
alaafin	Yr.	"Lord of the Royal Palace," title of the king of Oyo.
Allada	Fn.	Subkingdom of Dahomey.
antinomian	En.	Idea that each individual determines his or her own beliefs and moral code free from pressure from establishment authorities.

ashé	Yr.	Power, energy, blessings; energy of the universe; ritual power; also name of empowered material.
asiento	Sp.	From *asentar*, to put, set, or place; initiation ceremony to "make" or "crown" a priest; puts or "seats" the Orisha in the head of the devotee.
ason	Vd.	Sacred rattle, badge of priesthood in Vodou.
auto de fe	Sp.	Act of faith. Ritualized punishment used by the Inquisition in Spain.
aye	Yr.	Visible world. See *aiye*.
Ayiti	Cr.	Original spelling of name of the nation of Haiti.
Azaka	Vd.	Vodou deity of agriculture. Also Cousin Zaka.
babalawo	Yr.	"Father of secrets," priest of Orula/Orunmila, the owner of Ifa, the highest form of divination. Equivalent of Vodun *bokonon*.
babalosha	Yr.	"Father of Orisha," male priest.
Babaluaiye	Lk.	See *Shopona*. Also Babalu Ayie.
Bakongo	Kg.	Kongolese people.
banganga	Kg.	Plural of *nganga*, ritual specialists.
Baron Samdi	Vd.	Guede spirit in Vodou. See *Gede*.
Bas, La	Fr.	See *Eleggua*.
bata	Yr.	Double-headed drum used for sacred drum ceremonies. Consecrated in sets of three.
bembe	Lk.	Drum ceremony to invoke the Orisha. Also called *tambor*.
bokonon	Fn.	Diviner of Fa. Equivalent of Yoruba *babalawo*.
Bondye	Vd.	"Good God." High God in Vodou.
botanica	Sp.	Store selling religious goods, including the herbs and other materials needed for hoodoo and Santería religious practice.
cabildo	Sp.	Church chapter house, town council; in Cuba, the social clubs for *gente de color*.
Candomblé	Pt.	African-based religious tradition that developed in Brazil. Has many similarities to Santería.
Chango	Lk.	See *Shango*.
confradia	Sp.	Brotherhood, fraternity.
Cousin Zaka	Vd.	See *Azaka*.
Da	Cr.	See *Damballah Hwedo*.
Damballah Hwedo	Fn.	Rainbow serpent deity in Vodou. Also known as Aido-Hwedo, or Danbala Wèdo.

Danbala Wèdo	Vd.	Rainbow serpent deity in Vodou. Also known as Damballah Hwedo, Da.
deho	Fn.	Family shrine.
diloggun	Lk.	Sixteen, from Yr. *medilogun*; divination system using sixteen cowry shells.
ebo	Yr.	Sacrifice; offering or work given to Orisha or *egun*.
ebo eje	Yr.	Blood sacrifice.
egun	Yr.	The honored dead, the ancestors.
Eleggua	Lk.	Trickster Orisha, guardian of the crossroads, one of the warrior Orisha. Also known as Elegba, Elegbara, Eshu. Legba in Vodou; Limba, La Bas, Liba, and Lébat in Voudou.
Enle	Yr.	See *Erinle*.
Erinle	Yr.	Hunter and fisherman Orisha (also Eyinle, Enle).
Eshu	Yr.	Trickster Orisha often conflated with Eleggua.
experimentalism	En.	Willingness to welcome new religious beliefs and practices.
Eyinle	Yr.	See *Erinle*.
Ezili	Vd.	Deity of love, beauty, and sexuality.
Ezili Dantò	Vd.	Petro manifestation of Ezili. See *Ezili*.
Ezili Je-Rouge	Vd.	Petro manifestation of Ezili. See *Ezili*.
Fa	Fn.	Deity of divination. Equivalent of Yoruba Ifa.
fetish	En.	Object or practice pertaining to witchcraft. From the Portuguese *feitiço* and the Latin *factitius*, meaning an object made by humans.
fideism	En.	Belief in some sort of God figure.
Fon	Fn.	West African tribal group that established the Kingdom of Dahomey.
fuma	Kg.	Type of white stone.
Ga	Fn.	God of metal and war. See also *Ogun*.
gbà	Yr.	Agree to an assertion. Belief in what has been said.
gbàgbó	Yr.	Agreeing with what is heard; to believe.
gbetome	Fn.	Land of the living.
Gede	Vd.	Lord of the cemetery; also associated with sexual prowess and fertility. Head of Guede spirits.
gente de color	Sp.	"[Free] people of color." Name given to former slaves and their descendants in Cuba.
glossolalia	En.	"Speaking in tongues." The behavior where an individual speaks either in a language that is unknown to him or in a series of fluent speech-like syllables.

goofer dust	En.	Dirt from a gravesite.
Gran Brigit	Vd.	Guede spirit, wife of Baron Samedi.
Grand Zombi, La	Fr./Fn.	"The Great God." Snake deity in New Orleans Voudou.
Gu	Fn.	Also called Ga. See *Ogun*.
Guede spirits	Vd.	Pantheon of spirits associated with the lwa Gede.
guerreros, los	Sp.	Warrior Orisha Eleggua, Ogun, Ochosi, and Osun, which are usually received as part of a single ritual.
hacer el santo	Sp.	"To make the saint." See *asiento*.
hand	En.	See *toby*.
Heviosso	Fn.	Deity of thunder. Equivalent of Yoruba Shango.
hoho	Fn.	Deity that protects twins.
hoodoo	En.	African American magical system.
hungan	Fn.	"Chief for a vodun"; chief priest of Vodun congregation. Either male or female in Dahomey, male only in Haiti. Also *oungan*. See also *manbo*.
Ifa	Yr.	Divination system invoking the wisdom of Orula/Orunmila; performed only by a babalawo. Also another name for Orula/Orunmila (also known as Fa in Fon-based traditions).
Ifè	Fn.	Home of the Vodun and the "best" of the ancestors.
Ifè	Yr.	Premier Yoruba city, religious center.
igbàgbọ́	Yr.	Belief.
Iku	Yr.	Dead person; also the personification of death.
ilé	Yr.	Earth/town/household.
imọ̀	Yr.	Knowledge.
incubus	En.	(pl. incubi). Male demon that has sex with women and causes mental distress. See also *succubus*.
individualism	En.	Tendency to construct one's own religious beliefs and prefer personal experience of the holy.
Invisibles, les	Vd.	See *lwa*.
iyawo	Yr.	"Bride younger than speaker, wife." Literally junior wife. In Yoruba traditional religion and Santería, a new initiate of either sex (also *iyawo Orisha*).
iyawo Orisha	Yr.	"Wife of an Orisha." An initiated priest.
Jakuta	Yr.	Thunder deity whose worship was assimilated into that of Shango.
Kafou Legba	Vd.	Petro manifestation of Legba. See *Legba*.
kangu	Kg.	Liberty, salvation.
kariocha	Yr.	"To place the Orisha" (on/in the head). See asiento.

Kikongo	Kg.	Language of the Kongolese people.
kindoki	Kg.	Witchcraft powers.
Kreyòl	Cr.	Creole language of Haiti.
kutome	Fn.	Land of the dead.
Lébat	Fn.	See *Eleggua*.
Legba	Vd.	Vodou deity of gates and crossroads; also a trickster. Also Papa Legba. See also *Eleggua*.
Liba	Fn.	See *Eleggua*.
Limba	Fn.	See *Eleggua*.
Loa	Vd.	See *Lwa*.
loka	Kg.	To curse, conjure, or bewitch; also to excommunicate.
Loko	Vd.	Vodou deity, guardian of the fields and vegetation. Also Papa Loko.
Lukumí	Lk.	Creolized Yoruba language developed in Cuba; alternative name for Santería. Also Lucumí.
Lwa	Vd.	Deity in Vodou. Also Loa, les Mystere, les Invisibles.
madrina	Sp.	Godmother.
manbo	Fn.	Female chief priest in Haitian Vodun. See also *oungan*.
Marasa	Vd.	Divine twins.
Maroon, Saint	Fr.	Folk saint in New Orleans who protects runaway slaves.
matanza	Sp.	Blood sacrifice.
matrona	Sp.	Matron, queen, female leader in a cabildo.
Mawu-Lisa	Fn.	Twin creator gods of Fon. Mawu is female, Lisa male (similar to Yoruba Olodumare).
medilogun	Yr.	Twenty less four; sixteen. See *diloggun*.
Middle Passage	En.	That leg of the slave trade from Africa to ports in the Caribbean or along the eastern American coast.
minkisi	Kg.	Plural of *nkisi*.
mò	Yr.	To know.
Morts, les	Vd.	The dead, the ancestors.
muerto	Sp.	Dead person, usually used to designate the spirit of a dead person.
mukanda nkisi	Kg.	Holy Bible.
Mystere, les	Fr.	See *lwa*.
nacíon	Sp.	Nation. Grouping of Africans in Cuba according to their ethnic and cultural heritage.
na daho	Fn.	"Great princess." Senior daughter of the Fon king and head of the palace women.

ndoki	Kg.	(pl. kindoki). Spiritually evil or greedy person; witch or witchcraft in general.
Nesuhwe	Fn.	Series of Vodun cults that honor deified members of the royal family, many of their closest associates, and the spirits of magical monsters born to the family and called Tohosu.
nganga	Kg.	(pl. banganga). Religious specialist, priest.
nganga a nkisi		
nzambi a mpungu	Kg.	Holy priest of God Almighty, Catholic priest.
nganga nzo a nkisi	Kg.	Priest of the (Catholic) church or of the grave.
nkisi	Kg.	(pl. minkisi). Ritual object with otherworldly power; "fetish cults" in European correspondence.
nsanda	Kg.	Tree whose bark is pounded and woven into cloth.
nzambi	Kg.	Soul, spirit, ancestor, God.
nzambi a mpungo	Kg.	God Almighty
nzo a nkisi	Kg.	Holy house, church; also grave.
oba	Yr.	"Ruler," sometimes translated "king"; chiefly title.
Obaluaiye	Yr.	See *Shopona*.
Obatala	Yr.	"Ruler of the white cloth," wisest and oldest of the Orisha.
Obba	Yr.	River Orisha and first wife of Shango (also spelled Oba, but should not be confused with oba, a ruler).
Ocha	Lk.	Contraction of Orisha, used to designate both the religion (see *Regla de Ocha*) and its deities.
odu	Yr.	Letter or number determined by either diloggun or Ifa divination.
Oduduwa	Yr.	White Orisha, often named as creator of human-kind. Also first king and father of the Yoruba people.
Ogou	Vd.	Deity of iron. Similar to Yoruba Ogun.
Ogou Ferary	Vd.	Petro manifestation of Ogou. See *Ogou*.
Ogun	Yr.	Orisha of iron, a blacksmith, one of the warrior Orisha (Gu or Ga among the Fon, Ogou in Haiti).
òjat	Vd.	Thick almond and sugar syrup made for Danbala.
Olodumare	Yr.	Great God, deity behind the Orisha. Olodumare is only propitiated through the Orisha. Also known as Olorun and Olofi, although these are often considered separate members of a divine trinity reminiscent of the Christian trinity. Similar to Fon Mawu-Lisa.
Olofi	Lk.	Supreme ruler, title of Olodumare.
Olokun	Yr.	Orisha of the depths of the ocean.

olorisha	Yr.	"Owner of Orisha," priest of Orisha religion.
Olorun	Lk.	Owner of heaven, title of Olodumare.
Oluwa	Yr.	See *Shopona*.
òótọ́	Yr.	Truth.
opele	Yr.	Divination chain used by a babalawo.
opon Ifa	Yr.	Ifa divination board.
Ori	Yr.	Head, personal destiny, one's personal Orisha.
Orisa	Yr.	See *Orisha*.
Orisha	Yr.	Deities of the Yoruba traditional religion and Santería. Also orisa (Yr.), oricha (Sp.).
Orishala	Yr.	"The great Orisha" (also Oshala). White Orisha often conflated with Obalata.
Orula	Lk.	Deity of divination, owner of Table of Ifa. Also known as Orunmila.
orun	Yr.	Invisible world, heaven, sky. Opposite of aiye, the visible world.
Orunmila	Yr.	Deity of divination, owner of Table of Ifa. Sometimes call Ifa and known in Santería as Orula.
Oshun	Yr.	Orisha of rivers and sweet water, love, children, and the pleasures of life (also Ochun).
Osun	Yr.	Protector Orisha, one of the warrior Orisha.
Ouidah	Fn.	See *Whydah*.
oungan	Cr.	Male chief priest in Haitian Vodun. Also hungan. See also *manbo*.
Oya	Yr.	Orisha of the whirlwind, owner of the cemetery.
Papa Legba	Vd.	See *Legba*.
Papa Loko	Vd.	See *Loko*.
Petwo	Vd.	Vodou pantheon based on Kongo cosmology. Violent, "hot" spirits.
plaçage	Fr.	Marriage-like arrangement between European men and free African-heritage women in New Orleans.
polymorphism	En.	Engaging in several unrelated religious traditions at the same time.
ponto de segurar	Pt.	"Securing points," cords used to wrap nkisi-like objects in Brazil.
pragmatism	En.	Expectation that religion will provide practical benefits in one's life.
prenda	Sp.	"Pledge, jewel." Nkisi-like pot or kettle used in the Cuban religion of Palo Monte.

prêtsavann	Cr.	"Bush priest" who leads Catholic prayers at Vodou rituals.
protestantization	En.	Attempt by non-Christian religious traditions to take on Protestant Christian forms in order to fit better into American culture.
Rada	Vd.	Vodou pantheon based on Dahomey and Yoruba cosmology. Gentle, "cool" lwa.
Regla de Ocha	Sp./Yr.	"Way or rule of the Orisha," also known as Santería.
Sagbata	Fn.	Smallpox deity, first-born son of Mawu-Lisa and elder brother of Xevioso. See also *Shopona.*
Santería	Sp.	Conventionally translated as "way of the saints"; common name for followers of Orisha religion in Cuba and the US. Also Regla de Ocha, Lukumi, Ifa.
santero/a	Sp.	"Maker or seller of saints." Within Santería refers to a devotee, more properly only to an initiated priest.
santo/a	Sp.	"Saint." Used in Santería to refer to the Catholic saints associated with the Orisha; often used as generic term referring to the Orisha themselves. More properly should be translated "holy one" rather than "saint."
Sapata	Fn.	See *Shopona.*
Shango	Yr.	Fourth king of Oyo, Orisha of thunder and lightning (Chango in Cuban Santería). Equivalent of Vodun Heviosso, Xevioso.
Shopona	Yr.	Orisha of the infectious diseases, especially smallpox and HIV/AIDS. Also known as Sopona, Babaluaye, Obaluaiye, Oluwa. Equivalent of Vodun Sapata, Sagbata.
simbi	Kg.	Water spirits. In Vodou, deity of springs and ponds who facilitates communication between the living and the dead.
sinuka	Fn.	Gourd vessel for making offerings to deities and ancestors.
succubus	En.	(pl. succubi). Female demon that has sex with men and causes impotence and mental distress. See also *incubus.*
tambor	Sp.	Drum ceremony to invoke the Orisha. Also called bembe.
toby	En.	Type of conjure bag used in hoodoo. Also called trick, hand.

Tohosu	Fn.	Spirits of magical monsters born to the royal family and honored as vodun. See also *Nesuhwe*.
tolerance	En.	Willingness to accept that others are following a different spiritual path and a willingness to work with them on common causes.
trick	En.	See *toby*.
Vaudoux	Fn.	See *Vodou*.
veve	Vd.	Figure representing a lwa.
Vodou	Fn.	Name given to West African religion of the same name in Haiti, based on the name of the deities, the loa/lwa, the vodou. Also Voodoo, Voudou, Vodoun, Voudoun, Vaudoux, Vaudoo.
Vodoun	Fn.	See *Vodou*.
vodun	Fn.	Deities of the traditional Fon religion.
vodunon	Fn.	"Mother of Vodun." Male or female priest responsible for taking care of a vodun shrine.
vodunsi	Fn.	"Dependent or wife of the Vodun." Vodou initiate.
voodoo	Fn.	Americanized version of Vodou, often considered derogatory. See *Vodou*.
Voudou	En.	Name give to variant of Vodou developed in New Orleans. See *Vodou*.
wanga	Cr.	Nkisi-like spirit package used in Vodou.
Whydah	Fn.	Port city of Dahomey. Also Ouidah.
Xevioso	Fn.	Thunder deity and ruler of the seas. See also *Shango*.
Yemaya	Lk.	See *Yemoja*.
Yemoja	Yr.	"Mother whose children are like the fishes." Orisha of the ocean and maternal protection. Also Yemaya.
Zombi	Fn.	See *Grand Zombi, La*.
zombie	En.	Dead person who has been magically reanimated in order to work for a voodoo adept.
zumbi	Kg.	Ghost of the impiously buried dead doomed to wander aimlessly and haunt the living.

TIMELINE

Date	Location	Event
711	Europe	Moors from North Africa colonize Iberian Peninsula (Spain).
950	Africa	Yoruba-speaking people have thriving culture in northern Nigeria.
1076	Africa	Almoravids, a Berber-Muslim dynasty of North Africa, conquer Ghana.
1184	Europe	First ecclesiastical inquisition to root out heretics and witches established.
1333	Africa	Kingdom of Kongo founded.
1479	Europe	Alcáçovas Treaty allows Portuguese merchants to import African slaves into Spain.
1482	Africa	Portuguese build Fort Elmina in Ghana to buy slaves and gold.
1483	Africa	Portuguese sailors arrive on the Kongo coast.
1486	Europe	Witch-hunters' manual *Malleus Maleficarum* published.
1491	Africa	King of Kongo and his fellow nobility convert to Christianity and make Catholic Christianity religion of the state.
1492	Europe	Reconquest unites Spanish kingdoms of Castile and Aragon through the marriage of Isabella I of Castile and Ferdinand II of Aragon, ending the last remnant of Muslim control in Iberia.
1492	America	Christopher Columbus, sailing under a Spanish flag, makes landfall in the Caribbean and "discovers" the Americas.
1510	America	First shipment of slaves arrives in Haiti.

1517	Europe	Luther nails ninety-five theses to a church door, starting the Protestant Reformation.
1522	America	First slave uprising in Haiti.
1526	America	First blacks arrive in New Amsterdam as indentured servants.
1534	Europe	Church of England, under King Henry VIII, separates from Rome.
1564–1642	Europe	Galileo Galilei, physicist, mathematician, astronomer, and philosopher.
1573	America	First cabildo established in Cuba.
1575	Africa	Portuguese invade Angola and establish a colony there.
1591–1643	Europe/ America	Anne Hutchinson, leader of dissident church discussion group in Massachusetts Bay Colony.
1598	America	Don Juan Oñante leads five hundred men from Mexico to Pueblo and lands in present-day New Mexico to begin Spanish conquest of North America.
1600	Africa	Kingdom of Dahomey established.
1600	Africa	Oyo Empire established.
1607	America	First permanent English settlement in North America, Jamestown, founded.
1619	America	First slaves brought to Jamestown, Virginia.
1620	America	Pilgrims arrive at Plymouth Colony.
1620–1640	America	Puritans migrate to Massachusetts Bay Colony.
1624	Africa	Kikongo-language catechism published.
1636	America	Anne Hutchinson exiled to Rhode Island.
1688–1772	Europe	Emanuel Swendenborg, Swedish scientist, philosopher, and Christian mystic.
1680–1796	America	Black population of New York City buried in colonial African Burial Ground.
1692	America	Salem witch trials eventuate in the arrests of over 150 people as witches, the deaths of twenty-four, and the disruption of hundreds of lives.
1698	Africa	Oyo Empire invades Allada.
1700	America	Perpetual black slavery legal throughout Eastern Seaboard and in all thirteen colonies.
1700–1894	Africa	Kingdom of Dahomey.
1703–1791	Europe	John Wesley, Anglican cleric and Christian theologian, founder (with his brother Charles) of English Methodist movement.

1704	Africa	Dona Beatriz Kimpa Vita possessed by the spirit of Saint Anthony.
1706	Africa	Dona Beatriz Kimpa Vita and João Barro executed for heresy.
1712	America	First slave uprising in New York City.
1714–1770	Europe	George Whitefield, Anglican itinerant minister who helped spread the Great Awakening in Great Britain and the British colonies in North America.
1720	America	Enslaved Kongolese people begin arriving in United States in great numbers, landing principally in lowlands of South Carolina.
1724	Africa	Dahomey conquers and absorbs port city of Allada.
1727	Africa	Kingdom of Dahomey becomes an empire and a center for Atlantic slave trade after conquest of Allada and Whydah.
1730s–1740s	America	First Great Awakening.
1734–1815	Europe	Franz Anton Mesmer, German physician who developed theory of animal magnetism, mesmerism, later to become known as hypnotism.
1739	America	Stono Rebellion in South Carolina led by Kongolese slaves.
1740	Europe	John and Charles Wesley begin Methodist reform movement, based on a method of regular prayer, devotional reading, and contemplation that drew participants closer to God and led to a personal experience of religious conversion.
1740	America	George Whitefield preaches a series of revivals as part of the Great Awakening.
1741	America	Slave rebellion known as the Great Negro Plot in New York City.
1741	America	Jonathan Edwards gives his famous "Sinners in the Hands of an Angry God" sermon.
1744	Europe	Swedenborg's first vision and the beginning of his mystical period.
1760	America	Methodist lay preachers arrive in America and form societies in New York and Philadelphia and along the Atlantic Seaboard.
1763	America	Florida becomes a British colony.
1776	America	United States gains its independence from Great Britain.
1776	America	Wesleys recall American missionaries.

1783	America	Florida returns to Spanish rule as part of the Treaty of Paris that ended the American Revolutionary War.
1790–1849	America	Second Great Awakening, a wave of revivals, sweeps through "Burned-Over District" of New York and Cane Ridge, Kentucky, and eventually throughout the nation.
1791	America	Haitian Revolution begins with Vodou ritual offering to Ezuli Dantor.
1795	America	Point Coupée Conspiracy, slave revolt, in Louisiana.
1800	America	Gabriel's Plot, slave insurrection, in Virginia.
1800–1860	America	Second Great Awakening.
1801	America	Cane Ridge Revival, site of the largest camp meeting and one of the landmarks of the Second Great Awakening.
1801–1881	America	Marie Laveau, the Voudou Queen of New Orleans.
1803–1882	America	Ralph Waldo Emerson, lecturer, essayist, poet, and leader of the Transcendentalist movement.
1803	America	Napoleon Bonaparte unsuccessfully attempts to regain island of Haiti for France.
1804	America	Haitian declaration of independence creates the first independent black nation in the Americas.
1807	Europe	British nationals barred from slave trade, although some continued trading illegally.
1808	America	External slave trade banned in the United States.
1812	America	Denmark Vesey Conspiracy, attempted slave revolt, in South Carolina.
1816	America	African Methodist Episcopal Church founded.
1817	America	New Orleans city council sets aside Congo Square for free and enslaved African-heritage people to gather, trade, and entertain themselves.
1818–1858	Africa	Dahomey reaches peak in size, power, and prosperity during reign of King Gezo.
1822	America	Florida becomes a territory of the United States.
1826–1910	America	Andrew Jackson Davis, American Spiritualist, developer of "harmonial philosophy."
1831	America	Nat Turner slave rebellion in Virginia.
1831	America	Mount Auburn Cemetery, America's first landscaped or garden cemetery, founded in Boston.
1831–1833	America	French political thinker and historian Alexis-Charles-Henri Clérel de Tocqueville visits America and writes his famous *Democracy in America*.

1836	America	John Jay Smith Jr. founds the Laurel Hill Cemetery in Philadelphia.
1848	America	Fox sisters begin communicating with murdered peddler and go on to found the American Spiritualist movement.
1848	America	Seneca Fall Convention, America's first women's rights meeting, held.
1860	America	Concordat with Rome returns Catholic clergy to Haiti.
1861–1865	America	US Civil War to prevent secession of Southern states and eventually to free American slaves.
1863	America	Emancipation Proclamation frees American slaves.
1867	America	Last legal slave ship arrives in Cuba, marking the end of the Middle Passage between Africa and the Americas.
1884	America	Cedar Lawn Cemetery, first crematorium in America, founded in Lancaster, Pennsylvania.
1885	Africa	King Leopold II of Belgium formally acquires rights to the Congo territory as his private property at the Conference of Berlin in 1885.
1886	Africa	Great Britain charters Royal Niger Company to consolidate British control of modern Nigeria.
1886	America	Slavery abolished in Cuba.
1887–1927	America	Mother Leafy Anderson, Spiritualist and founder of the Spiritual church movement in New Orleans.
1888	America	Margaret (Maggie) Fox repudiates Spiritualism, claiming she and her sister were frauds. Less than a year later, she recants these claims.
1890	America	African Methodist Episcopal (AME) Zion Church founded.
1894–1960	Africa	Kingdom of Dahomey becomes a part of French West Africa.
1898	America	Cuba declares independence from Spain.
1906	America	William J. Seymour founds the Apostolic Faith Mission, starting the Azusa Street Revival movement.
1908	Africa	Belgium takes control of Congo as a colony.
1910–1940	America	Great Migration in the United States as African Americans leave the rural south for northern cities.
1915–1934	America	American troops occupy island of Haiti.

1920s	America	Mother Leafy Anderson founds loose confederation of African American Spiritual churches in New Orleans.
1922	America	National Colored Spirituals Association splits from white-controlled National Spiritualists Association of Churches.
1930	Africa	Emperor Haile Selassie, first black king in modern times, crowned in Ethiopia.
1959	America	Cuban Revolution installs Fidel Castro as president.
1960	Africa	Nigeria gains its independence from United Kingdom.
1960	Africa	Belgium Congo gains independence to become Republic of the Congo.
1960–1975	Africa	Independent Republic of Dahomey founded.
1965	Africa	Republic of the Congo renamed Democratic Republic of the Congo.
1970	America	Oyotunji Village, an African-style community dedicated to the redemption and restoration of African culture in North America, established in South Carolina.
1971	Africa	Democratic Republic of the Congo renamed Republic of Zaire.
1974	America	Church of the Lukumi Babalu Aye established in Florida.
1975	Africa	The People's Republic of Benin created from the former Republic of Dahomey.
1980	America	Mariel boatlift brings thousands of Cubans to United States.
1993	America	Church of the Lukumi Babalu Aye wins Supreme Court case concerning right to engage in animal sacrifice against the city of Hialeah, Florida.
1997	Africa	Republic of Zaire reclaims its name of Democratic Republic of the Congo.

ADDITIONAL READINGS

CHAPTER 1. A MOST RELIGIOUS NATION

Butler, Jon. *Awash in a Sea of Faith: Christianizing the American People*. Cambridge, MA: Harvard University Press, 1990.

Frazier, E. Franklin. *The Negro Church in America*. New York: Schocken Books, 1963.

Genovese, Eugene D. *Roll, Jordan, Roll: The World the Slaves Made*. New York: Vintage Books, 1975.

Raboteau, Albert J. *Slave Religion: The "Invisible Institution" in the Antebellum South*. New York: Oxford University Press, 1978.

Sobel, Mechal. *The World They Made Together*. Princeton, NJ: Princeton University Press, 1989.

Thornton, John. *Africa and Africans in the Making of the Atlantic World, 1400–1680*. Cambridge: Cambridge University Press, 1992.

CHAPTER 2. JESUS IS MY BOSOM FRIEND: THE DEVELOPMENT OF AMERICAN RELIGION

Armstrong, Karen. *A History of God: The 4,000-Year Quest of Judaism, Christianity, and Islam*. New York: Ballantine Books, 1993.

Butler, Jon. *New World Faiths: Religion in Colonial America*. New York: Oxford University Press, 2008.

Frey, Sylvia R., and Betty Wood. *Come Shouting to Zion: African American Protestantism in the American South and British Caribbean to 1830*. Chapel Hill: University of North Carolina Press, 1998.

Raboteau, Albert J. *Slave Religion: The "Invisible Institution" in the Antebellum South*. New York: Oxford University Press, 1978.

Wills, Garry. *Head and Heart: American Christianities*. New York: Penguin Press, 2007.

CHAPTER 3. AFRICAN CHRISTIANITY: KINGDOM OF KONGO

Heywood, Linda M., ed. *Central Africans and Cultural Transformations in the American Diaspora*. New York: Cambridge University Press, 2002.

Hilton, Anne. *The Kingdom of Kongo*. Edited by John D. Hargreaves and George Shepperson. Oxford Studies in African Affairs. New York: Oxford University Press, 1958.

Thornton, John K. *The Kongolese Saint Anthony: Dona Beatriz Kimpa Vita and the Antonian Movement, 1684–1706*. Cambridge: Cambridge University Press, 1998.

Young, Jason R. *Rituals of Resistance: African Atlantic Religion in Kongo and the Lowcountry South in the Era of Slavery*. Baton Rouge: Louisiana State University Press, 2007.

CHAPTER 4. THE DEAD ARE NOT DEAD

Ariès, Philippe. *The Hour of Our Death*. New York: Oxford University Press, 1981.

Berry, Jason. *The Spirit of Black Hawk: A Mystery of Africans and Indians*. Jackson: University Press of Mississippi, 1995.

Braude, Ann. *Radical Spirits: Spiritualism and Women's Rights in Nineteenth-Century America*. Bloomington: Indiana University Press, 2001.

Thompson, Robert Farris. *Flash of the Spirit: African and Afro-American Art and Philosophy*. New York: Random House, 1984.

Weisberg, Barbara. *Talking to the Dead: Kate and Maggie Fox and the Rise of Spiritualism*. New York: HarperSanFrancisco, 2004.

Wicker, Christine. *Lily Dale: The True Story of the Town That Talks to the Dead*. New York: HarperSanFrancisco, 2002.

CHAPTER 5. CHILDREN OF ODUDUWA: THE OYO EMPIRE

Bascom, William. *The Yoruba of Southwestern Nigeria*. New York: Holt, Rinehart, and Winston, 1969.

Bloom, Harold. *The American Religion: The Emergence of the Post-Christian Nation*. New York: Simon & Schuster, 1992.

Stuckey, Sterling. *Slave Culture: Nationalist Theory and the Foundations of Black America*. New York: Oxford University Press, 1987.

Taves, Ann. *Fits, Trances, and Visions: Experiencing Religion and Explaining Experience from Wesley to James*. Princeton, NJ: Princeton University Press, 1999.

CHAPTER 6. THEN WHY NOT EVERY MAN?

Bloom, Harold. *The American Religion: The Emergence of the Post-Christian Nation*. New York: Simon & Schuster, 1992.

Breslaw, Elaine G. *Tituba, Reluctant Witch of Salem: Devilish Indians and Puritan Fantasies*. New York: New York University Press, 1996.

Evans-Pritchard, E. E. *Witchcraft, Oracles, and Magic among the Azande* (abridged). Oxford: Clarendon Press, 1983.

Long, Carolyn Morrow. *Spiritual Merchants: Religion, Magic, and Commerce*. Knoxville: University of Tennessee Press, 2001.

Peach, Lucinda Joy. *Women and World Religions*. Upper Saddle River, NJ: Prentice Hall, 2002.

CHAPTER 7. CHILDREN OF THE LEOPARD: KINGDOM OF DAHOMEY

Bay, Edna G. *Wives of the Leopard: Gender, Politics, and Culture in the Kingdom of Dahomey*. Charlottesville: University of Virginia Press, 1998.

Herskovits, Melville J. *Life in a Haitian Valley*. New York: Alfred A. Knopf, 1937.

Hochschild, Adam. *King Leopold's Ghost: A Story of Greed, Terror, and Heroism in Colonial Africa*. Boston: Houghton Mifflin Company, 1998.

CHAPTER 8. THAT VOODOO THAT YOU DO

Brown, Karen McCarthy. *Mama Lola: A Vodou Priestess in Brooklyn*. Berkeley: University of California Press, 1991.

Deren, Maya. *Divine Horsemen: The Living Gods of Haiti*. New Platz, NY: McPherson, 1983. First published 1953.

Evans–Pritchard, E. E. *Witchcraft, Oracles and Magic among the Azande* (abridged). Oxford: Clarendon Press, 1983.

Long, Carolyn Morrow. *A New Orleans Voudou Priestess: The Legend and Reality of Marie Laveau*. Gainesville: University Press of Florida, 2006.

Ward, Martha. *Voodoo Queen: The Spirited Lives of Marie Laveau*. Jackson: University Press of Mississippi, 2004.

CHAPTER 9. NEW AFRICAN BRANCHES

Clark, Mary Ann. *Santería: Correcting the Myths and Uncovering the Realities of a Growing Religion*. Westport, CT: Praeger Publishers, 2007.

Cox, Harvey. *Fire from Heaven: The Rise of Pentecostal Spirituality and the Reshaping of Religion in the Twenty-First Century*. Reading, MA: Addison-Wesley Publishing Company, 1995.

Murphy, Joseph M. *Working the Spirit: Ceremonies of the African Diaspora*. Boston: Beacon Press, 1994.

Pinn, Anthony B. *Varieties of African American Religious Experience*. Minneapolis, MN: Augsburg Fortress Publishers, 1998.

Prothero, Stephen. *God Is Not One: The Eight Rival Religions That Run the World—And Why Their Differences Matter*. New York: HarperOne, 2010.

BIBLIOGRAPHY

Abimbola, Wande. *Ifá: An Exposition of Ifá Literary Corpus.* New York: Athelia Henrietta Press, 1997.

Adams, Eric. "Religion and Freedom: Artifacts Indicate That African Culture Persisted Even in Slavery." *Omni* 16, no. 2 (1993): 8.

Albanese, Catherine L. *A Republic of Mind and Spirit: A Cultural History of American Metaphysical Religion.* New Haven, CT: Yale University Press, 2007.

Anderson, Jeffrey E. *Hoodoo, Voodoo, and Conjure: A Handbook.* Folklore Handbooks. Westport, CT: Greenwood Press, 2008.

Argyle, W. J. *The Fon of Dahomey: A History and Ethnography of the Old Kingdom.* Oxford: Clarendon Press, 1966.

Ariès, Philippe. *The Hour of Our Death.* New York: Oxford University Press, 1981.

———. "The Reversal of Death: Changes in Attitudes toward Death in Western Societies." In *Death in America*, edited by David E. Stannard, 134–58. Philadelphia: University of Pennsylvania Press, 1974.

Armstrong, Karen. *A History of God: The 4,000-Year Quest of Judaism, Christianity, and Islam.* New York: Ballantine Books, 1993.

Baer, Hans A. *The Black Spiritual Movement: A Religious Response to Racism.* Knoxville: University of Tennessee Press, 2001.

Barnes, Sandra T. "Africa's Ogun Transformed: Introduction to the Second Edition." In *Africa's Ogun: Old World and New*, edited by Sandra T. Barnes, xiii–xxi. Bloomington: Indiana University Press, 1997.

Bascom, William. *The Yoruba of Southwestern Nigeria.* New York: Holt, Rinehart, and Winston, 1969.

Bay, Edna G. *Asen, Ancestors, and Vodun: Tracing Changes in African Art.* Urbana: University of Illinois Press, 2008.

———. *Wives of the Leopard: Gender, Politics, and Culture in the Kingdom of Dahomey.* Charlottesville: University of Virginia Press, 1998.

Beckmann, David M. "Trance: From Africa to Pentecostalism." *Concordia Theological Monthly* 45, no. 1 (1974): 11–26.

Blakey, Michael L. "The New York African Burial Ground Project: An Examination of Enslaved Lives, a Construction of Ancestral Ties." *Transforming Anthropology* 7, no. 1 (1998): 53–58.

Blauvelt, Martha Tomhave. "Women and Revivalism." In *Woman and Religion in America: The Nineteenth Century*, edited by Rosemary Radford Ruether and Rosemary Skinner Keller. San Francisco: Harper & Row, 1981.

Bloom, Harold. *The American Religion: The Emergence of the Post-Christian Nation.* New York: Simon & Schuster, 1992.

Boadle, Anthony. "Yoruba Deity Worshipers Open Congress in Havana." Nigerian Village Square. http://nigeriavillagesquare.com/forum/main-square/926-yoruba-deity-worshipers-open-congress-havana.html.

Bourguignon, Erica. *Possession.* San Francisco: Changler & Sharp Publishers, 1976.

Brandon, George. *Santería from Africa to the New World: The Dead Sell Memories.* Bloomington: Indiana University Press, 1993.

Braude, Ann. *Radical Spirits: Spiritualism and Women's Rights in Nineteenth-Century America.* Bloomington: Indiana University Press, 2001.

Breen, T. H. "Creative Adaptations: Peoples and Cultures." In *Colonial British America: Essays in the New History of the Early Modern Era*, edited by Jack P. Greene and J. R. Pole, 195–232. Baltimore: Johns Hopkins University Press, 1984.

Breslaw, Elaine G. *Tituba, Reluctant Witch of Salem: Devilish Indians and Puritan Fantasies.* New York: New York University Press, 1996.

Britannica, s.v. "Voodoo." www.britannica.com.proxy.yc.edu/bps/dictionary?query=voodoo.

Broadhead, Susan Harlin. "Slave Wives, Free Sisters: Bakongo Women and Slavery 1700–1850." In *Women and Slavery in Africa*, edited by Claire C. Robinson and Martin A. Kline. Madison: University of Wisconsin Press, 1983.

Brooks, David, and Gail Collins. "Does It All Come Down to Medicare?" In *Opinionator*, a blog in the *New York Times*. May 25, 2011. http://opinionator.blogs.nytimes.com/2011/05/25/does-it-all-come-down-to-medicare/.

Brown, Karen McCarthy. *Mama Lola: A Vodou Priestess in Brooklyn.* Berkeley: University of California Press, 1991.

Brown, Kenneth L., and Doreen C. Cooper. "Structural Continuity in an African-American Slave and Tenant Community." *Historical Archaeology* 24, no. 4 (1990): 7–10.

Butler, Jon. *Awash in a Sea of Faith: Christianizing the American People.* Cambridge, MA: Harvard University Press, 1990.

———. *New World Faiths: Religion in Colonial America.* New York: Oxford University Press, 2008.

Christianity Today. "Santería Holds Cuba in Thrall." January 12, 1998. www.christianitytoday.com/ct/1998/january12/8t1023.html.

Clark, Mary Ann. *Where Men Are Wives and Women Rule: Santería Ritual Practices and Their Gender Implications.* The History of African-American Religions, edited by Stephen Angell and Anthony Pinn. Gainesville: University Press of Florida, 2005.

Cox, Harvey. *Fire from Heaven: The Rise of Pentecostal Spirituality and the Reshaping of Religion in the Twenty-First Century.* Reading, MA: Addison-Wesley Publishing Company, 1995.

Cox, Robert S. *Body and Soul: A Sympathetic History of American Spiritualism.* Charlottesville: University of Virginia Press, 2003.

Crapanzano, Vincent. *Case Studies in Spirit Possession.* Edited by Vincent Crapanzano and Vivian Garrison. New York: John Wiley & Sons, 1977.

Creel, Margaret Washington. *"A Peculiar People": Slave Religion and Community-Culture among the Gullahs.* New York: New York University Press, 1988.

Cultural Orientation Resource Center. "Cuban Immigration to the United States." In *Cubans—Their History and Culture: Refugee Fact Sheet No. 12.* Washington, DC: Cultural Orientation Resource Center, 2004.

Dawkins, Richard. *The Selfish Gene.* Oxford: Oxford University Press, 1989.

Deren, Maya. *Divine Horsemen: The Living Gods of Haiti.* New Platz, NY: McPherson, 1983. First published 1953.

Drewal, Henry John. "Interpretation, Invention, and Re-Presentation in the Worship of Mami Wata." *Journal of Folklore Research* 25, no. 1–2 (1988): 101–139.

Drewal, Henry John, III, John Pemberton, and Roland Abiodun. "The Yoruba World." In *Yoruba: Nine Centuries of African Art and Thought,* edited by Allen Wardwell, 13–43. New York: The Center for African Art, 1989.

Du Bois, W. E. B. *The Negro Church.* Atlanta: Atlanta University Press, 1903.

Edwards, Jonathan, W. H. Kimnach, K. P. Minkema, and D. A. Sweeney. *The Sermons of Jonathan Edwards: A Reader.* New Haven, CT: Yale University Press, 1999.

Egerton, Douglas R. "A Peculiar Mark of Infamy: Dismemberment, Burial, and Rebelliousness in Slave Societies." In *Mortal Remains: Death in Early America,* edited by Nancy Isenberg and Andrew Burstein, 149–60. Philadelphia: University of Pennsylvania Press, 2003.

Evans-Pritchard, E. E. *Witchcraft, Oracles, and Magic among the Azande* (abridged). Oxford: Clarendon Press, 1983.

Farmer, Laurence. "When Cotton Mather Fought the Small Pox." *American Heritage Magazine* no. 5 (1957).

Frazier, E. Franklin. *The Negro Church in America.* New York: Schocken Books, 1963.

Frey, Sylvia R., and Betty Wood. *Come Shouting to Zion: African American Protestantism in the American South and British Caribbean to 1830.* Chapel Hill: University of North Carolina Press, 1998.

Garfinkel, Harold. *Studies in Ethnomethodology.* Englewood Cliffs, NJ: Prentice-Hall, 1967.

Genovese, Eugene D. *Roll, Jordan, Roll: The World the Slaves Made.* New York: Vintage Books, 1975.

Glassman, Sallie Ann. *Vodou Visions: An Encounter with Divine Mystery.* New York: Villard, 2000.

Gomez, Michael Angelo. *Exchanging Our Country Marks: The Transformation of African Identities in the Colonial and Antebellum South.* Chapel Hill: University of North Carolina Press, 1998.

Gorer, Geoffrey. *Death, Grief and Mourning in Contemporary Britain*. London: Cresset Press, 1965.

Greenhouse, Linda. "High Court Is Cool to Sacrifice Ban." *New York Times*, November 5, 1992, 25, col. 21.

Hall, Gwendolyn Midlo. *Slavery and African Ethnicities in the Americas*. Chapel Hill: University of North Carolina Press, 2005.

Hallen, B., and J. O. Sodipo. *Knowledge, Belief, and Witchcraft*. London: Ethnographica, 1986.

Halsall, Paul. "Sojourner Truth: 'Ain't I a Woman?,' December 1851." *Internet Modern History Sourcebook*. 1997. http://www.fordham.edu/halsall/mod/sojtruth-woman.asp.

Herskovits, Melville J. *Dahomey: An Ancient West African Kingdom*. 2 vols. Evanston: Northwestern University Press, 1967.

———. *Life in a Haitian Valley*. New York: Alfred A. Knopf, 1937.

———. *The Myth of the Negro Past*. Boston: Beacon Press, 1990. First published 1941.

Herskovits, Melville J., and Frances S. Herskovits. *An Outline of Dahomean Religious Beliefs*. Memoirs of the American Anthropological Association 41. New York: Kraus Reprint Corporation, 1964.

Heywood, Linda M., ed. *Central Africans and Cultural Transformations in the American Diaspora*. New York: Cambridge University Press, 2002.

Hilton, Anne. *The Kingdom of Kongo*. Oxford Studies in African Affairs, edited by John D. Hargreaves and George Shepperson. New York: Oxford University Press, 1958.

Holloway, Joseph E. *Africanisms in American Culture*. Bloomington: Indiana University Press, 1990.

Horton, Robin. *Patterns of Thought in African and the West: Essays on Magic, Religion and Science*. Cambridge: Cambridge University Press, 1993.

Jacobsen, Douglas G. *Thinking in the Spirit: Theologies of the Early Pentecostal Movement*. Bloomington: Indiana University Press, 2003.

James, William. *The Varieties of Religious Experience*. New York: Penguin Classics, 1985. First published 1902.

Klein, Herbert S. "Angelicanism, Catholicism, and the Negro Slave." In *Slavery in the New World: A Reader in Comparative History*, edited by Laura Foner and Eugene D. Genovese, 138–66. Englewood Cliffs, NJ: Prentice-Hall, 1969.

Klieman, Kairn A. *"The Pygmies Were Our Compass": Bantu and Batwa in the History of West Central Africa, Early Times to c. 1900 CE*. Social History of Africa, edited by Allen Isaacman and Jean Allman. Portsmouth, NH: Heinemann, 2003.

Kramer, Heinrich, and James Sprenger. *The Malleus Maleficarum*. Translated by Rev. Montague Summers. New York: Dover Publications, 1971. First published 1948.

Kucich, John. *Ghostly Communication: Cross-Cultural Spiritualism in Nineteenth-Century American Literature*. Hanover, NH: Dartmouth College Press, 2004.

Laguerre, Michel S. *Voodoo and Politics in Haiti*. New York: St. Martin's Press, 1989.

LaPlante, Eve. *American Jezebel: The Uncommon Life of Anne Hutchinson, the Woman Who Defied the Puritans*. San Francisco: HarperSanFrancisco, 2003.

Law, Robin. *The Kingdom of Allada*. Leiden, The Netherlands: CNWS Publications, 1997.

Lawal, Babatunde. "From Africa to the Americas: Art in Yoruba Religion." In *Santería Aesthetics in Contemporary Latin American Art*, edited by Arturo Lindsay, 3–37. Washington, DC: Smithsonian Institution Press, 1996.

Leonard, Bill J. *Baptists in America*. New York: Columbia University Press, 2005.

Leonard, Todd Jay. *Talking to the Other Side: A History of Modern Spiritualism and Mediumship*. New York: iUniverse, 2005.

Levine, Daniel M., and Ann Gleig. "New Age Movement." In *African American Religious Cultures*, edited by Anthony B. Pinn, 265–73. Santa Barbara, CA: ABC-CLIO, 2009.

Long, Carolyn Morrow. *A New Orleans Voudou Priestess: The Legend and Reality of Marie Laveau*. Gainesville: University Press of Florida, 2006.

———. *Spiritual Merchants: Religion, Magic and Commerce*. Knoxville: University of Tennessee Press, 2001.

MacGaffey, Wyatt. "Twins, Simbi Spirits, and Lwas in Kongo and Haiti." In *Central Africans and Cultural Transformation in the American Diaspora*, edited by Linda M. Heywood, 211–26. Cambridge: Cambridge University Press, 2002.

Mather, Cotton. *The Negro Christianized. An Essay to Excite and Assist That Good Work, the Instruction of Negro-Servants in Christianity: [Four Lines of Scripture Texts]*. Boston: B. Green, 1706.

McDannell, Colleen. *Material Christianity: Religion and Popular Culture in America*. New Haven, CT: Yale University Press, 1995.

Métraux, Alfred. *Voodoo in Haiti*. New York: Schocken Books, 1972. First published 1959.

Morgan, Philip D. "The Cultural Implication of the Atlantic Slave Trade: African Regional Origins, American Destinations and New World Developments." In *Routes to Slavery: Direction, Ethnicity, and Mortality in the Transatlantic Slave Trade*, edited by David Eltis and David Richardson, 122–45. Portland, OR: Frank Cass, 1997.

Morris, Brian. *Religion and Anthropology: A Critical Introduction*. Cambridge and New York: Cambridge University Press, 2006.

Newman, Richard S. *Freedom's Prophet: Bishop Richard Allen, the AME Church, and the Black Founding Fathers*. New York: New York University Press, 2008.

Olupona, Jacob K., and Terry Rey, eds. *Orisa Devotion as World Religion: The Globalization of Yoruba Religious Culture*. Madison: University of Wisconsin Press, 2007.

Oyewùmí, Oyerónké. *The Invention of Women: Making an African Sense of Western Gender Discourses*. Minneapolis and London: University of Minnesota Press, 1997.

Parrish, Lydia, Creighton Churchill, and Robert MacGimsey. *Slave Songs of the Georgia Sea Islands*. Hatburo, PA: Folklore Associates, 1965.

Peach, Lucinda Joy. *Women and World Religions*. Upper Saddle River, NJ: Prentice Hall, 2002.

Pew Research Center for People and the Press. "Question Search." http://people-press.org/question-search/?qid=1663013&pid=51&ccid=51.

Pierson, William Dillon. *Black Yankees: The Development of an Afro-American Subculture in Eighteenth-Century New England*. Amherst: University of Massachusetts Press, 1988.

Pinn, Anthony B. *Varieties of African American Religious Experience*. Minneapolis, MN: Augsburg Fortress Publishers, 1998.

Pitts, Walter F. *Old Ship of Zion: The Afro-Baptist Ritual in the African Diaspora*. New York: Oxford University Press, 1993.

Prothero, Stephen. *God Is Not One: The Eight Rival Religions That Run the World—and Why Their Differences Matter*. New York: HarperOne, 2010.

Raboteau, Albert J. *Slave Religion: The "Invisible Institution" in the Antebellum South*. New York: Oxford University Press, 1978.

Rey, Terry. "Habitus and Hybridity: A Bourdieuian Interpretation of Syncretism in Afro-Catholic Religion." Talk presented at the African Studies Association conference, New Orleans, LA, 2004.

———. "Kongolese Catholic Influences on Haitian Popular Catholicism: A Socio-historical Exploration." In *Central Africans and Cultural Transformation in the American Diaspora*, edited by Linda M. Heywood, 265–88. Cambridge: Cambridge University Press, 2002.

Riordan, Liam. "Passing as Black/Passing as Christian: African-American Religious Autonomy in Early Republican Delaware." *Pennsylvania History* 64, special supplemental issue (Summer 1997): 207–29.

Roediger, David R. "And Die in Dixie: Funerals, Death, and Heaven in the Slave Community 1700–1865." *Massachusetts Review* 22 (1981): 163–83.

Ruether, Rosemary R. "Christianity." In *Women in World Religions*, edited by Arvind Sharma, 207–33. New York: State University of New York Press, 1987.

Saint-Méry, Médéric Louis-Elie Moreau de. *Description Topographique, Physique, Civile, Politique et Historique de la Parti Française de l'Isle Saint-Domingue*. Paris: Société de l'historire des colonies françaises, 1958. First published 1797.

Smart, Ninian. *Worldview: Cross-Cultural Exploration of Human Beliefs*. New York: Scribner's, 1983.

Smith, Jonathan Z. "Religion, Religions, Religious." In *Critical Terms for Religious Studies*, edited by Mark C. Taylor, 269–84. Chicago: University of Chicago Press, 1998.

Smith, Mark M. "Time, Religion, Rebellion." In *Stono: Documentating and Interpreting a Southern Slave Revolt*, edited by Mark M. Smith, 108–23. Columbia: University of South Carolina Press, 2005.

Sobel, Mechal. *The World They Made Together*. Princeton, NJ: Princeton University Press, 1989.

Soyinka, Wole. "The Tolerant Gods." In *Orisa Devotion as World Religion: The Globalization of Yoruba Religious Culture*, edited by Jacob K. Olupona and Terry Ray, 31–50. Madison: University of Wisconsin Press, 2007.

———. "Wole Soyinka on Yoruba Religion: A Conversation with Ulli Beier." *Isokan Yoruba Magazine*, Summer 1997. www.yoruba.org/Magazine/Summer97/File93.htm.

Stannard, David E. *The Puritan Way of Death: A Study in Religion, Culture, and Social Change.* New York: Oxford University Press, 1977.

Stuckey, Sterling. "African Spirituality in Colonial New York, 1700–1770." In *Inequality in Early America*, edited by Carla Gardina Pestana and Sharon V. Salinger, 160–81. Hanover, NH: University Press of New England, 1999.

———. *Slave Culture: Nationalist Theory and the Foundations of Black America.* New York: Oxford University Press, 1987.

Sweet, James H. "The Evolution of Ritual in the African Diaspora: Central African *Kilundu* in Brazil, St. Domingue, and the United States, Seventeenth–Nineteenth Centuries." In *Diasporic Africa: A Reader*, edited by Michael A. Gomez, 64–80. New York: New York University Press, 2006.

Taves, Ann. *Fits, Trances, and Visions: Experiencing Religion and Explaining Experience from Wesley to James.* Princeton, NJ: Princeton University Press, 1999.

Thompson, Robert Farris. "Divine Countenance: Art and Altars of the Black Atlantic World." In *Divine Inspiration: From Benin to Bahia*, edited by Phyllis Galembo, 1–17. Albuquerque: University of New Mexico Press, 1993a.

———. *Face of the Gods: Art and Altars of Africa and the African Americas.* New York: The Museum for African Art, 1993b.

———. *Flash of the Spirit: African and Afro-American Art and Philosophy.* New York: Random House, 1984.

———. "Hip Hop 101." In *Droppin' Science: Critical Essays on Rap Music and Hip Hop Culture*, edited by William Eric Perkins, 211–18. Philadelphia: Temple University Press, 1996.

Thornton, John K. *Africa and Africans in the Making of the Atlantic World, 1400–1680.* Cambridge: Cambridge University Press, 1992.

———. "African Dimensions of the Stono Rebellion." *American Historical Review* 96, no. 4 (1991): 1101–14.

———. *The Kongolese Saint Anthony: Dona Beatriz Kimpa Vita and the Antonian Movement, 1684–1706.* Cambridge: Cambridge University Press, 1998.

———. "On the Trail of Voodoo: African Christianity in Africa and the Americas." *The Americas* 44, no. 3 (1988): 261–78.

———. "Religious and Ceremonial Life in the Kongo and Mbundu Areas, 1500–1700." In *Central Africans and Cultural Transformations in the American Diaspora*, edited by Linda M. Heywood, 71–90. New York: Cambridge University Press, 2002.

Tocqueville, Alexis de. *Democracy in America.* Translated by Henry Reeve. New York: D. Appleton and Company, 1904.

Vanhee, Hein. "Central African Popular Christianity and the Making of Haitian Vodou Religion." In *Central Africans and Cultural Transformation in the American Diaspora*, edited by Linda M. Heywood, 243–64. Cambridge: Cambridge University Press, 2002.

Voltaire, François-Marie de. *Philosophical Dictionary.* Translated by Theodore Besterman. London: Besterman, 1972.

Walker, Sheila S. "Introduction: Are You Hip to the Jive? (Re)Writing/Righting the Pan-American Discourse." In *African Roots/American Cultures: Africa in the Creation of the Americas*, edited by Sheila S. Walker, 1–44. Lanham, MD: Rowman & Littlefield Publishers, 2001.

Ward, Martha. *Voodoo Queen: The Spirited Lives of Marie Laveau*. Jackson: University Press of Mississippi, 2004.

Wells, Robert V. "A Tale of Two Cities: Epidemics and the Rituals of Death in Eighteenth-Century Boston and Philadelphia." In *Mortal Remains: Death in Early America*, edited by Nancy Isenberg and Andrew Burstein, 56–67. Philadelphia: University of Pennsylvania Press, 2003.

Wills, Garry. *Head and Heart: American Christianities*. New York: Penguin Press, 2007.

Winch, Julie. *The Elite of Our People: Joseph Wilson's Sketches of Black Upper-Class Life in Antebellum Philadelphia, Pennsylvania*. Philadelphia: Pennsylvania State University Press, 2000.

World Values Survey. http://www.worldvaluessurvey.org/.

Young, Jason R. *Rituals of Resistance: African Atlantic Religion in Kongo and the Lowcountry South in the Era of Slavery*. Baton Rouge: Louisiana State University Press, 2007.

INDEX

Afonso I, 50

Africa, place of the clergy, 20

African: Christianity in the Delaware valley, 32; ideas of witchcraft, 124; philosophical ideas, 112; prestige structure, 133

African Americans: historic burial practices, 72; and Christianity, 184; clues to historic daily life, 14; religiosity, 31; view of God, 45

African Burial Ground of the City of New York, 14

African Methodist Episcopal Church, 32

African religions: whiteness and blackness, 148; patterns of, 16; religious sensibilities, 34

African revelatory pronouncements, 146; secret societies, 45; destruction of spiritual systems, 13; ideas about revelations, 18

Africanisms in American religions, 43

afterlife: Kongolese, 84; Spiritualist, 84–85

Age, 140

Aguda (Afro-Brazilians), 135

Agwe, 158

ahosi (wives of the king), 138

ahovi (children of the king), 138

Aido-Hwedo, 140

Allada, 134

Allen, Richard, 32

altar-making, Yoruba, 100

amazons in Dahomey, 139

American: Africanisms in religion, 43; deists, 36; gnosticism, 111; hoodoo, 164; ideas of witchcraft, 126; occupation of Haiti, 164; religious sensibilities, 2; religious values, 3; religious diversity, 1700–1800s, 30; revelatory pronouncements, 146; Spiritualist movement, 77; transcendentalists, 36

ancestors: in Fon religion, 142; in Kongolese thought, 256

Angola, 2; religion in slave trade, 57; map of, 49

Anthony, Saint: Kongo, 59; Voudou, 163

Apolonia Mafuta, 60–61, 125

Apostolic Faith Mission, 185

Arius, view of God, 23

Arminian form of Calvinism, 29, 38

Arminius, Jacob: view of God, 29

ashé (power), 142

atheistic view of God, 26

Azaka, 158

Azusa Street Revival, 185

babalawo, 95
baptism: in African American religion, 147; as death-and-rebirth experience, 147; Kongolese, 55
Baron Samdi, 158
Barro, João, 63
belief, 115; English language, 113; validating, 114; Yoruba language (*igbàgbǫ́*), 115
bembe (drum ritual), 176
Bethel Church, Philadelphia, 32, 78
Beyond, 77
black: heathenism, 183; mediumship, 81; religiosity, 31; typology of religious groups, 170
blackness in African religions, 148
Bloom, Harold, 111
bokonon (diviner), 145
Bondye (Good God), 157
burial practices of enslaved African Americans, 72
burned-over district, 79

cabildos, 91, 171
calabash of existence: Fon, 144; Yoruba, 91
Calvin, John, view of God, 24
Calvinism, Arminian, 28, 29
Calvinist view of God, 28
Camisards, 179
Cane Ridge revival, 41
cannibalism, 126
Carroll, Charles, excavation of home, 14
Castro, Fidel, 172
catechism: Fon, 193n4; Kongolese, 57
categories of spirits. *See* spirits
Catholic saints: in Orisha Religion, 172; in Voudou, 163–64
cemetery: Laural Hill, 75; lawn, 75. *See also* Saint Louis Cemetary One
charms, 165
children of the palace, 137, 138
Christian dogma, importance, 42
Christianity of African Americans, 184

Church of the Lukumi Babalu Aye (CLBA), 176
colonial European ideas of witchcraft, 122
colonists, as pre-Enlightenment thinkers, 152
common graves, 69
communion form of religion, 17
Congo Square, 162
congregational independence, 30
conjure, 164; bags, 165; bottles, 165; as minkisi, 165
conversion: Anglican policy, 33; of blacks, 26, 32; of the enslaved, 6, 10; experiences, 40-41; importance of visions, 147; stages of, 28
cosmology: Fon, 143–44; Kongo, 52–53; Vodou, 56; Yoruba, 91–96, 97
Cotton, John, 188
Cousin Zaka, 158
creation story, Kimpa Vita, 63
Crossing Over, 77
Cuba: *cabildos*, 91; history, 90, 171–72; revolution, 91
cult of Fa (Ifa), 145
cultures contributing enslaved peoples, 7

Dahomey: amazons, 139; history of, 132; map, 133; militarism, 134; monarchy, 137; princesses, 138; slave trading, 136; wives of king, 137; women in society, 136
daily life of African Americans in the late seventeenth century, 14
Dambala, 140, 158
Danbala, 158
Davis, Andrew Jackson, 80
death, ideas about: 1700s, 70; African, 71–72; colonial and early Revolutionary periods, 68; early modern period, 70; medieval Europe, 70; nineteenth century, 76; Puritans, 70

death-and-rebirth experience, 147

deho (family shrine), 143

deism: in America, 36; view of God, 24

Deren, Mara, 159

destiny: in Fon religion, 145; in Yoruba religion, 97–99

destruction of African spiritual systems, 13

divination, 98; Fon system of, 145

doctrine of total depravity, 28

Don Petro, 159

Dona Beatriz Kimpa Vita. *See* Kimpa Vita, Dona Beatriz

Douglass, Fredrick, 79

Du Bois, W. E. B., 185

Edward, Jonathan, 22; "Sinners in the Hands of an Angry God," 38

Edwards, John, 77

Elegba, 94

Enlightenment religion, 25

enthusiasm: Anglican churches, 34; Methodist, 37; Wesley's interpretation, 40

Erzili, 158

Eshu, 94

European: burial practices, 69; ideas of witchcraft, 122; place of the clergy, 20; prestige structure, 132; revelatory pronouncements, 18, 146; stereotypes of Africa, 45, 131, 148

evangelicals, 1860s, 42

Evans-Pritchard, E. E., 124

experimentalism, 2, 187

Fa (Ifa) cult, 145

Fa (Vodou), 97

female piety, 118

female role models in Christianity, 117

fideism, 129

First Amendment protection of Orisha Religion, 176

Fon: ancestors, 142; cosmology, 143–44; culture, 135; destiny, 145;

divination system, 145; people, 132, 135; pragmatic and eclectic culture, 141–42; religion, 11; religion in war planning, 135; sacrifice, 139

forms of religion. *See under* religion

Four Moments of the Sun, 52

Fox, Catherine and Margaret, 78

free people of color, 161

fundamentalism, 187

gbà (agree to an assertion), 114

gbàgbó (to believe), 115

gbetome (land of the living), 144

Gede, 158

gender, 117; natural attitude toward, 104; possession, 194n3; as prestige structure, 104; in Yoruba society, 104

glossolalia (speaking in tongues), 178, 185

gnosis: in religion, 116, viewpoint, 111

God Is Not One (Prothero), 177

goofer dust, 166

Gran Brigit, 158

grave as *nkisi*, 54, 55, 72

gravesites, African American, 74

Great Awakening: First, 38; Second, 39

Gu, 95, 140

Haiti: American occupation of, 167; history of, 153; Kongolese influences, 155; revolution, 90, 154; Vodou, 4153

The Hammer of the Witches, 124

hands, 165

harmonial philosophy, 80

head-on-the-ground position, 183

heathenism, black, 183

henotheism, 141

Henrique of Kongo, 50

Henry VIII, 27

Herskovits/Frazier debate, 11

history of God among European Christians, 23–25

history of: Cuba, 90–91, 171–72;
    Dahomey, 132–34; Haiti, 153–54;
    Kongo, 48–50; Orisha religion, 172–
    76; Vodou, 154, 156; Voudou, 160–
    62; Yoruba, 88–91
hoodoo, 128, 164
hungan (the chief for a Vodun), 144
hush arbor, 180
Hutchinson, Anne, 119, 188–89

Ifa, 95; as name of American Yoruba
    religion, 171. *See also* Orisha
    Religion
Ifè, in Fon cosmology, 144
Ile-Ife, 88
individualism, 2
inner light, 26
Innocent VIII, 123
Inquisition, 123, 139
Invention of Women (Oyĕwùmí), 104
iyawo (bride), 101, 105

Jackson, Rebecca Cox, 81
Jansenists, 179
Jesus, in Kimpa Vita's view, 61

Kikongo, 54; catechism, 57; use for
    Christian concepts, 54
Kimpa Vita, Dona Beatriz, 59–64, 159,
    163; execution, 63; pregnancy, 63
Kimpasi society, 60
kindoki (witchcraft), 54
Kingdom of Dahomey. *See* Dahomey
Kingdom of Kongo. *See* Kongo
knowledge: English language, 112–13;
    Yoruba language (*imò*), 114–15; of
    Christianity in Kongo, 57
Knowledge, Belief and Witchcraft (Hallen
    and Sodipo), 112
Kongo: history of, 48, 50; influences in
    Haiti, 155; literacy, 48; map, 49;
    religion in slave trade, 51; religious
    history, 50

Kongolese: in American colonies, 51;
    baptism, 55; catechism, 57;
    cosmology, 52; deity, 52; knowlege
    of Christianity, 57; Little Anthonys,
    62; priests, 52; prophets, 62; Stono
    Rebellion, 64; traditional religion,
    52; view of ancestors, 56
Kongolese Saint Anthony. *See* Kimpa
    Vita, Dona Beatriz
kutome (land of the dead), 144

La Grand Zombi, 162, 164
Laurel Hill Cemetery, 75
Laveau, Marie, 160
lawn cemetery, 75
leadership positions among women, 120
Legba, 94, 140, 158
Levi Jordan Plantation, 14
literacy, Kongolese, 48
Little Anthonys, 62
Louisiana Writers' Project, 162
Lukumi Church of Orishas, 176
Lukumí. *See* Orisha religion
Luther, Martin, 124; view of God, 24
Lwa, 158; Petwo, 159; Rada, 158

*Malleus Maleficarum. See The Hammer of
    the Witches*
manbo (Vodou priest), 157
manipulation form of religion, 17
Marasa, 159
Mariel boat lift, 91, 172
Marron, Saint, 163–64
Mather, Cotton: *The Negro
    Christianized*, 32; small pox
    vacinations, 96
maps: Kingdom of Dahomey, 133;
    Kingdoms of Kongo and Angola,
    49; Oyo Empire, 89
Mawu-Lisa, 140
mediumship, Spiritualist, 84
memes, 148, 166; voodoo, 166;
    zombification, 168

Mesmer, Franz, 80
mesmerism, 80
Methodist: enthusiasm, 37; explosion, 36; movement, 37
mò (to know), 114
monarchy, Dahomey, 137
Mr. Splitfoot, 78

na daho (great princess), 138
The Negro Christianized (Mather), 32
Nesuhwe (royal Vodun), 140
New Orleans: slave origins, 161; Voudou, 160;
New York African Burial Ground of the City, 14
nganga (priest), 52
nkisi (ritual object), 52, 54, 72
Nok culture, 88
nzambi (spirit), 52, 167

Obatala, 95
Obba, 96
Ocha. *See* Orisha religion
Oedipus, 99
Ogou, 95, 158
Ogun, 95, 140
oko (husband), 24
Old Splitfoot, 78
Olodumare, 94
Olofi, 94
omo (child), 105
òótó (truth), 114
openness to revelation, Fon, 146
ori (destiny), 97
Orisha religion, 170–71; and Catholic saints, 172; communities, 175; First Amendment protection, 176; history of, 185; music, 177; origins, 172; possession trance, 176; re-Africanization, 176; in the United States, 175
Orisha, 93–96; as husband, 105
Orishala, 95

Orunmila, 95
Oshala, 95
Oshun, 96
oungan (Vodou priest), 157
Oya, 96
Oyĕwùmí, Oyèrónké, 104
Oyo, 88, 90; map of, 89
Oyotunji Village, 176

pantheons, Vodun, 140
Papa Legba, 158
Papa Loko, 158
papal bull of Innocent VIII, 123
Parham, Charles Fox, 185
Patterns of Thought in Africa and the West (Horton), 16
Pedro I, 61
Pentecostalism, 185–86; characteristics of, 185; compared to Kongolese religious culture, 187; differences from fundamentalists, 185; empiricism, 186; movement, 178; social gospel, 186
Peter, Saint, in Voudou, 163
Petro, Don, 159
Petwo Lwa, 13, 157; origins, 13
philosophical ideas, African, 112
Pilgrims, 27
Pinkster Festival, 79
plaçage, 161
place of the clergy: in Africa, 20; in Europe, 20
polymorphism, 2, 55–56, 130, 183
ponto de segurar (securing points), 165
possession trance, 98, 101–102, 176; in ring shout, 181; as prophecy, 146
possession, conscious, 102
Poughkeepsie Seer. *See* Davis, Andrea Jackson
Praagh, James Van, 77
pragmatism, 3; in religion, 146

praise house, 180

prenda, 165

prestige structures: African, 133; European, 132

prêtsavann (bush priest), 157

priest as wife, 105

priests of Vodun, 144, 146

primal spirituality, 187

princesses in Dahomey, 138

prophecy: African ideas, 58; control of, 146; European ideas, 58; Fon, 145; validation, 116

prophets, Kongolese, 60, 62

prosperity gospel, 111

pure forms of religion, 17

Puritans, 27

queen mother in Dahomey, 138

Slave Religion (Raboteau), 43

Rada Lwa, 157, 158

Randolph, Paschal Beverly, 81

re-Africanization of Orisha religion, 176

rebellious women, 118–19

Regla de Ocha. *See* Orisha religion

religion: and gender, 117; definitions, 15; diversity in American, 30; different forms of, 17; Fon, 139; in America, 27; Kongo, 52; of the heart, 25; Orisha, 171; in West Africa, 110

religious: activity, description, 15; experiences, 115–16; indifference to in America, 30; intolerance of, 185; music, Yoruba, 189; pragmatism, 146, 191; roles for women, 117, 119, 121; syncretism, 154; tolerance: 129, 188; values, American, 3; viewpoint, universalist, 129;

revelation, 18; revelatory pronouncements, 146

revivals: Southern, 121. *See also* Cane Ridge revival

ring shout, 181

rituals, Vodou, 160

roles for religious women: European, 117; Yoruba, 119

Romantic movement, 36; view of God, 26

"The Roughcast," Bethel Church, 33

royal Vodun, 140

sacred spaces, Yoruba, 100

sacrifices among Fon, 139, 141

Sagbata, 140

Saint Louis Cemetery One, 164

Saint Thomas's African Episcopal, 78

saints: in Orisha Religion, 172; in Voudou, 163–164

Salem witch trials, 77, 127

salvation, 129

Salve Antoniana, 61

Santería. *See* Orisha religion

second funeral, 72

Second Great Awakening, 39–43

secrecy in African religions, 5

secret societies, 18, 45, 147; Kimpasi, 60

secularism, 26

Seneca Falls Convention, 79

Seymour, William J., 185

Shango, 95, 140

Shopona, 95, 140

"Sinners in the Hand of an Angry God," 38

skills brought by Africans, 8

slave: conversions, 6, 10, 40; gravesites, 74; origins, New Orleans, 160

Slave Religion (Raboteau), 43

Smith, John Jay, Jr., 127

social gospel movement, 111

social gospel, 186

South Carolina: Kongolese center of North America, 64

Soyinka, Wole, 189–90

spirit rapping, 78

spirits: categories of, 156; Petwo, 157; Rada, 157
spiritual ecstasy as possession trance, 181
Spiritualism, 76; claims of fraud, 85; doctrines, 83, famous participants, 82; mediumship, 84; summer camps, 85
spirituals, 182
stages of conversion, 28
stereotypes of Africa, 131
Stono Rebellion, 64
Summerland, 80, 83, 84
superstition, description of, 152
Swedenborg, Emanuel, 80
syncretism, 44, 154, 172; and religious purity, 173

tambor (drum ritual), 177
Tituba, 77, 127
tobies, 165
Tohosu (magical monsters), 140
tolerance, 3, 129
total depravity: doctrine of, 28
trance as religious activity, 103; possession, 98, 102; shamanic, 102; types of, 102
transcendentalism, 36
tricks, 165
Truth, Sojourner, 130
typology of black religious groups, 170

Union Church of Africans, 32, 79
universalist, religious viewpoint, 129; theology, 111

vacinations, 95
validating: beliefs, 114; prophecy, 116
Vaudoux, 155–56
vestry, 31
view of evil, West and West Central African, 110
view of God: African American, 45; Arminian, 29; Arius, 23; atheist, 26; Calvinist, 28; deist, 24; European, 109; Kongolese, 110; Romantics, 26; secularist, 26
visions in African American religion, 147
Vodou: cosmologies, 156; gods, 158; history of, 154–56; religion in Haiti, 151, 153; rituals, 160
Vodun: as spiritual beings, 139; eclectic and flexible, 141; mobility, 141; pantheons, 140; priests, 144, 146; royal, 140
vodunon (mother of a Vodun), 144
vodunsi (wife of a Vodun), 144
voodoo: as cultural meme, 148, 166; description, 151, 154; in popular imagination, 131; as witchcraft, 127
Voudou, 160; eclectic mix of beliefs and practices, 163; history of, 160; religion in New Orleans, 151; saints, 163–64
wanga, 165

Wesley, John, 179
whiteness in African American religious experience, 148
Whitfield, George, 37
Whydah, 134
Winthrop, John, 119, 188
witch trials, Salem, 77, 127
witchcraft, 20, 122; African view, 124–26; Amerian view, 126–28; European view, 23, 122, 124; Kongolese, 54; substance, 125; as voodoo, 127
wives in Dahomey palace, 137
wives of the king, 138–39
women: and religion, 117; in Christianity, 117; Dahomean society, 136; leadership positions, 120; rebellious, 15, 118; religious participation, Yoruba, 120; roles, 19, 117, 119, 146

Writers' Project. *See* Louisiana Writers' Project

Xevioso, 140

Yemoja, 96
Yoruba: altar-making, 100; cosmology, 91–96, 97; culture, 173; destiny, 88; flexible and incorporative gender, 104; gods, 93–94; history, 88; knowledge, 114; map of, 89; Orisha, 93–94; Oyo empire, 90; sacred spaces, 100; roles for women, 119; tolerance in traditional religion, 189

zombie, 167–68; meme, 148–49; zombification, 168
Zombi, La Grand. *See* La Grand Zombi
zumbi (ghost), 72, 167

CPSIA information can be obtained at www.ICGtesting.com
Printed in the USA
BVOW072025060512

289394BV00002B/1/P